Dr Hankey is Associate Professor of Classics at King's College and Dalhousie University, Halifax, Nova Scotia.

OXFORD THEOLOGICAL MONOGRAPHS

OXFORD THEOLOGICAL MONOGRAPHS

God In Himself

Aquinas' Doctrine of God
as Expounded in
the *Summa Theologiae*

W. J. HANKEY

OXFORD UNIVERSITY PRESS

1987

Oxford University Press, Walton Street, Oxford OX2 6DP

Oxford New York Toronto
Delhi Bombay Calcutta Madras Karachi
Petaling Jaya Singapore Hong Kong Tokyo
Nairobi Dar es Salaam Cape Town
Melbourne Auckland

and associated companies in
Beirut Berlin Ibadan Nicosia

Oxford is a trade mark of Oxford University Press

Published in the United States
by Oxford University Press, New York

British Library Cataloguing in Publication Data
Hankey, W. J.
God in himself: Aquinas' doctrine of
God as expounded in the Summa theologiae.
—(Oxford theological monographs)
1. Thomas, Aquinas, Saint. Summa theologiae
I. Title
230'.2   BX1749.T6
ISBN 0-19-826724-X

Library of Congress Cataloging-in-Publication Data
Hankey, W. J.
God in Himself.
(Oxford theological monographs)
Bibliography: p.
Includes index.
1. God—History of doctrines—Middle Ages, 600—1500.
2. Thomas, Aquinas, Saint, 1225?—1274. Summa theologica.
I. Title. II. Series.
BT100.T4.H36 1987   231   86-28572
ISBN 0-19-826724-X

Set by Joshua Associates Limited, Oxford
Printed and bound in Great Britain by
Biddles Limited, Guildford and King's Lynn

TO JAMES ALEXANDER DOULL

... τοῖς φιλοσοφίας κοινωνήσασιν · οὐ ... πρὸς
χρήμαθ' ἡ ἀξία μετρεῖται, τιμή τ' ἰσόρροπος οὐκ
ἂν γένοιτο, ἀλλ' ἴσως ἱκανόν, καθάπερ καὶ πρὸς
θεοὺς καὶ πρὸς γονεῖς, τὸ ἐνδεχόμενον.

(Aristotle, *Eth. Nic.* ix. 1)

ACKNOWLEDGEMENTS

IN the course of writing this book I have incurred many debts. The Governors of Pusey House, the University of King's College, and the Social Sciences and Humanities Research Council of Canada have all supported me financially. I am grateful to my colleagues in the Classics Department of Dalhousie University and at King's who assumed my work while I was on leave, to St Peter's College, Oxford, for making me a member of their Society, and to the Governing Body of St Cross College, Oxford, for giving me a place in their Common Room. The Bodleian Library, Pusey House Library, and the Library of Blackfriars in Oxford, the collections of the Augustinianum, the Angelicum, and the Vatican in Rome, of the Bibliothèque du Saulchoir in Paris, of the Universitas S. Pauli in Ottawa, and of the Pontifical Institute of Mediaeval Studies in Toronto have been indispensable.

Several organizations have given me the opportunity to present preliminary versions of my ideas and to benefit from support, advice, and contradiction. Such benefits have accrued from my paper for the 1977 Bonn Congress of the Société Internationale pour l'Étude de la Philosophie Médiévale which has now been published in their proceedings (Miscellanea Mediaevalia 13/2, Berlin/New York, 1981), as also from my communication for the Eighth International Conference on Patristic Studies held in Oxford in 1979 which was published in the issue of *Dionysius* for that year. The Editors of *Dionysius* kindly published further articles in the volumes for 1980, 1982, and 1985. A paper delivered for me by Professor C. J. Starnes appeared in the *Atti del Congresso Internazionale di Studi Boeziani* (Pavia, 5–8 October 1980), edited by L. Obertello and published during 1981 in Rome. The Pontificia Accademia Romana di S. Tommaso d'Aquino e di Religione Cattolica heard a paper I delivered in September of 1980 and it is printed in the *Atti dell'VIII Congresso Tomistico Internazionale nel centenario dell'Enciclica 'Aeterni Patris' di Leone XIII e della fondazione dell'Accademia di S. Tommaso* edited by A. Piolanti (Vatican City, 1982). Other aspects of my work on Thomas have been presented in lectures or at colloquia sponsored by the Norman Sykes Society of Ripon College, Cuddesdon; the Philosophy Department and Queen's College, Memorial University, Newfoundland; the Philosophy Department of Georgia State University in Atlanta, Georgia; the Mediaeval Colloquium of the University of the South, Sewanee, Tennessee; the Harvard Divinity School; the Faculty of Divinity of Trinity College, Toronto, and the Lightfoot Society of Durham University. One of these papers was published in *The Thomist* for 1982. Finally the Sixth International Conference on Patristic, Mediaeval and Renaissance Studies, meeting at Villanova, Pennsylvania in September 1981, heard my paper entitled 'Theology as System and as Science: Proclus and Thomas Aquinas'.

My personal debts are enormous. My thesis supervisors, Professor Ian Macquarrie and Dr Anthony Meredit, SJ, were tolerant and encouraging. My colleagues in Halifax, Professors A. H. Armstrong, R. D. Crouse, and J. A. Doull, have helped at every stage. The assistance of Fathers L.-J. Bataillon, OP, of the Leonine Commission, of J. G. Bougerol, OFM, of the College of St Bonaventure at Grottaferrata, of H.-D. Saffrey, OP, of the CNRS, and of the Revd Professors A. Patfoort, OP, and G. Lafont, OSB, of the Angelicum and Anselmianum respectively, has placed resources at my disposal which I could never have provided for myself. Their help and much more is owed to Dr M.-O. Garrigues of the CNRS. Dr M. T. D'Alverney, Professor J. Trouillard, PSS, Fr B. de Margerie, SJ, Dr L. Minio-Paluello, Miss Jean Petersen, Professor Bruno Neveu, and Sir Richard Southern have also been generous. The Revd Professors D. J. M. Bradley of the Oratory of St Philip Neri and Georgetown University and E. R. Fairweather of Trinity College, Toronto, have been more than kind in assisting an enterprise of which they remain suspicious. The sufferings of Miss Joyce Brewis, Mrs Margaret Kirby, Miss Elizabeth Holder, and Dr Marcia Rodríguez, who, with Miss Anne Ashby, Dr Leofranc Holford-Strevens, and Mr John Waś of the Oxford University Press, cared for its production, have all contributed with these others to whatever merit it possesses.

CONTENTS

ABBREVIATIONS

Arch. hist. doct. lit. du Moyen Âge	*Archives d'histoire doctrinale et littéraire du Moyen Âge*
Comp. Theo.	Aquinas, *Compendium Theologiae*
De Div. Nat.	Eriugena, *De Divisione Naturae*
De Pot.	Aquinas, *Quaestiones Disputatae de Potentia*
De Sub. Sep.	Aquinas, *De Substantiis Separatis*
De Veritate	Aquinas, *Quaestiones Disputatae de Veritate*
Elements	Proclus, *The Elements of Theology*
En.	Plotinus, *Enneads*
In de Anima	Aquinas, *Sentencia libri de Anima*
In de Caus.	Aquinas, *Super librum de Causis Expositio*
In de Div. Nom.	Aquinas, *In librum Beati Dionysii de Divinis Nominibus Expositio*
In de Trin.	Aquinas, *Expositio super librum Boetii de Trinitate*
In Ethica	Aquinas, *Sententia libri Ethicorum*
In Meta.	Aquinas, *In duodecim libros Metaphysicorum Aristotelis Expositio*
In Phys.	Aquinas, *In octo libros Physicorum Aristotelis Expositio*
In Post. Anal.	Aquinas, *In Aristotelis libros Posteriorum Analyticorum Expositio*
In Sent.	Aquinas, *Scriptum super libros Sententiarum Magistri Petri Lombardi*
Nic. Eth.	Aristotle, *Nicomachean Ethics*
Plat. Theo.	Proclus, *The Platonic Theology*
Rev. sc . ph. th.	*Revue des sciences philosophiques et théologiques*
ScG	Aquinas, *Summa contra Gentiles*
ST	Aquinas, *Summa Theologiae*

INTRODUCTION

WHAT could justify something more on the first questions of the
Summa Theologiae of Thomas Aquinas? The delayed official celebra-
tions of the centenary of Leo XIII's encyclical 'Aeterni Patris' are now
five years past.[1] This and subsequent papal declarations meant that,
for a considerable period only recently ended, more scholarly careers
and more effort were devoted to the teaching of St Thomas than to
any other philosophical and theological doctrine. Yet the quantity and
enthusiasm of the work is just the problem. Such a massive expendi-
ture was made only because the scholars, theologians, and philosophers had been able to identify the 'mind of St Thomas' with their own
urgent concerns and prevailing perspectives. One fears that the teaching of Thomas, who was invoked to bless every enterprise of philosophical theology which sought—and some which fled—official
ecclesiastical approbation in the Roman Church for nearly a century,
was somewhat manhandled and pushed out of shape in the process.[2]

[1] The encyclical is published in St Thomas Aquinas, *Opera Omnia* (Leonine), i
(Rome, 1882), pp. iii–xvi. There is an English translation in St Thomas Aquinas, *Summa
Theologica*, 22 vols., i (London, 1911), pp. ix–xxxiii. On the character, background, and
consequences of the encyclical, there are now the eight volumes of the proceedings of
the congress organized by the Pontificia Accademia di S. Tommasso: *Atti dell'VIII
Congresso Tomistico Internazionale*, ed. A. Piolanti, Studi tomistici 10–17 (Vatican City,
1981–2), in which my 'Pope Leo's Purposes and St Thomas' Platonism' appears, in vol.
viii (1982), pp. 39–52, and A. Piolanti, *Il tomismo filosofia cristiana nel pensiero di Leone XIII*.
Most of the papers at the Eighth Congress, like those at the earlier congresses, had
more to do with the politics of the Roman Church than with St Thomas—or indeed with
an objective appreciation of the encyclical. A critical piece is J. Hennessey, 'Leo XIII's
Thomistic Revival: A Political and Philosophic Event', *The Journal of Religion*, 58
Supplement (1978), S185–S197, which stresses Leo's 'fortress mentality'. Also useful
are: G. A. McCool, 'Twentieth-century Scholasticism', ibid., S198–S221; id., *Catholic
Theology in the Nineteenth Century* (New York, 1977); F. van Steenberghen, *Introduction à
l'étude de la philosophie médiévale*, Philosophes médiévaux 18 (Louvain/Paris, 1974),
pp. 54ff.; R. F. Harvanek, 'History and "Aeterni Patris"', *Notes et Documents, Institut
International 'J. Maritain'*, v, 16 (July–Sept., 1979), 1–12.

[2] To appreciate the massiveness of the neo-Thomist enterprise, one need only con-
sult the gigantic bibliography: *Bulletin thomiste*, i–xii (1924–65), rédaction et administra-
tion Le Saulchoir; continued as *Rassegna di letteratura tomistica, nuova serie del Bulletin
thomiste*, ed. Pontificia Università s. Tommaso d'Aquino (Rome), which began publication in 1969 (Naples) with the literature for 1966. The latest volume (xviii) treats the
literature for 1982. The proceedings of the various Thomistic congresses are indicative,
for example: *Atti del Congresso Internazionale Tommaso d'Aquino nel suo settimo centenario*, 9
vols. (Naples, 1975–8). Two articles therein are critical of how in carrying out Pope Leo

Now that official ardour has cooled, or at least become divided and less effective, may there not be, as Anthony Kenny has suggested, new opportunities for looking at Thomas more disinterestedly and with greater historical accuracy?

The aim of this book, to look at the structure of a section of Thomas's work in a historical view, may be given reason by other considerations. The preoccupation of the Thomist revival since the nineteenth century has been with ontology. Questions about structure were largely subordinate to the quest for a distinct doctrine of being. *Esse*, the absolutely simple act of being, was identified as the highest philosophical notion in Aquinas' system, providing his theology with its rational intelligibility.

The reaction against Thomism has partly been in order to replace ontology with henology, to substitute a science of the One for a science of being as the philosophical logic of theology. It happens that the same late Hellenistic philosophical and theological tradition which was most concerned to give absolute priority to the One is that which was most consumed by the problems of structuring theology. The study of these thinkers, awakened and immensely forwarded by E. R. Dodds's edition and translation of the *Elements of Theology* of Proclus in 1933,[3] has been the area of the prehistory of medieval scholasticism most advanced in the last decades. By attending to the Neoplatonic background of the structure of the initial questions of the *Summa Theologiae*—the ones most distorted by the abstraction of a philosophical ontology from the rest of his giant system—it is hoped to occupy territory less trampled than others, to restore somewhat the shape of a portion of the *Summa*, and to exploit current theological and philosophical interests as well as much present historical enterprise.

The progress of the studies set in motion by Professor Dodds was interrupted by the Second World War and it is only now that they have advanced far enough to yield much fruit for the interpretation of the history of medieval theology and philosophy. Stephen Gersh has applied their results to the earliest part in his *From Iamblichus to*

XIII's anti-modern purposes Thomist philosophy assumed the shape of the Cartesianism it attacked: see O. Blanchette, 'Philosophy and Theology in Aquinas: On Being a Disciple in our Day', ii (1976), pp. 427–31 and J. Owens, 'Value and Person in Aquinas', vii (1978), pp. 56–62. Acute on the subject is J. Pieper, *The Silence of St. Thomas: Three Essays*, trans. D. O'Connor (London, 1957), p. 54. See also my 'Pope Leo's Purposes' and 'Aquinas' First Principle: Being or Unity?', *Dionysius*, 4 (1980), 133–72.

[3] Oxford, 1933; 2nd edn., Oxford, 1963. All citations are from the second edition.

Eriugena,[4] but Thomas, whose relation to Neoplatonism is primarily through these later forms—he read none of the work of Plotinus—has hardly begun to be reconsidered in this reworking.

Two results of recent Neoplatonic scholarship are essential to the correction of the dominant anti-Platonic tendency of the Thomism of the Leonine revival.[5] First, there is the possibility of locating crucial features of the content of Thomas's system within the Neoplatonism which he inherited: Aquinas' doctrine of the soul—its structure, the relation of the physical world to its knowledge—the significance of his turn towards Aristotle, the relation of religious symbols and practices to philosophical intellection, and most importantly the origins of his teaching about being. Secondly, we are now better able to understand Thomas's interest in questions of structure and order, and to judge what genre he is adapting to his theological purposes. For these two results we are dependent on the scholarship of Pierre Hadot and of Henri Saffrey.

Professor Hadot has uncovered the character of Porphyry's modification of Plotinus and has indicated something of how his elevation of being toward the Neoplatonic One has been transmitted in the Latin theological and philosophical schools. Father Saffrey has taught us about another, perhaps more influential Neoplatonic tradition, that which originated in Iamblichus' reaction against the doctrine of his teacher Porphyry, and which was systematized by Proclus. Having

---

[4] S. Gersh, *From Iamblichus to Eriugena: An Investigation of the Prehistory and Evolution of the Pseudo-Dionysian Tradition*, Studien zur Problemgeschichte der antiken und mittelalterlichen Philosophie 8 (Leiden, 1978). His earlier work, *KINHΣIΣ 'AKINHTOΣ: A Study of Spiritual Motion in the Philosophy of Proclus* (Leiden, 1973), is essential for the historical background of the principles Aquinas uses to structure his *Summa Theologiae*.

[5] On the anti-Platonic tendency and the reasons for it, see my 'Pope Leo's Purposes' and 'Making Theology Practical: Thomas Aquinas and the Nineteenth Century Religious Revival', *Dionysius*, 9 (1985), 85–127. Leo XIII wanted a philosophical theology which could 'speak to an intellectual world in which science and philosophy had become independent and even opposed to ecclesiastical theology, and ... it should bring philosophy, and the political and social life thought to be based thereon, back within the control of and into subordination to ecclesiastical theology and authority.... On the other hand, the systematic and synthetic unity of Neoplatonism, taken together with the incompatibility of Platonic anti-empirical idealism with the nineteenth-century view of modern science, prevented both dialogue with natural science and the separation of science and philosophy and of natural and revealed theology' ('Pope Leo's Purposes', p. 42). Pierre Colin, 'Contexte philosophique de la restauration du thomisme en France à la fin du xixᵉ siècle', *Atti dell'VIII Congresso Tomistico Internazionale*, ed. A. Piolanti, ii, pp. 57–64, shows the similarity between what motivated the Thomistic revival in France and the neo-Kantianism of the period.

edited Thomas's commentary on the *Liber de Causis*, which is Proclan doctrine (and even contains propositions of Proclus' *Elements*) mediated through the Arabs, he has gone on to edit the *Platonic Theology* of Proclus (with the assistance of L. G. Westerink). We are indebted to him for showing the objective connections between the writings of pseudo-Dionysius the Areopagite and Proclus, for displaying the character of later Neoplatonic systematic anthropology and spirituality, and most recently for indicating the links between these and Proclus' establishment of theology as science.

The scholars of the Thomist revival have been correct to identify an ontology of *esse* in Aquinas. In the *Summa Theologiae*, as elsewhere, within the treatment of the divine simplicity, St Thomas denies the composition of essence and existence in God.[6] Rather the absolute simplicity of God requires that both be united in his *esse*. He does teach that from a certain perspective good is a higher name for God than being: 'In causation then the good precedes the existent as end precedes form; and, for this reason, in any list of names designating divine causality, good will precede existent.'[7] Moreover, Thomas knows the identification of the One and good in Platonism.[8] Yet,

---

[6] St Thomas Aquinas, *Summa Theologiae*, Commissio Piana, editio altera emendata (Ottawa, 1953), I, 3, 4, hereafter identified as *ST* (references without indication of title are to the *Summa Theologiae* in this edition); id., *De Ente et Essentia, Opera Omnia* (Leonine) xliii (Rome, 1976), cap. iv, pp. 375–7; id., *Quaestiones Disputatae de Potentia*, new edn., ed. P. M. Pession, *Quaestiones Disputatae*, 2 vols., ii (Turin/Rome, 1964), II, vii, 2, hereafter abbreviated *de Pot.* and without volume number; id., *Summa contra Gentiles, Opera Omnia* (Leonine) xiii–xv (Rome, 1918–30), I, 21–2, hereafter abbreviated *ScG*; id., *Compendium Theologiae, Opera Omnia* (Leonine) xlii (Rome, 1979), i, cap. ix, 'Quod Deus est simplex', cap. x, 'Quod Deus est sua essentia', cap. xi, 'Quod Dei essentia non est aliud quam suum esse', hereafter abbreviated *Comp. Theo.*; id., *De Substantiis Separatis, Opera Omnia* (Leonine) xl, *Pars* D–E (Rome, 1968), ix, p. D57, lines 104–7: 'Cum enim necesse sit primum principium simplicissimum esse, necesse est quod non hoc modo esse ponatur quasi esse participans, sed quasi ipsum esse existens'. This last work is indicated as *De Sub. Sep.*

[7] 'Et sic in causando bonum est prius quam ens, sicut finis quam forma; et hac ratione, inter nomina significantia causalitatem divinam, prius ponitur bonum quam ens', *ST* I, 5, 2 *ad* 1.

[8] Thomas recognizes that 'ipsum Unum et ipsum Bonum separatum' is the 'summum et primum rerum Principium' for the Platonists; see his *Super librum de Causis Expositio*, ed. H.-D. Saffrey, Textus Philosophici Friburgensis 4/5 (Fribourg/Louvain, 1954)—which we abbreviate as *In de Caus.*—prop. 3 and prop. 4, and treats them as identical in accord with Proclus, prop. 13 of the *Elements* (cf. also Dodds's comment, pp. 199–200). But he does not seem to know the doctrine of *Plat. Theo.* II, 6, that the First is One, as principle of procession, and Good, as principle of reversion. For at *In de Div. Nom.* = *In librum Beati Dionysii de Divinis Nominibus Expositio*, ed. C. Pera (Turin/Rome, 1950)—XIII, iii, 989 and elsewhere, agreeing with Dionysius, he treats the One as cause of return: 'divina Unitas est virtuosior omni unitate, omnia relinquentes in ipsam

actuality is a higher perspective than causation, and so later in the *Summa*, when Aquinas reflects on the knowledge of the divine substance attained in his *de divinis nominibus* of questions 3 to 11, and lays down the rules for applying names to God, he determines that *esse* is the highest of them: 'this name, *Qui est* . . . is the most proper name of God'.[9] This is the teaching from which a philosophy has been extracted in the last century.

However, the newly uncovered facts relating to the source and transmission of Thomas's ontology of *esse* overthrow the Thomist representation of the significance of his teaching.[10] It is of revolutionary import that the anti-Christian Neoplatonist Porphyry, uniting the One and the first intelligible triad, identified the One and εἶναι.[11] It is also significant that he is the source of this doctrine in the Christians Victorinus, Augustine,[12] and Boethius,[13] and that thus it was held well before Thomas. Indeed Thomas is only one in the long line of interpreters of the crucial early texts in Boethius which convey it to the

convertimur . . . finis enim et terminus ad rationem unius pertinere videntur'. The good is treated in a similar way, e.g. ibid. I, iii, 94. One and good are also thought of equally as belonging to God's character as source.

[9] 'hoc nomen Qui est . . . est maxime proprium nomen Dei', *ST* I, 13, 11. On the priority of activity cf. *In de Div. Nom.* v, i, 634 ff. and *In de Caus.*, prop. 18 and also props. 3 and 12.

[10] Étienne Gilson puts the Thomist position strongly and clearly in all his many works on Thomas. *Being and Some Philosophers*, 2nd edn. (Toronto, 1952) is written for a wide audience; *Les Tribulations de Sophie* (Paris, 1967), was originally written for *Seminarium*, a journal for Roman seminaries, and provides an account of the degree to which the ontology of *esse* was accepted as Thomas's teaching. My 'Aquinas' First Principle', 'Pope Leo's Purposes', and 'Making Theology Practical', argue that it is the common doctrine of various contemporary Thomist schools—realist, transcendental, and those in the middle.

[11] See P. Hadot, 'Dieu comme acte d'être dans le néoplatonisme. A propos des théories d'É. Gilson sur la métaphysique de l'Exode', *Dieu et l'être: exégèses d'Exode 3, 14, et de Coran 20, 11–24*, ed. Centre d'études des religions du livre, CNRS, Études augustiniennes (Paris, 1978), pp. 57–63; see the 'présentation' by P. Vignaux in *Dieu et l'être*; and also P. Hadot, 'L'être et l'étant dans le néoplatonisme', *Études néoplatoniciennes*, ed. J. Trouillard *et al.* (Neuchâtel, 1973), pp. 27–39.

[12] For endeavours to show that Thomas and Augustine share a similar doctrine of God's *esse*, cf. É. zum Brunn, 'L'exègese augustinienne de "Ego sum qui sum" et la "métaphysique de l'Exode"' and 'La "métaphysique de l'Exode" selon Thomas d'Aquin' in *Dieu et l'être*, pp. 141–64, 245–69, and J. F. Anderson, *St. Augustine and Being* (The Hague, 1965). On his relation to Porphyry, cf. P. Hadot, *Porphyre et Victorinus*, Études augustiniennes, 2 vols. (Paris, 1968), i, pp. 24 ff. and É. zum Brunn, 'La dialectique du "magis esse" et du "minus esse" chez saint Augustin', *Le Néoplatonisme*, Colloques internationaux du CNRS, Royaumont, 1969 (Paris, 1971), pp. 373–80.

[13] P. Hadot, *Porphyre et Victorinus*, i, pp. 490 ff. and 'La distinction de l'être et de l'étant dans le *De Hebdomadibus* de Boèce', *Die Metaphysik im Mittelalter*, 2 vols, ed. P. Wilpert, Miscellanea Mediaevalia 13 (Berlin, 1963), ii, pp. 147–53.

Middle Ages.[14] Finally, it is important that it is Porphyry, not a common scriptural revelation, that stands behind the similar teaching in Arab Neoplatonists like Avicenna.[15] Avicenna and Thomas both maintained that God was the simple act of being and that, in contrast, existence and essence were distinct in creatures.[16] Indeed Avicenna may be one of Thomas's sources of the Porphyrian tradition. If these considerations destroy the notions that Thomas's ontology, his philosophy of *esse*, is unique, or Christian, or a 'metaphysic of Exodus', or reflects the Aristotelian rather than the Platonist side of his thought, the historical investigations used to establish these judgements are not therefore useless. What served to distinguish Thomas from Aristotle in this regard—Thomas was thought to have been able to grasp the import of Exod. 3: 14 because of the Aristotelian direction of his thought, though his 'existential' philosophy of being was contrasted with Aristotle's 'essentialism'[17]—in fact rather serves to distinguish his position as Neoplatonic as opposed to Aristotelian. Indeed, the characteristics meant to place Thomas and Avicenna together in the tradition of Exodus rather serve to identify their common filiation from Porphyry.[18]

---

[14] P. Hadot, '"*Forma Essendi*"; interprétation philologique et interprétation philosophique d'une formule de Boèce', *Les Études classiques* 38 (1970), 143–56.

[15] See P. Thillet, 'Indices porphyriens dans la théologie d'Aristote' and S. Pines, 'Les textes arabes dit plotiniens et le courant "porphyrien" dans le néoplatonisme grec' in *Le Néoplatonisme*, pp. 293–302, 303–13.

[16] On the Arabic teaching, cf. A. Rachid, 'Dieu et l'être selon Al-Farabi: le chapitre de "l'être" dans le Livre des Lettres', *Dieu et l'être*, pp. 186 ff. For a list of similarities and differences between the teaching of Thomas and Avicenna (according to Thomas), cf. G. C. Anawati, 'Saint Thomas d'Aquin et la *Métaphysique* d'Avicenne', *St. Thomas Aquinas, 1274–1974: Commemorative Studies*, ed. A. A. Maurer, 2 vols. (Toronto, 1974), i, pp. 458–9, and M. L. Colish, 'Avicenna's Theory of Efficient Causation and its Influence on St. Thomas Aquinas', *Atti del Congresso Internazionale Tommaso d'Aquino nel suo settimo centenario*, 9 vols. i (Naples, 1975), p. 297, n. 3.

[17] É. Gilson, *History of Christian Philosophy in the Middle Ages* (London, 1955), p. 365 and elsewhere. This is a very common theme for contemporary Thomists. A most useful piece of scholarship to emerge from this enterprise is J. Owens, *The Doctrine of Being in the Aristotelian Metaphysics* (Toronto, 1951)—but see criticism by J. D. Beach, 'Separate Entity as the Subject of Aristotle's *Metaphysics*', *The Thomist*, 20 (1957), 75–95 and by L. Elders, 'Le Commentaire sur le quatrième livre de la *Métaphysique*', *Atti del Congresso Internazionale Tommaso d'Aquino nel suo settimo centenario*, i (Naples, 1975), pp. 203–14.

[18] See those listed by É. Gilson in '*Quasi Definitio Substantiae*', *Commemorative Studies*, ed. A. A. Maurer, i, pp. 125–6. Some recent studies of Thomas do take account of the Neoplatonic origins of his doctrine of being: M. D. Jordan, 'The Grammar of *Esse*', *The Thomist*, 44 (1980), 1–26; Klaus Kremer, *Die neuplatonische Seinsphilosophie und ihre Wirkung auf Thomas von Aquin*, Studien zur Problemgeschichte der antiken and mittelalterlichen Philosophie 1 (Leiden, 1966); F. van Steenberghen, *Introduction à l'étude de la philosophie médiévale*, pp. 100–1; F. J. Ruello, 'La mystique de l'Exode', *Dieu et l'être*,

At least as important as the philosophical ideas Aquinas derives from Neoplatonism are its formalism and the theological literary genre it created. The movement toward a systematizing of the diverse dialogues and separate treatises of Plato and Aristotle respectively pre-dates Neoplatonism.[19] But the complete encompassing of the whole circuit of reality within theology, together with its explicit, formal ordering into one system, is specifically the work of Proclus.[20] Iamblichus arranged Plato's dialogues into a systematic schema, a project which came to masterful fruition in Proclus' *Platonic Theology*, but Proclus' *Elements of Theology* is an explicit formal system of reality beginning from the One and ending, in the last of its 211 propositions, with the soul altogether descended into the temporal world.[21]

pp. 213–43; C. Fabro, *Participation et causalité selon s. Thomas d'Aquin*, Chaire card. Mercier 2 (Louvain/Paris, 1961). Pierre Aubenque, 'Les origines néoplatoniciennes de la doctrine de l'analogie de l'être', *Néoplatonisme: mélanges offerts à Jean Trouillard*, Les Cahiers de Fontenay 19–22 (Fontenay-aux-Roses, 1981), p. 66, maintains that Gilson's Thomist Christian existentialism is overthrown by Pierre Hadot's researches.

[19] On Aristotle, cf. L. Minio-Paluello, 'La tradition aristotélicienne dans l'histoire des idées', *Actes du Congrès de Lyon 1958, Association Guillaume Budé* (Paris, 1960), pp. 166–85. On Plato, see R. T. Wallis, *Neoplatonism* (London, 1972), pp. 136ff. On the differences between Classical and Hellenistic structures in philosophy, there is P. Hadot, 'Les divisions des parties de la philosophie dans l'Antiquité', *Museum Helveticum*, 36 (1979), 201–23. His 'Exercices spirituels antiques et "philosophie chrétienne"', in his collected articles *Exercices spirituels et philosophie antique*, Études augustiniennes (Paris, 1981), pp. 59–74, relates the parts of philosophy among the Platonists to the stages of the spiritual life: 'L'éthique correspond à une première purification, la physique correspond au détachement définitif du sensible et à la contemplation de l'ordre des choses; la théologie correspond enfin à la contemplation du principe de toutes choses' (p. 71).

[20] There are several dimensions to the Proclan synthesis. On the religious impulse and its relation to the scientific aspect, see H.-D. Saffrey, 'Quelques aspects de la spiritualité des philosophes néoplatoniciens, de Jamblique à Proclus et Damascius', *Rev. sc. ph. th.* 68 (1984), 169–82. On reconciling the philosophical traditions as well as the dialogues of Plato, cf. Dodds, *Elements*, p. xviii, Saffrey, 'La *Théologie platonicienne* de Proclus, fruit de l'exégèse du *Parménide*', *Revue de théologie et de philosophie*, 116 (1984), 1–12, and his introduction to his edition of *The Platonic Theology*. Jean Trouillard, 'Les fondements du mythe selon Proclos', *Le Mythe et le symbole de la connaissance figurative de Dieu*, ed. S. Breton *et al.*, Philosophie 2 (Paris, 1977), pp. 11–37 and Saffrey, 'L'Hymne IV de Proclus, prière aux dieux des Oracles chaldaïques', *Néoplatonisme: mélanges offerts à Jean Trouillard*, pp. 297–312, add the mythical element.

[21] See Introduction to Proclus, *Théologie platonicienne*, ed. H.-D. Saffrey et L. G. Westerink, Collection des Universités de France, 4 vols. of 6, i (Paris, 1969), pp. lx–lxxv. J. M. P. Lowry, *The Logical Principles of Proclus' ΣΤΟΙΧΕΙΩΣΙΣ ΘΕΟΛΟΓΙΚΗ as Systematic Ground of the Cosmos*, Elementa, Schriften zur Philosophie und ihrer Problemgeschichte 13 (Amsterdam, 1980), is an attempt to exhibit the inclusiveness of Proclus' system, to demonstrate its originality and to defend his project. A. Charles-Saget, *L'Architecture du divin: mathématique et philosophie chez Plotin et Proclus*, Collection d'études anciennes (Paris, 1982), considers the problems of unifying mathematical form

His system has a form appropriate to its content. It is a view of a spiritual world with its elements and levels carefully separated and subordinated, encompassing everything from spirit utterly transcendent and unmoved to a form which must turn toward sensible matter to perfect its life, and the whole requiring a powerful divine motion running downward and back to draw its dispersed parts in return toward the unity from which they had come out. Plotinus shows no interest in such a formal system. His treatises begin very obviously from individual questions and even current problems and Porphyry is unable to unite form and content in schematizing Plotinus' works. It is Proclus' invention which the medieval *summae* recreate.

Thomas follows Iamblichus' school in the doctrines belonging to this literary development and he is imbued with its formalizing and systematizing spirit. In his Aristotelian and other commentaries, he not only looks at the content through Neoplatonic spectacles, but, indifferent to its own form, he divides and restructures it into a systematic chain of arguments. The greatest fruit of this spirit in him is his *Summa Theologiae*.[22] It is, like the *Elements* of Proclus, an explicit, consistently formalized system containing the complete circuit of reality. It begins by justifying itself because of the formal inadequacies of the available writings on the subject. It proceeds to show how what belongs to its object, God, in himself and as principle and end of all things, can be unified under one formal consideration, the *revelabilia*, in order to produce a science. The whole immense content is divided into components organized in a single form, the *quaestio*, itself a product of the endeavour both to understand and to remain faithful to the conflicting authorities which also characterizes our Neoplatonists

and philosophical content, of reconciling the requirements of system with tradition and authority, and of maintaining the continuity of the discursive within the apophatic framework of Neoplatonic divinity.

[22] In ch. I, I attempt to show why the structure of theology determined by the *Sentences* of Peter Lombard was unsatisfactory to Aquinas and thus why the *Commentary on the Sentences* could not be his final system. Difficulties about the *Summa contra Gentiles* because of its apologetic stance are also discussed. His remaining extant system (incomplete) is the *Compendium Theologiae*. But its structure is determined by the needs of piety. The *Compendium* shows its intention for piety not only by its organization around the virtues of faith, hope, charity but also because it is meant for Frater Reginald 'semper pre oculis . . . habere'. It imitates Christ, who compresses the divine immensity 'nostra brevitate assumpta', 'propter occupatos sub brevi summa humane salutis doctrinam conclusit' (I, cap. i, p. 83). Thus the Lord's Prayer and the Apostles' Creed are important to its structure as Thomas indicates and as his editors agree: *Compendium Theologiae* I, cap. i and introduction, pp. 6–7.

after Plotinus.[23] The *Summa Theologiae* embraces every level of reality from God to prime matter, what is given to man in creation, what he does in his freedom, and what completes his freedom in grace. It includes time and eternity and time's beginning and end.

All of this is not to deny that much stands between Proclus' *Elements of Theology* and Thomas's *Summa Theologiae*, and the differences will be prominent at many particular points. In any case the *Elements* could not have been the direct inspiration of the *Pars Prima* of the *Summa*, which is what we shall mainly consider. But there are connections via the pseudo-Dionysius. Thomas had a direct knowledge of Dionysius and there is also the important influence of the *De Divisione Naturae* and the *De Fide Orthodoxa* of Dionysius' followers Eriugena and John of Damascus on the formation of the *summa* as a theological literary genre for the High Middle Ages.[24]

Proclus, mediated by Dionysius, also provides Thomas with a second genre, that for treating God in himself in the *Summa Theologiae*. For the treatise may be regarded as a *de divinis nominibus*.[25] This form was Christianized by Dionysius, but the very first tract *de divinis nominibus* is contained in the *Platonic Theology* of Proclus, which Dionysius was imitating and transforming.[26] The originality of Proclus has been discovered by the editors of the *Platonic Theology*. What they call a 'traité des attributs divins' is an exposé uncovering, enumerating, and organizing the essential divine characteristics.[27] Such a treatise is not to be found among either the classical or Neoplatonic predecessors of Proclus.

A comparison of the treatises is too large a task to be undertaken here but a few points may be noted. For the three thinkers, the

---

[23] For the pagan Neoplatonists, cf. A. H. Armstrong, 'Tradition, Reason and Experience in the Thought of Plotinus', *Atti del Convegno internazionale sul tema Plotino e il Neoplatonismo in Oriente e in Occidente, Roma, 1970* (Rome, 1974) = *Plotinian and Christian Studies*, xvii; id., 'Pagan and Christian Traditionalism in the First Three Centuries A.D.', *Studia Patristica* xv, ed. E. A. Livingstone, Texte und Untersuchungen 128 (Berlin, 1984), pp. 414–31; and id., 'Philosophy, Theology and Interpretation: the Interpretation of Interpreters', *Eriugena: Studien zu seinen Quellen: Vorträge des III. internationalen Eriugena-Colloquiums, Freiburg im Breisgau, 27.–30. August 1979*, ed. W. Beierwaltes, Abhandlungen der Heidelberger Akademie der Wissenschaften 1980, 3 (Heidelberg, 1980), pp. 7–14. Also there are H.-D. Saffrey, 'Quelques aspects de la spiritualité' and 'La *Théologie platonicienne* de Proclus'.

[24] See chs. I and II below.

[25] T. C. O'Brien in St Thomas Aquinas, *Summa Theologiae*, 60 vols., vii (Blackfriars, 1976), pp. xxiff.

[26] Saffrey and Westerink, *Plat. Theo.* i, pp. lxiii, cxci–cxcii.

[27] Ibid., p. cxc.

discovery of the names involves a dependence on authority. Proclus derives his from Plato's dialogues.[28] Dionysius will not presume to speak or conceive of the Godhead anything which is not revealed in Holy Scriptures.[29] The relation of Thomas's argument at different stages to various kinds of authority—scriptural, ecclesiastical, philosophic—is complex. In principle, the Trinitarian names are known only through scriptural revelation. In fact, his use of the *quaestio* involves the citation of both scriptural and other authority throughout the *de deo* of the *Summa Theologiae*.[30] However, the form Proclus uses to relate his treatise to its sources means that he is more limited in arranging it logically than these successors. For 'the attributes are classed according to the Platonic dialogues in which they appear'.[31] No comparable principle confines Dionysius or Thomas.

Aquinas exposes with great acuity the principles organizing Dionysius' treatise. He perceives that Dionysius begins with 'good' as a name[32] and employs an *exitus–reditus* structure in drawing the exposition back to its source by means of the names 'perfect' and 'one'.[33] Thomas knows the Proclan conception by which these names, 'good' and 'one', are identified. He notes that the author moves from the more to the less generic in relating the names.[34] He calls these

---

[28] Saffrey and Westerink, *Plat. Theo.* i, pp. lxii–lxiii, clxxxviii.

[29] καθόλου τοιγαροῦν οὐ τολμητέον εἰπεῖν οὔτε μὴν ἐννοῆσαί τι περὶ τῆς ὑπερουσίου καὶ κρυφίας θεότητος παρὰ τὰ θειωδῶς ἡμῖν ἐκ τῶν ἱερῶν λογίων ἐκπεφασμένα, *De Div. Nom.* i, 1 (PG 3, 585A).

[30] The corpus of Thomas's treatment of our natural knowledge of the divine persons (*ST* I, 32, 1) begins 'Dicendum quod impossibile est per rationem naturalem ad cognitionem Trinitatis divinarum Personarum pervenire', and ends by quoting Dionysius. On reason and revelation in Thomas's consideration of the Trinity in the *Summa Theologiae*, cf. R. L. Richards, *The Problem of an Apologetical Perspective in the Trinitarian Theology of St. Thomas Aquinas*, Analecta Gregoriana 131 (Rome, 1963), and ch. VII below.

[31] *Plat. Theo.* i, p. lxii.

[32] 'in hoc libro intendit exponere divina Nomina quibus manifestantur processiones Dei in creaturas. Principium autem commune omnium harum processionum bonum est. . . . Et ideo primo, agit in hoc 4° de Bono', *In de Div. Nom.* IV, i, 261. On the principles of order in Dionysius, cf. E. Corsini, *Il trattato de Divinis Nominibus dello Pseudo-Dionigi e i commenti neoplatonici al Parmenide* (Turin, 1962). Unity has also the nature of principle, cf. *In de Div. Nom.*, II, ii, 135: 'cum omnis multitudo rerum a Principio primo effluant, primum Principium, secundum quod in se consideratur, unum est'; ibid., 143, 'unum habet rationem principii'; also XIII, ii, 135, and text cited.

[33] See n. 8 above; because things return to their source, the last names are perfect and one. 'Sed circa ordinem rerum in finem, duo sunt consideranda, scilicet providentia gubernantis et ordinantis in finem . . . et ipse finis ad quem res per providentiam et gubernationem perveniunt et hoc pertinet ad 13° capitulum, in quo agitur de perfecto et uno', *In de Div. Nom.* IV, i, 265.

[34] Speaking of the name 'wisdom', which follows 'goodness', 'being', and 'life': 'Est

Platonic principles and in fact they are generally used also by Proclus. Thomas employs them in forming his own treatise, though not exclusively, and its structure has important differences from those of either Proclus or Dionysius, despite a fundamental formal continuity.

As if leaping over the intermediary, Thomas begins like Proclus—as opposed to Dionysius—by establishing the existence of his divine subject, and in fact, for both, the first argument is from motion.[35] (Our editors mistakenly state: 'tout traité des attributs divins commence toujours par une ou plusieurs démonstrations de l'existence de dieu'.)[36] But there is a great difference between this aspect of Proclus' treatise and subsequent Christian ones. Proclus demonstrates τὸ εἶναι τοὺς θεούς,[37] which is sharply contrasted with the ὕπαρξις of the One.[38] If they were identified, he would be following Porphyry not Iamblichus. The Christians and Arabs cannot make this distinction. One alternative is to avoid speaking of God as existing in himself. For Dionysius[39] and Eriugena,[40] God's existence is not in himself but in

autum considerandum quod semper in posterioribus priora salvantur. Bonum autem, secundum quod prius dictum est, quantum ad causalitatem est prius quam ens, quia bonum etiam ad non entia suam causalitatem extendit, ens autem ad plura se extendit quam vita et vita quam sapientia, quia quaedam sunt quae non vivunt et quaedam vivunt quae non cognoscunt', *In de Div. Nom.* VII, i, 697; cf. also IV, i, 263; V, i, 606–11, etc. An extended discussion of his attitude to this Platonic teaching is found in *In de Caus.*, prop. 12.

[35] *ST* I, 2, 3 and *Plat. Theo.* i, 14ff.

[36] *Plat. Theo.* i, p. cxc.

[37] *Plat. Theo.* i, 13 (i, p. 59, lines 18–19).

[38] *Plat. Theo.* ii, 2 (especially ii, 22–3) and ii, 4 (ii, p. 31, lines 7–8 and 15–16). 'Existence in the specific sense of ὕπαρξις must inevitably be prior to activity' (p. 101). It is 'a general term for "existence (entity)" at various levels of reality, ... it is therefore applied right up to the One', S. E. Gersh, *ΚΙΝΗΣΙΣ*, pp. 32–3. On the history of ὕπαρξις, cf. P. Hadot, *Porphyre et Victorinus*, pp. 489–90: 'L'originalité de la doctrine ontologique de Porphyre, c'est identifier l'ὕπαρξις avec l'εἶναι μόνον ...' (p. 490).

[39] μᾶλλον δὲ οὔτε ἐστίν, ἀλλ' αὐτός ἐστι τὸ εἶναι τοῖς οὖσι (*De Div. Nom.* V, 4; PG3, 817D). Cf. also *De Div. Nom.* 955Dff., Gersh, *From Iamblichus*, pp. 153ff. (esp. p. 153, n. 131), and J. D. Jones, 'The Ontological Difference for St Thomas and Pseudo-Dionysius', *Dionysius*, 4 (1980), 119–32. Unfortunately in this latter article there is little relation between Jones's quotations from Thomas's *Expositio* and its text; none the less his report of the doctrine is correct. C. Andresen, 'The Integration of Platonism into Early Christian Theology', *Studia Patristica* XV, ed. E. A. Livingstone, Texte und Untersuchungen 128 (Berlin, 1984), pp. 399–413, provides a good account of the recent scholarship on how pagan hypotheses become Christian names for Dionysius.

[40] 'Non est igitur οὐσία, quia plus est quam οὐσία; et tamen dicitur οὐσία, quia omnium οὐσιῶν, id est essentiarum, creatrix est', *De Div. Nat.* i, 15 (PL 122, 464B), ed. I. P. Sheldon-Williams with L. Bieler, *Periphyseon, de divisione naturae*, Script. lat. Hiberniae 7, 9, 11 (Dublin, 1968–81), i, p. 86, lines 29–31. Cf. also *De Div. Nat.* i, 3 (443A–443B), p. 38, lines 19–25 where Eriugena cites Dionysius as an authority. W. Beierwaltes, '*Negati Affirmatio*, or the World as Metaphor: A Foundation for Medieval

his effects. This is the strongly negative sense of naming through effects. Though, for Thomas, naming God from effects is necessary because we do not see his essence directly in this life, none the less the names taken from creatures are properly and affirmatively predicated of God.

The two major divisions of Thomas's treatise *de deo* (*qq.* 2–43) originate in the Dionysian mediation of Proclan Neoplatonism. The first is the distinction of the *de deo uno* (*qq.* 3–26) from the *de deo trino* (*qq.* 27–43). This has its origin in Dionysius' division of treatises on the divine names between one on the names belonging to the unity of the Trinity and another on those names proper to the persons considered severally.[41] Thomas's second division is that of the *de deo uno* between a consideration of God's substance (*qq.* 3–11) and of his operations (*qq.* 14–27). This derives from a Neopolatonic form of Aristotle's distinction between the first and second acts of the soul which St Thomas first finds in Dionysius and later identifies as Proclan.[42] So it seems that both the theological literary genres employed by Aquinas, and elements of the structure he gives them, originate in one of the streams of late Greek Neoplatonism.

Our brief and condensed report on a few of the results of recent Neoplatonic scholarship indicates how much it illuminates the back-

Aesthetics from the Writings of John Scotus Eriugena', *Dionysius*, 1 (1977), 133–4, and John Macquarrie, *In Search of Deity: An Essay in Dialectical Theism* (London, 1984), ch. 7, provide accounts of the doctrine.

[41] See *De Div. Nom.* ii, 2 (PG 3, 640A) and *De Mystica Theologica*, iii (PG 3, 1032D–1033a), and Thomas's comments at *In de Div. Nom.* II, i, 108; II, i, 126; II, ii, 153. V. Lossky, 'Apophasis and Trinitarian Theology', *In the Image and Likeness of God*, ed. J. H. Erikson and T. E. Bird (St Vladimir's Seminary, 1974), p. 26, supposes that Dionysius never wrote the second treatise, but C. Andresen, 'The Integration of Platonism', pp. 404–5, supposes it was suppressed by those Christians seeking to assimilate his teaching to orthodoxy. On Thomas and Dionysius regarding the divisions of theology, see my 'The *De Trinitate* of St. Boethius and the Structure of the *Summa Theologiae* of St. Thomas Aquinas', *Atti del Congresso Internazionale di Studi Boeziani*, ed. L. Obertello (Rome, 1981), pp. 367–75.

[42] Aristotle, *De Anima* ii, 1, 412ª 22–3 distinguishes two forms of activity. For Thomas's use of this distinction in a form 'inconnue d'Aristote, . . . élaborée à l'aide de Denys: la perfection seconde, ou ultime, toujours mise en parallèle avec la perfection première ou nature (ou essence)', see É. H. Wéber, *Dialogue et dissensions entre saint Bonaventure et saint Thomas d'Aquin à Paris (1253–1273)*, Bibliothèque thomiste 41 (Paris, 1974), pp. 463–5. When announcing how he will structure a section of the *Summa*, Thomas observes: 'secundum Dionysium, xi cap. *De Angel. Hier.* tria inveniuntur in substantiis spiritualibus, scilicet essentia, virtus et operatio', *ST* I, 75, *prol.* In *De Sub. Sep.*, cap. xx, p. D79, lines 307–9, Thomas recognizes this doctrine as Proclan: 'Unde et Proclus dicit quod "omnis intellectus in aeternitate substantiam habet, et potentiam et operationem".' Cf. also *In de Caus.*, prop. 2, p. 14, line 25, p. 15, line 1. The source is *Elements*, prop. 169.

ground of Thomas's greatest systematic work. It also points to the important relation between his proof for God's existence and his subsequent argument. Thus it somewhat justifies the disproportionate dimensions of our consideration of a single question, 'de Deo an sit', in what follows.

Partly as a result of the impact of these historical studies and the possibilities for philosophy and theology which they recall, but partly also in response to their perception of the contemporary necessities of thought, some Catholic theologians have endeavoured to revive and develop a Christian Neoplatonism. What attracts them to this ancient tradition and what primarily characterizes it for them is its being a negative theology. The person who has developed the historical, systematic, and contemporary aspects of this Plotinian and post-Plotinian Neoplatonism most completely is the Frenchman Jean Trouillard.[43] But just as the greatest historians, philosophers, and theologians in the service of the Thomist ontology were French—men like É. Gilson, J. Maritain, M.-D. Chenu—so Father Trouillard is surrounded in France by a constellation of historians[44]—Édouard des Places, A. M. J. Festugière, H.-D. Saffrey, P. Hadot—and philosophers and theologians like H. Duméry,[45] S. Breton,[46] J.-L. Marion,

---

[43] A bibliography of Father Jean Trouillard, PSS, is to be found in *Néoplatonisme: mélanges offerts à Jean Trouillard*, Les Cahiers de Fontenay, 19–22 (Fontenay-aux-Roses, 1981). Since then his *La Mystagogie de Proclus*, Collection d'études anciennes (Paris, 1982), has appeared. A partial bibliography and consideration of the significance of his early work can be found in A. Charles, 'La raison et le divin chez Proclus', *Rev. sc. ph. th.* 53 (1969), 458–82. A. H. Armstrong's piece in the Trouillard festschrift includes a short appreciation of his influence.

[44] The festschrift for Father Édouard des Places, SJ, contains a bibliography: cf. *Études platoniciennes, 1929–1979*, Études préliminaires aux religions orientales dans l'empire romain 90 (Leiden, 1981). Since then we have his 'Les Oracles chaldaïques et Denys l'Aréopagite', *Néoplatonisme: mélanges offerts à Jean Trouillard*, pp. 291–5, and 'La théologie négative de Pseudo-Denys, ses antécédents platoniciens et son influence au seuil du Moyen-Âge', *Studia Patristica*, xvii(1), ed. E. A. Livingstone (Oxford, 1982), pp. 81–92. For our purpose his great use is on the connections between the use of myth as scripture by the pagan Neoplatonists and the authority of Scripture for Dionysius and his followers. Father A. M. J. Festugière has edited *La Révélation d'Hermès Trismégiste* and the commentaries of Proclus on the *Timaeus* and the *Republic*. A bibliography will be found in *Memorial A. J. Festugière*, ed. H.-D. Saffrey, Cahiers d'Orientalisme 10 (Geneva, 1984).

[45] Of special interest for our purposes are Henri Duméry, 'Le néant d'être', *Les Études philosophiques* (July–Sept. 1973), pp. 315–27 and 'L'Être et l'Un', *Miscellanea Albert Dondeyne*, Bibliotheca Ephemeridum Theologicarum Lovaniensium 35 (Louvain, 1974), pp. 313–50. Cf. Y. Labbé, 'Le problème de Dieu dans la philosophie de la religion de H. Duméry', *Rev. sc. ph. th.* 55 (1971), 393–431.

[46] Stanislas Breton was editor with other members of L'Association des Professeurs de Philosophie des Facultés Catholiques de France of an important seven-volume series, 'Recherches de philosophie', published between 1962 and 1971 by Les Éditions

G. Lafont, and P. Aubenque.[47] Together they represent a considerable force in current French Catholic intellectual life. Among the Germans and the English the most devoted advocates of the reconsideration of Neoplatonism for the purposes of Christian thinking are W. Beierwaltes,[48] A. H. Armstrong,[49] and Stephen Gersh. However, two recent books by Anglican theologians must also be mentioned: A. Louth, *The Origins of the Christian Mystical Tradition: From Plato to Denys* (Oxford, 1981) and John Macquarrie, *In Search of Deity: An Essay in Dialectical Theism* (London, 1984). The second of these is especially significant as it is part of the author's Heideggerian critique of Western ontological theism and even, within this perspective, specifi-

du Cerf. His article in vol. vi, *Saint Thomas d'Aquin aujourd'hui*, 'L'idée de transcendental et la genèse des transcendentaux chez saint Thomas d'Aquin' (pp. 45–74), anticipates M. D. Jordan's article cited above (n. 18). His 'Le théorème de l'Un dans les *Éléments de Théologie* de Proclus', *Rev. sc. ph. th.* 58 (1974), 561–83, and 'Actualité du néoplatonisme' in *Études néoplatoniciennes*, ed. J. Trouillard (Neuchâtel, 1973), pp. 110–26, are arguments for the contemporary soundness of characteristic Neoplatonic positions. His *Être, monde, imaginaire* (Paris, 1976) is Heideggerian. Cf. Y. Labbé, 'Logique, métaphysique et théologie, deux ouvrages de Stanislas Breton', *Rev. sc. ph. th.* 56 (1972), 252–64.

[47] Jean-Luc Marion conducts a critique of Thomas as a metaphysical ontologist adopting a completely Heideggerian standpoint. For him a theology of being must be replaced by one of love. See his *Dieu sans l'être: hors-texte*, Communio (Paris, 1982) and 'La vanité d'être et le nom de Dieu', *Analogie et dialectique: essais de théologie fondamentale*, ed. P. Gisel et Ph. Secretan, Lieux théologiques 3 (Geneva, 1982), pp. 17–49. There is a critical response: René Virgoulay, 'Dieu ou l'être? Relecture de Heidegger en marge de J.-L. Marion, *Dieu sans l'être*', *Recherches de science religieuse*, 72, 2 (1984), 163–98. Ghislain Lafont, 'Le *Parménide* de Platon et saint Thomas d'Aquin: l'analogie des noms divins et son arrière-plan néoplatonicien', *Analogie et dialectique*, pp. 53–80, is a good piece of synthetic scholarship and is, like his 'Écouter Heidegger en théologien', *Rev. sc. ph. th.* 67 (1983), 371–98, moderate, endeavouring to find places in theology both for ontology and the critique of metaphysics. Father G. Lafont, OSB, praises Pierre Aubenque's 'Plotin et le dépassement de l'ontologie grecque classique', *Le Néoplatonisme*, Colloques internationaux du CNRS, Royaumont, 1969 (Paris, 1971), pp. 101–8. The list of philosophical theologians here provided is by no means complete.

[48] See W. Beierwaltes, *Proclus: Grundzüge seiner Metaphysik* (Frankfurt am Main, 1965) and *Identität und Differenz* (Frankfurt am Main, 1980). His 'Image and Counterimage: Reflections on Neoplatonic Thought with Respect to its Place Today', *Neoplatonism and Early Christian Thought: Essays in Honour of A. H. Armstrong*, ed. H. J. Blumenthal and R. A. Markus (London, 1981), pp. 236–48 has substantial sections on both Heidegger and Hegel.

[49] The movement in Professor Armstrong's relation to the official theology of the Roman Catholic Church is evident in the various editions of *Introduction to Ancient Philosophy* and in the articles collected in *Plotinian and Christian Studies*, Variorum Reprints Collected Studies 103 (London, 1979). The position at which he has arrived is strongly presented in his piece for the Trouillard festschrift and in 'Some Advantages of Polytheism', *Dionysius*, 5 (1981), 181–8 and in his Editorial Comment which begins the *Dionysius* volume. His festschrift, *Neoplatonism and Early Christian Thought*, indicates his influence.

cally of St Thomas. That something of the same may be moving Andrew
Louth is suggested by the importance of H. G. Gadamer for him.[50] It is
significant for the history of Thomism that some of the Roman Catho-
lics listed, such as Fathers Trouillard and Breton and Professor Armstrong, are clearly reacting against Thomism. Thus, Professors
Trouillard, Breton, and Marion, among others, are endeavouring to
construct a henology to replace its ontological metaphysics.

Of the various 'essentialisms' opposed to the ontology of *esse*,
henology appeared to Thomists to be the most dangerous. It involved
for them all the pantheistic and other errors of pagan Neoplatonism
and its modern idealist counterparts. It is an extraordinary reversal,
then, to find that immediately with the decline of the official ontological Thomism there is an assertion of henology as a basis for Catholic
theology. But more ironic yet, part of the appeal of henology is that it,
not Thomism, is now conceived to be exempt from Heidegger's criticism of onto-theo-logy.[51] Both sides accept the same standard; the
question is what falls under it. Also henology, which understands the
first principle as the One above being, seems able to lead men to
worship a God who, as not being, satisfies what is sought in the contemporary phenomenon of Christian atheism. Further, since what is
below the One is self-constituted, henology provides the room which
ontology does not for modern freedom. This judgement that the
priority of essence threatens freedom is also, of course, part of existentialism, but perhaps it belongs there more to the side of it seen in
Sartre than that in Heidegger.

---

[50] See Andrew Louth, *Discerning the Mystery: An Essay on the Nature of Theology* (Oxford, 1983).

[51] S. Breton, *Être, monde, imaginaire*, p. 10; id., 'Le théorème de l'Un', 580ff.; J. Trouillard, 'Théologie négative et auto-constitution', pp. 320–1; H. Duméry, 'Le néant', 315, all endeavour to get beyond the problems of onto-theo-logy generally exem-plified by Thomism or Thomas. P. Aubenque, 'Plotin et le dépassement de l'ontologie grecque classique', regards both the Plotinian and Porphyrian (Thomistic) alternatives as escaping Heidegger's critique of onto-theo-logy. J. D. Jones, 'The Ontological Dif-ference' compares Aquinas with Dionysius from the Heideggerian perspective and finds Thomas lacking. Thomas is too 'essentialist'. '. . . it is Pseudo-Dionysius and not Aquinas who radically goes beyond an essentialistic way of thinking be-ing. For in my view a radical overcoming of essentialistic metaphysics requires not only that essence be subordinated to *esse* . . . such an overcoming requires that *esse* not be thought as a being or as subsisting in itself' (p. 126). 'Aquinas . . . uses the essentialist language and constantly makes crucial distinctions based on such language. Thus while one needs to depart considerably from traditional interpretations of Pseudo-Dionysius to compre-hend his understanding of be-ing, it seems one must engage in an Heideggerian retrieve of monumental proportions to get Aquinas to say that *esse* is not an *ens* and is not to be thought as *per se subsistens*' (pp. 128–9).

All these considerations give some reason for looking at Thomas's *Summa Theologiae* taking account of the logic of later Neoplatonism. Nothing like a complete treatment is yet possible. Our tools are insufficiently exact for a judgement of the transformations the tradition underwent in reaching St Thomas. We do not possess, for example, a proper critical text of his commentary on the *De Divinis Nominibus* of the pseudo-Dionysius—the most authoritative source of the Proclan Neoplatonism for Thomas. Dionysius' work had a quasi-biblical authority as he accepted throughout the Middle Ages as a disciple of St Paul.[52]

Moreover, the philosophical and theological structure of the henological reaction to ontological Thomism is itself one-sided and does not itself provide a logic through which we may understand the structure of the *Summa Theologiae*.[53] The extreme negative theology of the tradition coming to Thomas from Iamblichus, Proclus, and Dionysius is only one of the post-Plotinian Neoplatonisms to which Thomas is indebted. A more than one-sided account of Thomas's *Summa* and its sources requires equally a consideration of what he owes to the Porphyrian interpretation of Plotinus against which Iamblichus and his followers were reacting. If this is also taken into account, some sense of the real inner tension, both doctrinal and structural, of Thomas's system may emerge. This involves an appreciation of the priority of being in St Thomas as well as of the priority of the unity and simplicity of God. An ontological existentialism too exclusively dominated Thomism through the middle of this century. It is no true corrective to swing entirely to a henology, though this better understands the negative theology in Thomas's *summae*. Our interpretation will suggest that Thomas himself may not be claimed for one or the other of the sides in this debate. His synthesis has perhaps a wider appeal than recognized, although it remains to be seen whether the tensions necessary to this breadth are genuinely held together within his thought.

Despite these caveats, historical and philosophical, both contemporary scholarship and theological directions make possible, as well as necessary, study of the *Summa Theologiae* which appreciates its

[52] J. Durantel, *S. Thomas et le pseudo-Denis* (Paris, 1919) is the classic work. It catalogues and evaluates all 1,700 citations of Dionysius by Thomas—more than of any other author. A very useful short piece on Thomas and Dionysius is T. C. O'Brien, 'The Dionysian Corpus', appendix 3, in St Thomas Aquinas, *Summa Theologiae*, 60 vols, xiv (Blackfriars, 1975), pp. 182–93.

[53] Cf. my 'Aquinas' First Principle', esp. 168–72.

Neoplatonic character. What precedes our modest and partial study is an examination of the work which established the prevailing structure of High Medieval theology—Peter Lombard's *Sentences*. Our purpose is to see what is exceptional about the structure and order of matters in St Thomas's last and greatest systematic work.

Still another justification is required before we set out. What reason can be given for ending with question 45 and thus at the beginning of the consideration of creation and indeed only part way through a sub-section of it? Questions 1 to 45 correspond to no division of the *Summa Theologiae* made by St Thomas. The rationale is found in the same late Neoplatonic logic which will be used to illumine the structure of these questions. It is characterized by the elaborate and extensive use of the *exitus–reditus* form. Indeed, the crucial modification of theological structure and content made by St Thomas relative to his pagan predecessors lies in applying this circular motion to the inmost reaches of divinity. In order to exhibit his use of this form, it is necessary to include the whole *exitus* in principle. Thus, we must reach creation, yet for logical completeness we need not, and so that we may contain our investigation we must not, descend to creatures in particular.

I

Sub ratione dei: the *Sentences* of Peter Lombard and the Structure of Theology

PART of the justification given the *Summa Theologiae* in its prologue is that the necessities of theological teaching cannot be adequately provided when the teacher of Catholic truth must follow the order which expositing another book requires. Besides the Bible, the book whose order dominated the teaching of theology in the High Middle Ages and beyond was the *Sentences* of Peter Lombard. The discovery of what alterations to the traditional order of High Scholastic theology St Thomas thought necessary so that it might conform to the 'ordo disciplinae' and be carried forward 'secundum quod materia patietur' requires a comparison of the structure of these two works.[1]

The *Sentences* had been explicitly recommended by the Lateran Council in 1215 and, from about 1230, it was the official textbook for theological instruction. It maintained this position even beyond the Middle Ages.[2] Indeed, though scholars, and its own prologue, suggest

---

[1] *ST* I, *prol.*: *ordo disciplinae* is both the order of teaching and the necessary objective order of the content: M.-D. Chenu, *Toward Understanding St. Thomas*, revised translation of *Introduction à l'étude de saint Thomas d'Aquin* (Montreal/Paris, 1950) with authorized corrections and bibliographical additions by A.-M. Landry and D. Hughes, Library of Living Catholic Thought (Chicago, 1964), brings out its ambiguity: 'St. Thomas uses the words: *ordo disciplinae*. In point of fact the construction of such an order is required by the very object of science. The latter does not surrender itself to the mind apart from that hidden order without which the most exact formulae would be, scientifically speaking, shapeless and inpenetrable matter' (p. 301). For a history of *disciplina* cf. G. R. Evans, *Old Arts and New Theology* (Oxford, 1980), pp. 96ff.

[2] Per Eric Persson, *Sacra Doctrina: Reason and Revelation in Aquinas*, trans. R. Mackenzie (Oxford, 1970), p. 6. The popularity of the *Sentences* may be gathered from the list of commentaries: F. Stegmueller, *Repertorium Commentariorum in Sententias Petri Lombardi* (Würzburg, 1947); also V. Doucet, *Commentaires sur les Sentences, supplément au répértoire de F. Stegmueller* (Ad Claras Aquas, Quaracchi, 1954) which goes up to Luther and beyond. Essential is J. de Ghellinck, *Le mouvement théologique du XIIᵉ siècle: études, recherches et documents*, 2nd edn., Museum Lessianum, sect. hist. 10 (Bruges, 1948), pp. 213–49. E. R. Fairweather, *A Scholastic Miscellany: Anselm to Ockham*, Library of Christian Classics 10 (London, 1956), gives a nice summary of de Ghellinck. Cf. also A. M. Landgraf, *Einführung in die Geschichte der theologischen Literatur der Frühscholastik* (Regensburg, 1948),

that Thomas intended the *Summa Theologiae* 'to take the place of Lombard's *Sentences* as an elementary introduction to dogmatics for divinity students',[3] it had no such success in the Middle Ages. Thomas's *Summa* was more used than his own *Commentary on the Sentences*,[4] but it remained an experiment which did not gain authority outside a limited school.[5] It may be that his designating the *Summa* for 'incipientes' implies that his *Sentences* commentary continued to be for him proper magisterial theology, but this is made more doubtful by H.-F. Dondaine's argument that his supposed second version of that commentary was only a piece of patchwork sewn together by a disciple. Although the controversy continues with L. E. Boyle's response to Fr Dondaine, there is no question of the discovery of the text of a commentary produced by Thomas himself at Rome just a year before he began the *Prima Pars* of the *Summa Theologiae*, but of a student's 'reportatio' of Thomas's lectures.[6] In any case, the alterations in

and its revision: *Introduction à l'histoire de la littérature théologique de la scholastique naissante*, ed. A.-M. Landry, Université de Montréal, Publ. de l'Institut d'études médiévales 22 (Montreal/Paris, 1973).

[3] Per Eric Persson, *Sacra Doctrina*, p. 7.

[4] Judging by the number of surviving MSS discovered to date; see J. A. Weisheipl, *Friar Thomas d'Aquino: His Life, Thought and Works* (Oxford, 1975), pp. 358, 360–1. This list gathers in everything before printing, and the domination of the *Summa Theologiae* in the earlier period might be less than for the whole period; still it is clearly in the majority.

[5] The Dominican order soon rallied round Thomas's teaching and used the *Summa* to expound it, but outside it was far different; see F. J. Roensch, *Early Thomistic School* (Dubuque, 1964). Even within the order, the *Summa*'s structure did not immediately conquer that of the *Sentences*: Albert the Great in his *Summa*, written after Thomas's death, follows the order of Alexander's *Summa*; cf. M.-M. Gorce, 'Le problème des trois Sommes: Alexandre de Halès, Thomas d'Aquin, Albert le Grand', *Revue thomiste* 26 (1931), 293–301. 'The first comprehensive work of the Thomist school . . . rather awkwardly follow[ed] the plan of the *Sentences* [the *Defensiones* of John Capreolus]', Fairweather, *A Scholastic Miscellany*, p. 228. Cajetan 'primus in scholis explicavit Summam Theologiam sancti Thomae loco Sententiarum', R. Garrigou-Lagrange, *De Deo Uno* (Paris, 1938), p. 12.

[6] The issue is discussed by M. Grabmann, *La Somme théologique de saint Thomas d'Aquin*, trans. of *Einführung in die Summa des hl. T. von Aquin* (Freiburg i. B., 1919/Paris, 1925), p. 91; Chenu, *Toward Understanding St. Thomas*, p. 300; and Weisheipl, *Friar Thomas*, pp. 216–17; there is an extensive literature on the subject but the debate has been raised to a new level by H.-F. Dondaine, '"Alia lectura fratris Thomae"? (*Super I Sent.*)', *Mediaeval Studies*, 42 (1980), 308–36. Fr. Dondaine has discovered the supposed second commentary of Thomas on the *Sentences*: 'un manuscrit du Super primum Sententiarum, qui fait mention d'une alia lectura fratris Thomae' (308). L. E. Boyle, '"Alia Lectura Fratris Thome"', *Mediaeval Studies*, 45 (1983), 418–29, concludes that whoever wrote this piece 'was one of those select students of Santa Sabina in 1265–6 to whom Thomas lectured on the first book of the *Sentences* before embarking a year later on the *prima pars* of his *Summa Theologiae*' (428–9).

the *Summa* to the order of theology fixed by the *Sentences* are so closely
bound up with Thomas's own doctrine that it seems hard to believe
that he would ever want to write another *Sentences* theology.

The popularity of the *Sentences* stems in part from its limitations as
theology. It is a textbook—a collection of texts.[7] A great deal of room is
left for the commentator to develop his own thought:

There is very little or hardly any metaphysics, the philosophical data are frag-
mentary or badly assimilated, there are frequent (and often intentional) cases
of indecision in thought. But the exposition ... is rich in content for the
period, and assembles its materials in a relatively brief and convenient organic
whole.... [There is an] absence of long drawn out digressions, [it] goes
forward accurately, is clear in its plan, alert to dialectical discussions, careful
in noting all opinions, sufficiently impersonal to give free play to comment by
other teachers, and rigorously orthodox.[8]

The development of both *lectio*, or exposition, and *quaestio* as tech-
niques of commentary increased the freedom for the expositor
implicit in the character of the work.[9] But, despite Thomas's
relation to Lombard having been mediated by Alexander, or his
contemporary, who produced the organizing 'distinctions',[10] and

---

[7] For the sources cf. Peter Lombard, *Sententiae in IV Libris Distinctae*, editio tertia, 2
vols., Spicilegium Bonaventurianum 4, 5, i (Ad Claras Aquas, Grottaferrata, 1971),
p. 119*. J. Pieper, *Scholasticism: Personalities and Problems of Medieval Philosophy*, trans.
R. and C. Winston (London, 1961), p. 98, calls it '... a systematically organized Augustinian breviary.... It contains one thousand texts from the works of Augustine; these
works make up nearly four fifths of the whole.' In consequence Lombard is placed by
the author of the *Summa philosophia* in the third rank of theologians, 'those that are
called "makers of Summaries" (*multique moderniores scriptores, quos summarum vocant confec-
tores*)', É. Gilson, *History of Christian Philosophy*, p. 267. He removes most of the philosophical speculation in his sources (ibid., p. 314). This lack of originality is honestly
derived from its model, John Damascene's *The Source of Knowledge*. Its 'third part [was] a
collection of texts taken from his predecessors and arranged in systematic order, about
the fundamental truths of the Christian religion. This third part ... was to serve as a
model for the *Book of Sentences* of Peter Lombard.... John Damascene did not claim to
do any original work in philosophy but to organize a handy collection of philosophical
notions useful to the theologian' (ibid., p. 91).

[8] Fairweather, *A Scholastic Miscellany*, pp. 226–7, quoting and translating de Ghellinck.

[9] On this see M.-D. Chenu, *S. Thomas d'Aquin et la théologie*, Maîtres spirituels 17
(Paris, 1959), p. 179; id., *La Théologie au douzième siècle*, Études de phil. médiévale 45
(Paris, 1957), and G. R. Evans, *Old Arts*. On the specific character of Thomas's develop-
ment of the *quaestio*, see Grabmann, *La Somme théologique*, p. 80.

[10] The editors of the *Sentences* write: 'Quaestionem profundius indagantes, conclu-
dere coacti sumus Magistrum Alexandrum primum Distinctiones introduxisse sive tan-
quam ab ipso inventas sive, quod multo minus probabile est, ut sumptas ab alio
magistro anonymo et huc usque ignoto' (*Sententiae in IV Libris Distinctae*, p. 144*). Cf.
Alexander of Hales, *Glossa in Quatuor Libros Sententiarum Petri Lombardi*, i (Ad Claras
Aquas, Quaracchi, 1951), pp. 33*, 65*, 102*, 107*–9*.

Bonaventure,[11] his own *Commentary* was still confined by the main features of the Lombard's structure.

Thomas analyses the structure of the *Sentences* accurately. There are two fundamental divisions. The first is into things, 'res', and signs, 'signa'.[12] The last of the four books is about signs, the earlier, things. The three initial books are again divided. The first, 'de mysterio Trinitatis' concerns things to be enjoyed, 'frui'; the second, 'de rerum creatione et formatione corporalium et spiritualium et aliis pluribus eis pertinentibus' is of things to be used, 'uti'. Book Three, 'de incarnatione Verbi, aliisque ad hoc spectantibus' is of those things which order the useful to the enjoyable.[13] Book Four is entitled 'de sacramentis et signis sacramentalibus'. According to Thomas the first three books have an *exitus–reditus* structure; the exit is described in the first two, the return in the third.[14]

The *Summa Theologiae* gathers Books One and Two of the *Sentences* into the *Prima Pars*, which considers God and his works.[15] The *Secunda Pars* organizes around man all the virtues and vices scattered through the books of the *Sentences*.[16] The *Tertia Pars* combines Books Three and Four by treating Christ, his sacraments, and our end.[17] Thomas is

---

[11] See É. H. Wéber, *Dialogue et dissensions*, pp. 18 and 223, and compare the comment of Thomas on the *prologus* with that of Bonaventure; cf. Bonaventure, *Commentaria in IV Libros Sententiarum Magistri Petri Lombardi, Opera Theologica Selecta*, editio minor, 5 vols., i (Quaracchi, 1934), *prooemium*, pp. 1–6.

[12] 'potest dividi secundum intentionem Magistri, quod in prima determinat de rebus, et in secunda de signis et hoc in quarto', St Thomas Aquinas, *Scriptum super libros Sententiarum Magistri Petri Lombardi*, ed. nova R. P. Mandonnet et M. F. Moos (Paris, 1929–47), I, *d.* ii, *div. text.*, p. 57.

[13] 'Item prima in tres: in prima de fruibilibus, in secunda de utibilibus, et secundo libro, in tertia de his quae ordinant utibilia ad fruibilia, quae etiam partim sunt utibilia, partim fruibilia, et hoc in tertio libro', ibid. Lombard is explicit that both divisions derive from Augustine. On how Augustine employs this ordering principle, cf. O. O'Donovan, '*Usus* and *Fruitio* in Augustine, *De Doctrina Christiana* I', *Jour. of Theo. Studies*, 33 (1982), 361–97.

[14] 'Unde in prima parte determinat de rebus divinis secundum exitum a principio; in secunda secundum reditum in finem et hoc in principio tertii', *In Sent.* I, *d.* ii, *div. text.*, p. 57.

[15] 'primo tractabimus de Deo', *ST* I, 2, *prol.* '... postquam praedictum est de exemplari, scilicet de Deo et de his quae processerunt ex divina potestate secundum eius voluntatem', *ST* I–II, *prol.*

[16] 'secundo, de motu rationalis creaturae in Deus', *ST* I, 2, *prol.* 'de homine, secundum quod et ipse est suorum operum principium quasi liberum arbitrium habens et suorum operum potestatem', *ST* I–II, *prol.*

[17] 'tertio de Christo, qui secundum quod homo via est nobis tendendi in Deum', *ST* I, 2, *prol.* 'Circa quam, primo considerandum occurrit de ipso Salvatore; secundo, de sacramentis eius, quibus salutem consequimur; tertio de fine immortalis vitae, ad quem per ipsum resurgendo pervenimus', *ST* III, *prol.*

not only rearranging the material of theology, since each of its parts and the whole also have a new logical principle. Man's freedom, because he is created in the divine image and has power over his own works, is made the foundation of the whole world of virtues and vices. In the Third Part, Christ both gives his sacraments their sanctifying power and determines their end and purpose as the means by which men come to share his resurrected life. And Thomas's 'de Deo' has a logic markedly different from Lombard's first book. He divides what in Peter Lombard is the 'de mysterio Trinitatis' into a *de deo uno* and a *de deo trino* and begins divinity with the unity. Then he moves the operations of God from their place in Lombard at the end of Book One to a new position between the substance of God and the three persons.[18]

Peter Lombard's material is largely drawn from Augustine and his explicit principles of organization are derived from him as well. Thomas's structural transformations depend upon principles outside Augustine's world. Changing the formal subject of theology from 'res et signa' to God—on which the simplification of the *Summa* is based— is, in part, a move toward Aristotelian science. The division of the *de deo* comes to Thomas through Dionysius and is Proclan in its philosophical origins. The step-by-step development from the unity of substance through the conceptual division of the operations to the real relation and opposition of the persons also has a late Neoplatonic logic behind it. The anthropology on which the *Secunda Pars* is founded draws on this source and the Greek Fathers, and the Christology of the *Tertia Pars* has similarly ingested later Greek patristic and philosophical sources.[19]

The shift from the psychological categories of Lombard in making God the centre of theology as its object seems to depend on a genuine move by Thomas in the direction of Aristotelian science. An Augustinian source is precluded.[20] Thomas's view can not come, without Aristotle's help, from the Proclan Neoplatonism of the *Liber de Causis* or of Dionysius, for which God in himself is above scientific knowledge.[21]

[18] 'Post considerationem eorum quae ad divinam substantiam pertinent, restat considerandum de his quae pertinent ad operationem ipsius', *ST* I, 14, *prol.* These are *qq.* 14–26.
[19] P. Faucon, *Aspects néoplatoniciens de la doctrine de saint Thomas d'Aquin* (Lille/Paris, 1975), is concerned with these sources of his doctrine of Christ.
[20] 'This order [of the *Sentences*] cannot have the objective breadth of speculative reaches that the plan of St. Thomas offers, because these Augustinian categories are centred on the psychology of man, not on the work of God as such', Chenu, *Toward Understanding St. Thomas*, p. 310.
[21] 'Pour lui, "l'inconnaissance de cette Suressentialité même qui dépasse raison,

God is one of the subjects of the science, which for Aristotle is alter-natively called metaphysics, first philosophy or theology.[22] This is also how the Philosopher is understood by Aquinas.[23] It is the movement toward Aristotle which allows Thomas to imitate Proclus and embrace the whole course of reality within theology's *exitus–reditus* frame-work.[24] Whereas, by Thomas's account, only the material belonging to *res* in Lombard's scheme could be given such a structure, in his own *Summa* the whole course of theology falls within it. 'All things are treated in sacred doctrine with reference to God; for its matter is either God himself or what is ordered to God as its principle and end. From whence it follows that God truly is the subject of this science.'[25] What is remarkable is both the lateness of this development for Chris-tian theology and the mixing of Aristotelian and Neoplatonic logics in this solution.[26] What explains the long delay is the necessity of uniting

pensée et essence, tel doit être l'objet de la science suressentielle". L'objet de la théo-logie ne peut être que Dieu', Ch.-A. Barnard, 'Les formes de la théologie chez Denys l'Areopagite', *Gregorianum*, 59 (1978), 41. Cf. *ST* I, 1, 7 *obj.* 1, drawn from Dionysius' disciple John of Damascus. The discursive treatment of the gods and all which reveals them in myth, of the philosophic tradition become a spirituality, and of religious prac-tice is, for Proclus and his school, theology as science. This school may be regarded as the founders of the genre in this restricted sense. Cf. H.-D. Saffrey, 'Quelques aspects de la spiritualité des philosophes néoplatoniciens'; W. J. Hankey, 'Theology as System and as Science: Proclus and Thomas Aquinas', *Dionysius*, 6 (1982), 91–2; and Jean Trouillard, 'Les fondements du mythe selon Proclos': 'La Théologie de Proclos est intégralement nocturne' (p. 14).

[22] J. Owens, *The Doctrine of Being in the Aristotelian Metaphysics*, pp. 152 ff.; id., 'Exis-tence and the Subject of Metaphysics', *Science et esprit*, 32 (1980), 255–69; É. Gilson, *Being and Some Philosophers*, p. 157, are sufficient to establish that God is a subject of metaphysics for Aristotle. The claim of Fr. Owens that separate entity or God is the subject rather than being is more doubtful, cf. J. D. Beach, 'Separate Entity'. The names of the science are given at *Metaphysics*, E, 1026ᵃ 19 and 1026ᵃ 24.

[23] See Endnote 1 p. 162 below.

[24] See the excellent article by Th. A. Audet, 'Approches historiques de la *Summa The-ologiae*', *Études d'histoire littéraire et doctrinale*, U. de Montréal, Publ. de l'Institut d'études médiévales 17 (Montreal/Paris, 1962), pp. 7–29.

[25] 'Omnia autem pertractantur in sacra doctrina sub ratione Dei, vel quia sunt ipse Deus, vel quia habent ordinem ad Deum, ut ad principium et finem. Unde sequitur quod Deus vere sit subiectum huius scientiae', *ST* I, 1, 7, *resp.* Cf. also *ST* I, 1, 3 *ad* 1, and I, 2, *prol.*

[26] If one sticks strictly to the exact form of the statement, *Deus* is the *subiectum* of this *scientia*, Thomas is probably its initiator among Christians. For a history of theology cf. E. Schillebeeckx, *Revelation and Theology*, trans. by N. D. Smith of 'Theology' in *Theologisch Woordenboek*, iii (1958) (London, 1967), ch. V. The objective and deductive character of theology thus understood is opposed by contemporary theologians who prefer to understand it more subjectively—it has to do with God in his self-communica-tion rather than in himself; cf. for example, K. Rahner's article 'Theology' in *Sacramen-tum Mundi: an Encyclopedia of Theology*, ed. K. Rahner *et al.*, 6 vols., vi (London, 1970), pp. 234–6. On the history see also Lawrence Dewan, '*Objectum*. Notes on the Invention

these two opposing logics so as to be able to achieve a theological science which, having God as its formal object, both treats the divine in itself and all else as ordered to God.

Theology for Aquinas, as for Aristotle, contains a definite knowledge of God, is demonstrative, and arrives at proper affirmative predication; although for both, our theology is presently only a limited participation in God's science, not the true possession of it. Our theology is subalternate to God's own science.[27] Yet, even with these qualifications, St Thomas has shifted theology definitely towards the objective pole in making God, rather than the relations to the revealed content of the Christian soul seeking salvation, the subject of divine science. This move toward Aristotle and away from Augustine is essential if a logic which can embrace all reality is to be found. This must be a divine logic.

Still, what may be found in Aristotle is not enough to explain Thomas's *Summa*. To find the missing elements we must turn to the theological systems of Proclus. Both Thomas and Proclus unite in a single, explicitly organized system what Aristotle divides between separate sciences, theoretical and practical. One of the features of Thomas's commentaries on Aristotle's books, which often make them clearer than the Philosopher could ever be, is Thomas's very definite conception of an Aristotelian system containing logical, substantially theoretical, and practical sciences hierarchically arranged. Thomas uses this to flesh out Aristotle's vague cross-references. Not only does Thomas differ from Aristotle in his conception of some parts of the system—for example, in Thomas, logic is contentless in a way unknown to Aristotle—but also Thomas understands the Philosopher in terms of a notion of philosophical organization tht Aristotle never

---

of a Word', *Arch. hist. doct. lit. du moyen âge* 48 (1981), 37–96, which traces the Platonist transformations of Aristotle which produced Aquinas' understanding of the object of science.

[27] For Aristotle, cf. *Metaphysica* A, 982^b 27–983^a 24 and *Nic. Eth.* x, 1178^a 2. Aquinas says 'Est ergo theologia scientia quasi subalternata divinae scientiae a qua accipit principia sua', *In Sent.* I, *prol.*, I, 3, *sol.* 2 (Mandonnet, p. 14). Cf. D. J. M. Bradley, 'Aristotelian Science and the Science of Thomistic Theology', *Heythrop Jour.* 22 (1981), 162–71. On man's participation in divine science, cf. St Thomas Aquinas, *In duodecim libros Metaphysicorum Aristotelis Expositio*, ed. M. R. Cathala et R. M. Spiazzi (Turin/Rome, 1964), I, iii, 61–8, pp. 19–20; *ST* I–II, 169, *ad* 3, and J. H. Walgrave, 'The Use of Philosophy in the Theology of Thomas Aquinas', *Aquinas and the Problems of His Time*, Mediaevalia Lovaniensia 5 (Louvain/The Hague, 1976), pp. 161–93; *In de Div. Nom.* I, i, 32 and I, i, 36, pp. 9–10; St Thomas Aquinas, *Sententia libri Ethicorum*, 2 vols., *Opera Omnia* (Leonine), xlvii, ii (Rome, 1969), x, 11, pp. 587–8 (hereafter: *In Ethica*).

made explicit.[28] Common to Proclus and Aquinas and necessarily absent from Aristotle is the idea that all knowledge is comprehensible within theology. It is true that for Aristotle the science of the wise man is a ruling science—though there are the difficulties about the relation between the sciences of the wise and of the politician.[29] It is also the case that being as being is not a particular form of what is and that this creates part of the great difficulty experienced in beginning the *Metaphysics*, for instance the confusion between first philosophy and the way of looking at knowledge in general which is found in the *Analytics*. Still, the reduction of philosophy, theoretical and practical, to theology is a development of the Neoplatonists, carrying further the work of the Stoics, which presupposes views of both subjectivity and external reality quite different from Aristotle's. This systematic theology is found in Proclus' *Elements of Theology*. His *Platonic Theology* also involves such a systematically total examination of reality in relation to the graduated forms of divinity.

Finally, both Proclan and Thomistic theology, as opposed to the Aristotelian, make God their starting-point. Indeed, both begin from simplicity or goodness as the first characteristic of divinity. This is rather the conclusion of Aristotle's *Metaphysics*. That God is for Aristotle the good as final cause and that he is not also given his place at the beginning of theology as the self-diffusive source and principle of all is a criticism of metaphysical theology made by both Proclus and Aquinas.[30]

The Aristotelian and Proclan theologies seem to fit neatly together so as to constitute Thomas's unification of theology as science of the first principle and as *summa* or systematic treatment of reality as a whole. Each contributed what the other lacked. Aristotle had not shown how what is other than the first emerged from it and is related to it. Proclus elevated the first into absolutely ineffable transcendence

---

[28] See e.g. Thomas's *prooemium* to his *In Aristotelis libros Posteriorum Analyticorum Expositio* in *In Aristotelis libros Peri Hermeneias et Posteriorum Analyticorum Expositio*, ed. R. M. Spiazzi (Turin/Rome, 1955), pp. 147–8; compare Thomas's commentary with Aristotle's text at *In Post. Anal.* I, xv, 133, p. 198; I, xvii, 145–6, pp. 203–4; I, xviii, 152, p. 207; I, xx, 171–2, pp. 214–15. On the nature of logic, see his comparisons of it with metaphysics at *In Post. Anal.* I, xx, 171–2 and *In Meta.* IV, iv,574, p. 160; in the latter he sets logic, as considering 'ens rationis', against philosophy, which treats 'ens naturae'.

[29] Cf. *Metaphysics*, A, 2 with *Nic. Eth.*, i, 2 and vi, 7.

[30] See Proclus, *In Timaeum*, i, 267, 4, and Dodds, *Elements*, p. 198. For Aquinas, cf. *In Sent.* I, *prol.*, pp. 2ff., *epil.*, p. 1092; *ScG* II, 4; IV, 1; St Thomas Aquinas, *Expositio super librum Boethii de Trinitate*, ed. B. Decker, Studien und Texte zur Geistesgeschichte des Mittelalters 4 (Leiden, 1959), *prol.*, p. 45, line 22 to p. 46, line 10; *In Meta.* III, i, 344, p. 97.

and so could not manifest what in the character of the principle makes it the intelligible source of reality. Treating these two theologies as complementary is not, however, the whole account. Aristotle's theology is affirmative, discursive, and demonstrative thought about the highest objects of intellectual intuition just because the highest is considered beside other objects of knowledge.[31] For Proclus, once the absolute source is given the proper elevation in which the true relationship of the finite to the One is manifest, it is also clear that the One is not to be known.[32] How successful Thomas is at drawing together what is opposed in Aristotle and Proclus as well as what is complementary cannot yet be our question. It is sufficient if we understand something of what is involved in his passing beyond Lombard's Augustinian conceptions when grounding the structure of his *Summa Theologiae*.

The divisions of the *de deo* we must consider again later, but a word is appropriate here about the interposing of the operations between the substance of God and the Trinity so as to lead the mind step by step from the unity of God to the divisions which lie within, and then without, his essence. The treatment of unity and Trinity in the first book of the *Sentences* is mixed.[33] It seemed unsatisfactory even to earlier followers[34] of the Lombard and to those usually called Augustinians[35]

[31] Metaphysics is established as wisdom (*Metaphysics*, i, 2) and as science (*Metaphysics*, iv, 1). Wisdom is science and intuitive reason; demonstration about the highest things (*Nic. Eth.*, vi, 7). Cf. *In Ethica*, vi, 5 (Leonine xlvii, ii, pp. 348–50).

[32] On this see J. Trouillard, 'Les fondements du mythe', pp. 13–14 and Pierre Hadot, 'Apophatisme et théologie négative', *Exercices spirituels et philosophie antique*, Études augustiniennes (Paris, 1981), pp. 185–93.

[33] The first place where Lombard treats anything equivalent to Thomas's consideration of the *essentia Dei* is at *Distinctio* viii, 'De proprietate et incommutabilitate et simplicitate Dei essentia', which occurs right in the middle of what Thomas would designate as 'ea quae pertinent ad distinctionem Personarum'.

[34] The first book of the *Sententiae Petri Pictaviensis*, ed. P. Moore, M. Dulong, and J. Garvin, 2 vols., Publications in Mediaeval Studies, The University of Notre Dame, 7, 11 (Notre Dame, Indiana, 1943 and 1950), is divided 'de Deo uno, de attributis divinis, de proprietatibus divinis, de Deo trino, de operationibus ad extra' (i, p. ix). Cf. also i, pp. 2 and 11 and ii, p. xxi. For a discussion of the relation to Lombard and the subsequent history of these revisions, cf. P. S. Moore, *The Works of Peter of Poitiers*, Publications in Mediaeval Studies, The University of Notre Dame (Notre Dame, Indiana, 1943), pp. 48–50.

[35] Alexander of Hales, *Summa Theologica*, 4 vols. (Ad Claras Aquas, Quaracchi, 1924–48) distinguishes within the '*Libri Primi Pars Prima*' between the inquisition '*de substantia divinae Unitatis*' and that '*de pluralitate divinae Trinitas*', and within the '*inquisitio prima*' of the '*Libri Primi Pars Secunda*' between the tract '*de nominibus essentialibus*' and that '*de nominibus personalibus*'. Bonaventure's *Itinerarium mentis in Deum*, *Opera Theologica Selecta*, v (Quaracchi, 1964), pp. 296–313, divides chs. 5 and 6 between a 'de deo uno' and a 'de deo trino' respectively.

who remained as faithful as possible to him. Thomas understands that, in such an arrangement, the purpose of placing the operations of knowing, power, and will at the end of the treatise[36] is to provide a transition to the procession of creatures.[37] But the logic of Thomas requires from his earliest works a different order: 'his approach ... consists in three simple steps, moving out from the oneness of the divine essence, to the plurality of the rationally distinct attributes, and finally to the plurality of the really distinct persons'.[38] And indeed, in a revision of the *Sentences'* commentary he introduces such an order into the structure of his consideration of one of the 'distinctions'.[39] As we shall see, placing the operations before the procession of persons and creatures enables a rational link to be made between the unity and the Trinity. The persons are understood through the internal activities of knowing and willing and the procession to creatures through the activity *ad extra* of power. The three operations and the three persons are related by a Proclan triad.[40] This connection was not accomplished in the *Summa contra Gentiles* either and the treatment of the Trinity there, separated by the entire remainder of the work from the *de deo uno*, is much more directly scriptural in its argumentation than is the *Summa Theologiae*'s consideration. The 'missionary' purposes of the *contra Gentiles* compel this, as it is Thomas's scheme to go through

[36] *Distinctio* is 'de quibusdam quae secundum substantiam de Deo dicuntur, quae specialem efflagitant tractatum, scilicet de scientia et praescientia et providentia et dispositione, praedestinatione, voluntate et potentia'. This gives the plan for the rest of *Liber* I.

[37] Thomas comments, I, *d.* ii, *div. textus*: 'Primus autem liber dividitur in duas partes ... in secunda determinantur attributa quaedam, ex quorum rationibus completur causalitas in divinis personis respectu productionis creaturarum, scilicet de scientia, potentia, voluntate infra, xxxv *distinct*' (Mandonnet, p. 57).

[38] R. L. Richards, *The Problem of an Apologetical Perspective in the Trinitarian Theology of St. Thomas Aquinas*, Analecta Gregoriana 131 (Rome, 1963), p. 64.

[39] See B. M. Lemaigre, 'Perfection de Dieu et multiplicité des attributs divins: Pourquoi s. Thomas a-t-il inséré la dispute des attributs divins (*I Sent.*, d. 2, q. 1, a. 3) dans son *Commentaire des Sentences*?', *Rev. sc. ph. th.* 50 (1966), 197–227.

[40] Dodds, *Elements*, p. 264: 'Goodness, Power and Knowledge constitute the primary divine triad (*Th. Pl.* I, xvi, 44), which prefigures in a seminal form the triad of the second hypostasis, Being, Life, and Intelligence (prop. 101)—δύναμις πάντων is already a standing definition of the One in Plot. (e.g. v, iii, 15).... The Procline doctrine reappears in ps.-Dion., who devotes separate chapters of the *Div. Nom.* to the praise of God as προών, as αἰώνιος ζωή and as κρυφία γνῶσις.' One might say it extends to Thomas as well where a source is Augustine (*ST* I, 39, 8 obj. 3). See *ST* I, 39, 8 *resp.* as follows: 'Potentia enim habet rationem principii. Unde habet similitudinem cum Patre caelesti, qui est principium totius divinitatis.... Sapientia vero similitudinem habet cum Filio caelesti, inquantum est Verbum, quod nihil aliud est quam conceptus sapientiae.... Bonitas autem, cum sit ratio et objectum amoris, habet similitudinem cum Spiritu divino, qui est Amor.'

the whole material accessible to reason before touching on what is only available to faith.[41] Consequently, it is only in the *Summa Theologiae* and the *Compendium Theologiae* that this logic is able to be carried through structurally. These considerations must make impossible the view that Thomas's thinking becomes less Dionysian after the *Commentary on the Sentences*.[42] Only after it can the full implications for theology of a gradual *exitus* and a complete *reditus* of reality from and to God be developed in form and content.

The anthropocentrism of St Thomas is astonishing and perhaps involves a conception of man's place which is unique and inimitable. This seems to be the view of Sir Richard Southern:

> Thomas Aquinas died in 1274 and, it is probably true that man has never appeared so important a being in so well-ordered and intelligible a universe as in his works. Man was important because he was the link between the created universe and the divine intelligence. He alone in the world of nature could understand nature. He alone could use and perfect nature in accordance with the will of God and thus achieve his full nobility.[43]

The results of this notion of the crucial mediatorial role of man are to be seen in the whole structure of the *Summa Theologiae* and especially in the reorganization of the *Secunda Pars*. The radical shift from Peter Lombard led M. Grabmann to call this point the most original, and

[41] There is a very extended controversy about Thomas's aims and how they provide a motive for the *Summa contra Gentiles*: see A. Gauthier's introduction to *Contra Gentiles*, 4 vols., i (Paris, 1961); F. van Steenberghen, *La Philosophie au XIIIe siècle*, Philosophes médiévaux 9 (Louvain/Paris, 1966), pp. 316–24; G. van Riet, 'La *Somme contra les Gentils* et la polémique islamo-chrétienne', *Aquinas and the Problems of his Time*, Mediaevalia Lovaniensia, 5 (Louvain/The Hague, 1976), pp. 156–60 and M. D. Jordan, 'The Modes of Thomistic Discourse: Questions for Corbin's *Le Chemin de la théologie chez Thomas d'Aquin*', *The Thomist*, 45 (1981), 87 n. 4. For the plan consequent on his missionary purposes, cf. *ScG* I, 9.

[42] T. Delvigne, 'L'inspiration propre du traité de Dieu dans le *Commentaire des Sentences* de saint Thomas', *Bulletin thomiste, Notes et communications* (1932), 119*–22*. É. zum Brunn, 'La "métaphysique de l'Exode" selon Thomas d'Aquin', *Dieu et l'être*, p. 253, reports this view but holds rather that his use of Aristotle's ways to God's being through sensible effects already alters the Augustinian logic of the *Sentences* and 'les voies dionysiennes sont intégrées à une épistémologie *sui generis*' (pp. 266–7). She makes a great deal of Thomas's reversal, after the *Sentences* commentary, of Augustine's placing of immutability after eternity; this change is owing to Thomas's Aristotelian ascent to God as the unmoved mover; ibid., pp. 250–1.

[43] R. Southern, *Medieval Humanism and Other Studies* (Oxford, 1970), p. 50. Cf. M.-M. Gorce, *L'essor de la pensée au Moyen Âge: Albert le Grand—Thomas d'Aquin* (Paris, 1933), on 'l'humanisme profond de la *Somme théologique*' (pp. xiv, 296ff.). F. J. Ruello, 'Réflexions sur les intentions et la méthode pédagogiques de saint Thomas dans la *Somme théologique*' (unpubl. thesis, Institut catholique de Paris, Faculté de philosophie, 1945) connects this humanism with the *ordo disciplinae* directed to the student's development.

indeed Thomas has moved beyond what may be found in Augustine.[44] It is in John Damascene that he finds that interpretation of the *imago dei* which gives theological authority to his way of proceeding.[45] This and other features suggest the influence of Proclan Neoplatonism, but, in fact, without Christian reformation, this tradition will not supply what we need to understand the elements from which Thomas constructed what was new in his final system. To grasp what is active at this point we shall need to get some hold on how Thomas unites Augustine and Dionysius. But first let us see how his view of man's place in the cosmos informs the structure of his *Summa Theologiae*.

Man's first appearance is in the *Prima Pars*, which belongs to God. There he is seen in his unfallen state; for the creation is present in this part as it is in God. The creation is in God as the caused is in the cause, and it is law abiding, that is, contained in God's government. But though the *Prima Pars* is especially God's part, man concludes it, because, uniting spiritual and material, he is sum of both these opposed aspects of God's creation and government.[46] It is in the *Secunda Pars* that man falls. The fall is his work, not God's, and this whole part is devoted to man's works as they may be distinguished from the divine.[47] God's being and his works had been considered together in the *Prima Pars*; but, because man is dependent, his being and his works are divided from one another. The *Tertia Pars* is also heavily weighted toward the human. Christ concludes theology because as man he is man's way of returning to the God of

---

[44] M. Grabmann, *La Somme Théologique*, p. 119; P. E. Persson, *Sacra Doctrina*, p. 245; M.-D. Chenu, 'S. Thomas innovateur dans la créativité d'un monde nouveau', *Atti del Congresso Internazionale Tommaso d'Aquino*, i (Naples, 1975), pp. 39–50, interprets the notorious novelty of St Thomas in terms of his positioning of man 'à la jointure de deux univers' accomplishing 'l'homogénéité de l'esprit et de la matière' (p. 43).

[45] *ST* I–II, *prol.* and also *ST* I, 93, 5 *obj.* 2 and I, 93, 9.

[46] *ST* I, 50, *prol.*; I, 75, *prol.*, I, 106, *prol.*

[47] It is significant that Lombard moves directly from man's creation to his fall: *Lib.* II, *d.* xvi, 'de homine facto ad imaginem Dei', *d.* xvii, 'de creatione animal, et de paradiso', *d.* xviii, 'de formatione mulieris, et de causis rerum', *d.* xix, 'de primo hominis statu ante peccatum', *d.* xxi, 'de invidia diaboli et modo tentationis', *d.* xxii, 'quae fuerit origo et radix primo peccati'. But Thomas divides the matter between the *Prima Pars* and the *Secunda Pars*. *Prima Pars* has a treatise on man as God's work (*qq.* 75 ff.), where man is considered according to his essential powers and his unfallen state (*qq.* 96 ff.). It is in the *Secunda Pars*, where he is 'suorum operum principium' (*prol.*) that his fall is considered—sin begins (i–ii, *qq.* 71 ff.), the fall (*qq.* 80 ff.). On this self-determination, though with an insufficient grasp of Thomas's assessment of the consequences and of how he deals with them in the *Tertia Pars*, cf. K. Wojtyła, 'The Structure of Self-determination as the Core of the Theory of the Person', *Atti del Congresso Internazionale Tomasso d'Aquino*, vii (Naples, 1978), pp. 37–44.

the *Prima Pars*, from whom in the *Secunda Pars* man had separated himself.

If the subject of the *Summa* is God, God in himself and as creator and governor, God freely sought and freely rejected by man, God as saviour, it is also about man. For, though man's intellectual powers are lower than those of angels, man has a dignity deriving from his complexity. Being a unity of body and soul, he joins the purely material and purely spiritual creations. As rational, irrational creatures are ordered to him; but, as corporeal and sensible, he has a part with them and so in heaven they will be given a glory to match his.[48] The human is taken into Christ as consummator and, by virtue of the personal union with God, mankind is better and more loved than the angels.[49] So the *Summa* is also the drama of man. Man as glorious sum of creation, man as fallen and making his own world, man united to God in Christ, the God-man. The movement of the *Summa* occurs in humanity: 'Turn us again, O Lord, and we shall be turned.'

The lack of such a concrete unity of universal and particular as well as of material and spiritual prevents any pagan Neoplatonic system achieving the completeness of *exitus* and *reditus* which Thomistic anthropocentrism permits.[50] Soul, not man, is where mind and matter meet for the Neoplatonists. Man as a particular instance of soul is found at the end, not in the centre of *The Elements of Theology*, and so the return is not actually seen to be accomplished. Though *exitus* and *reditus* are the movement of all reality except the One and provide its relation to the One, this pattern is not explicit in the overall organization of Proclus' theology. It is found rather in Christian works subsequent to it and influenced by it. The *Theological Tractates* of Boethius, the works of pseudo-Dionysius, as well as the *De Divisione Naturae* of Eriugena, which were all at least partly known to Thomas, have this pattern. Christianity is able to find in Christ's union of God and man a point upon which to move the universe, which fulcrum is lacking to the Neoplatonism supplying the philosophical logic for the development.[51]

[48] *ST* I, 20, 2 *ad* 3; *ScG* III (1), 81–3; *ScG* III (2), 112; *ScG* IV, 97; *Comp. Theo.*, i, 148.

[49] *ST* I, 20, 4 *ad* 2.

[50] Cf. H.-D. Saffrey, 'Théologie et anthropologie d'après quelques préfaces de Proclus', *Images of Man in Ancient and Medieval Thought, Studia Gerardo Verbeke ab amicis et collegis dicata*, ed. F. Boissier *et al.*, Symbolae 1 (Louvain, 1976), pp. 199–212.

[51] Cf. W. J. Hankey, 'The *De Trinitate* of St. Boethius'; id., 'The Place of the Proof for God's Existence in the *Summa Theologiae* of Thomas Aquinas', *The Thomist*, 46 (1982), 370–93; R. D. Crouse, '*Semina Rationum*: St. Augustine and Boethius', *Dionysius*, 4 (1980), 75–86, and P. Rorem, 'The Place of *The Mystical Theology* in the Pseudo-Dionysian Corpus', *Dionysius*, 4 (1980), 87–98; and ch. II below.

Overcoming the deficient humanism of Classical and Hellenistic paganism is a great Christian work partially completed by Augustine. One of the central problems, if not the main question, Augustine is attempting to work out in the *Confessions* is how the God, who finally becomes thinkable for him through a Platonic conception of immateriality, immutability, and eternity, can be the principle of the material temporal world. Within the solution to this question is also the satisfaction of his search to understand man's moral responsibility and his desire for salvation or unity with the principle. These are, from opposite sides, both questions about how spirit and matter can beheld together.[52]

The main answer given in the *Confessions* is man in Christ. Structurally this is indicated by the place of Book xi. In it the time-consciousness of the human soul is used as a transition between the temporal journey of Augustine to his eternal *patria* (Books i–ix) and the exegesis of the creation narrative in Genesis (Books xii–xiii). Time is possible because the now which is eternity becomes a unity divided between past, present, and future, a presence of past and future. Again, doctrinally the solution to the problem of how material temporal being can actually be one with God is the God-man, Jesus Christ. This living way overcomes the Platonic problem. The way up is the way down. The man, whose infancy is analysed in Book i, is baptized into Christ in Book ix, and is able to confess his sins in Book x because moral responsibility is discovered when the source of the material in the spiritual is known.[53] There is involved here a transformation of the cosmos of Plotinus and Porphyry parallel to Thomas's reinterpretation of the same feature in the world view of Proclus.

Thomas transforms a formula about the soul—'quasi horizon et confinium spiritualis et corporalis naturae'—from prop. 2 of the *Liber de Causis*, into a doctrine of man as sum of creation's elements.[54] In

[52] Cf. C. J. Starnes, 'Saint Augustine and the Vision of the Truth', *Dionysius*, 1 (1977), 85–126.

[53] Cf. R. D. Crouse, '*In Multa Defluximus: Confessions* X, 29–43; and St. Augustine's Theory of Personality', *Neoplatonism and Early Christian Thought*, ed. H. J. Blumenthal (q.v.), pp. 180–5; and E. G. T. Booth, 'St Augustine's *de Trinitate* and Aristotelian and neo-Platonist Noetic', *Studia Patristica*, xvi, ed. E. A. Livingstone, Texte und Untersuchungen 129 (Berlin, 1985), pp. 487–90. Dr Booth argues that Augustine's unambiguous reduction of the centre of self-knowledge and self-love from the level of the neo-Platonist hypostases to that of the individual human *mens'* (p. 489) is confirmed in the *de Trinitate* and involves a movement towards Aristotle.

[54] The text is found at *ScG* II, 68 and 81; cf. F. J. Ruello, 'Saint Thomas et Pierre Lombard', *San Tommaso: fonti e riflessi del suo pensiero*, ed. A. Piolanti, Studi tomistici 1 (Rome, n.d.), p. 202.

Plotinus, soul provides the medium between spiritual and material. It is the spiritual source of the unspiritual world and, through the self-recollection of soul, the divine hypostases are found. Thomas and Augustine are aware that crucial to the Christianizing of the Platonic cosmos is the abolition of the world soul. Man in Christ is the ultimate heir. This is the direction of Augustine's thought but he has not moved as far as Eriugena or Thomas. Aquinas brings this out rather nicely at *In de Causis*, prop. 3, p. 25, lines 9–14:

Haec etiam positio non est rata in fide, scilicet quod motus caeli sit ab anima; sed AUGUSTINUS hoc sub dubio relinquit in II° *Super Genesim ad litteram*. Quod autem sit a Deo dirigente totam naturam et quod corporalis creatura moveatur a Deo mediantibus intelligentiis sive angelis, hoc asserit AUGUSTINUS in *III° De trinitate* et GREGORIUS in *IV° Dialogorum*.

Common to Plotinus and Augustine, and separating them from Eriugena and Aquinas, is the conviction that man must turn inward toward his noetic soul in order to ascend to God. Dionysius provides his heirs with the Proclan view that, because the descent into the material of the human soul is complete, it has no alternative but to turn outward to move upward. The human body and the sensual are thus given a value even in this world which Christians had not hitherto adequately appreciated.[55] Because they lack this aspect of the philosophical means for fully valuing man's whole being, they retain something of Plotinus' misanthropy.

Plotinus found Gnostic anthropocentrism blasphemous and ridiculous. It was foolish for the human to compare itself to those far greater intellectual powers in the heavens with their spiritual bodies, the sun and the stars, and to imagine that the salvation of humans was the central concern of the cosmos.

Moreover, Augustine with his followers viewed humanity as replacing the number of angels which was lost by the fall of Satan with

[55] The great contribution of the Proclan Neoplatonism to this is a more optimistic view of matter than is found in Plotinus. It is not in itself evil; cf. on Plotinus, D. O'Brien, 'Plotinus on Evil: A Study in Matter and the Soul in Plotinus' Conception of Human Evil', *Le Néoplatonisme*, pp. 113–46; id., 'Plotinus and the Gnostics on the Generation of Matter', *Neoplatonism and Early Christian Thought*, ed. H. J. Blumenthal, pp. 108–23. There is indeed for Proclus a likeness between the simplicity of the One and that of formless matter; cf. A. Louth, *The Origins*, p. 162, and my 'Aquinas' First Principle', p. 149, nn. 76–80. Thus, the descent in emanation is good if it is carried to the extreme. Thomas has the Proclan re-evaluation of matter from Dionysius; cf. *In de Div. Nom.* IV, xiii–xxiii; and *ST* I, 48, 1 *sed contra*. Dionysius has it from Proclus, *De malorum subsistentia*: cf. Pera's notes to the *In de Div. Nom.* But neither Proclus nor Dionysius work out the consequences of this for anthropology; for Dionysius, cf. ch. II n. 61 below.

his hosts. In this framework man is valued only because of his intellectual soul. Augustine, Gregory the Great, Boethius, Anselm, and Peter
Lombard all hold this view, which is incompatible with the anthropocentrism of Thomas, and the tradition in western theology stemming
from Eriugena. Anselm and Gregory explicitly maintain that mankind
was created for the purpose of supplying the wanted numbers of lost
spirits. But those who follow Dionysius learn to construct a different
conception of man's place in the cosmos, using Greek Christian and
pagan sources as well as drawing on the accomplishments of Augustine. St Thomas never indicates having read the first great result of a
synthesis of Augustine and Dionysius, the *De Divisione Naturae* of
Eriugena, but he certainly used the *Dionysiaca*, which was full of the
doctrines, and fragments of the theological work of the man who first
translated Dionysius into Latin. In any case, twelfth-century enthu-
siasts of Eriugena like Honorius Augustodunensis made his teachings
part of the spiritual atmosphere. This more than Augustinian humanism inspired Aquinas to the great structural innovation which constitutes the *Secunda Pars*.[56]

If man in his independence, freedom, and sin provides the middle
of the Thomist theology, such a being can be reunited to its source,
and such a theology can be made complete only through what unites
God and man.[57] Christ forms the basis of the *Tertia Pars*, joining
what in the *Sentences* is divided between two books. He enables the
reditus and thus allows God to be the subject of the whole work as
both principle and end. Such a view of the relation of the Third Part
to the *Summa* as a whole is opposed to M.-D. Chenu's view that
there are two returns in the work, a natural one in the *Secunda Pars*,
and one through gracious history: 'The transition from *IIa* to the *IIIa
Pars* is a passage from the order of the necessary to the order of the
historical, from an account of structures to the actual story of God's
gifts.'[58]

Two difficulties attend this position. First, it depends upon an
opposition of the historical and the necessary which is not Thomas's.

[56] Complete citations for Plotinus, Augustine, and Augustine's followers are found in
W. J. Hankey, 'The Place of the Proof', p. 389. The evidence for Thomas's knowledge of
Eriugena is given in id. 'The *De Trinitate* of St. Boethius', pp. 371–2 and at ch. II, n. 74
below.

[57] 'Necesse est ut ad consummationem totius theologici negotii . . . de ipso omnium
Salvatore . . . nostra consideratio subsequatur', *ST* III, *prol.*

[58] Chenu, *Toward Understanding St. Thomas*, p. 315; cf. also his 'Création et histoire',
Commemorative Studies, ed. A. A. Maurer, ii, pp. 391–9.

Thomas is eager, like the ancients generally, to resolve the contingent into the essential—he is not an existentialist.

'For the Greek, the question of salvation was primarily a question of know-ledge, but it is not possible to have true knowledge of what is transient in his-tory, only of what is permanent and unchanging. Thomas's starting-point is essentially the same: everything in salvation depends on revelation, but revelation is conceived as the giving of an otherwise inaccessible knowledge of God. We can indeed, says Thomas, have a knowledge, *scientia, de rebus mobilibus* . . . but only on the assumption that we are aware of the immovable order that is presupposed by all motion and change and know how to refer such motion and change to *aliquid immobile*.[59]

Secondly, there is nothing optional about the so-called second return. There is no return in sacred doctrine without it. The very first article of the first question makes clear that a teaching based on revelation is necessary because 'man is ordered to God as to an end which exceeds the rational understanding'. The man of Thomas's *Secunda Pars* 'has freedom and power over his own works', but he is also fallen, and certainly this power cannot bring him to God, who is his end. Over and again Christ is called the *via*.[60] The whole argument is assimilated to the logic of *exitus et reditus* and it is to the traditions which transmit this logic to Thomas that we must be alert.

---

[59] P. E. Persson, *Sacra Doctrina*, p. 254; cf. also A. A. Maurer, *St. Thomas and Histori-city*, Aquinas Lecture 1979 (Milwaukee, 1979), and id., 'St. Thomas and Changing Truths', *Atti del Congresso Internazionale Tommaso d'Aquino*, vi (Naples, 1977), pp. 267–75. G. Lafont, *Structures et méthode dans la Somme Théologique de saint Thomas*, Textes et étude théo. (Paris/Bruges, 1961), ch. 1, considers Chenu's theory along with a number of other current positions and finds it unsatisfactory. A better approach than that of Father Chenu to relating emanationist and creationist structures is found in Jean Trouillard, 'Procession néoplatonicienne et création judéo-chrétienne', *Néoplatonisme: mélanges offerts à Jean Trouillard*, pp. 1–26, where he places Neoplatonic procession as a philoso-phical form within Christianity as a religion.

[60] *ST* I, 2, *prol.*; II, 101, 2; I, 113, 4; III, *prol.*; III, 2, 7; *Comp. Theo.* I, ii, 11–20, pp. 83–4; *De Rationibus Fidei ad Cantorem Antiochenum, Opera Omnia* (*Leonine*) xl, Pars B–C (Rome, 1968), cap. v, p. B62, gives the reasoning; *Super Evangelium S. Ioannis lectura*, ed. v revisa, cura P. Raphaelis Cai (Rome, 1952), xiv, ii, 1863–80. Thomas tells us that sensible things and virtuous life are also *viae*; but, unless these be radically distinguished from, and incorporated into, Christ, 'qui secundum quod homo, via est nobis tendendi in Deum', then there are at least three ways of return in the *Summa*.

II

Eadem via ascensus et discensus: the Place of the Proof of God's Existence[1]

THE proof of God's existence in the five ways of article 3, question 2, requires special attention, for its very presence in the *Summa* would seem to contradict Thomas's representation of the order and logic of sacred doctrine. Moreover, though according to Thomas this question is within the first section of the *Prima Pars*, the treatment of God's essence, it stands by itself. It is separated from the other questions which consider how God is and his operations: 'an Deus sit' is not the investigation of one of his predicates or attributes.[2] This becomes evident when the form of its title as well as the content of the question is compared with the subsequent questions in Thomas's treatise *de divinis nominibus*. Properly Aquinas initiates his discussion of them with question 3, 'de simplicitate Dei'.[3] So we start our structural analysis with a consideration of the place of the proof for God's existence in the *Summa*.

After enquiring whether God's existence is self-evident and whether it can be demonstrated, Thomas asks whether indeed God exists. He raises two objections to God's existence: firstly, the presence of evil in the world, and secondly, that nature, together with human will and reason, are sufficient to explain what we experience. Then, on the other side, he cites God himself. 'But, on the contrary, there is what is said in Exodus 3 by the person of God "I am who I am".'[4] Aquinas starts from what God in his own person says; he begins

---

[1] The substance of this chapter has been published as 'The Place of the Proof for God's Existence in the *Summa Theologiae* of Thomas Aquinas', *The Thomist*, 46 (1982), 370–93, but there are changes of form and an alteration of the content at a crucial point.

[2] E. Sillem, *Ways of Thinking about God* (London, 1961), p. 43.

[3] 'Circa essentiam vero divinam, primo considerandum est an Deus sit; secundo quomodo sit . . . tertio considerandum erit de his quae ad operationem ipsius pertinent . . .', *ST* I, 2, *prol.* These divisions correspond to question 2, questions 3 to 11, and questions 13 to 26 respectively. See *ScG* I, 9 as quoted n. 16 below.

[4] 'Sed contra est quod dicitur *Exod.* III ex persona Dei "Ego sum qui sum"', *ST* I, 2, 3 *sc.* For the significance of this theological beginning, cf. É. zum Brunn, 'La "métaphysique de l'Exode" selon Thomas d'Aquin', *Dieu et l'être*, pp. 245–69. Thomas wishes to avoid all ambiguity about the theological character of the *Summa* 'en mettant en tête de

treating God's existence from what we have been told. Faith seeks understanding but certainly need not commence with philosophical reason.[5] So Aquinas teaches that theology or sacred doctrine is a knowledge which begins from principles made evident to a higher form of cognition, namely that possessed by God and the blessed.[6]

The knowledge from which theology begins is God's own simple knowledge of himself, and all else in him,[7] communicated to the Prophets and Apostles who wrote the canonical books,[8] handed on to us through that Scripture, and summed up in the articles of the faith.[9] Because sacred theology begins with God's own self-revelation grasped by faith, it has a shape and order distinct from natural theology, the theology which is a part of philosophy.[10]

la "Somme de théologie" la parole "*Ego sum qui sum*", et en insistant sur le fait qu'elle est révélée "*ex persona Dei*" ' (p. 267).

[5] 'Dicendum quod argumentari ex auctoritate est maxime proprium huius doctrinae', *ST* I, 1, 8 *ad* 2. While what is able to be known rationally is not an article of the faith, but a preamble and presupposed to it, none the less, 'Nihil tamen prohibet illud quod secundum se demonstrabile est et scibile, ab aliquo accipi ut credibile, qui demonstrationem non capit', *ST* I, 2, 2 *ad* 1. Theology begins with the unity of God not because his unity is rationally grasped but because the one is by nature principle; cf. introduction, n. 32 and *In de Div. Nom.*, *proem*: 'Cuius unitatis et distinctionis sufficiens similitudo in rebus creatis non invenitur'; also, *In de Trin.*, *prol.* with my comment in 'The *De Trinitate*', p. 375.

[6] 'Et hoc modo sacra doctrina est scientia, quia procedit ex principiis notis lumine superioris scientiae, quae scilicet est scientia Dei et beatorem', *ST* I, 1, 2 *resp.*

[7] 'Soli autem Deo convenit perfecte cognoscere seipsum secundum id quod est. Nullus igitur potest vere loqui de Deo vel cogitare nisi inquantum a Deo revelatur. Quae quidem divina revelatio in Scripturis sacris continetur', *In de Div. Nom.* 1, i, 13. 'ut sic sacra doctrina sit velut quaedam impressio divinae scientiae, quae est una et simplex omnium', *ST* I, 1, 3 *ad* 2. 'Unde licet in scientiis philosophicis alia sit speculativa et alia practica, sacra tamen doctrina comprehendit sub se utramque, sicut et Deus eadem scientia se cognoscit, et ea quae facit', *ST* I, 1, 4 *resp.*

[8] 'Innititur enim fides nostra revelationi Apostolis et Prophetis factae qui canonicos libros scripserunt', *ST* I, 1, 8 *ad* 2. Vision of God is the ground of this revelation: the highest kind of rapture, contemplation of God 'in sua essentia' is given to Moses and Paul: 'Et satis congruenter, nam sicut Moyses fuit primus Doctor Iudaeorum, ita Paulus fuit primus Doctor Gentium', *ST* I–II, 175, 3 *ad* 1. See also *ST* I, 12, 11 *ad* 2. This is not, however, the usual method of divine revelation; generally the modes of human knowledge *in via* are respected and there is a special illumination of an object of sense or imagination; cf. P. Benoit, 'Saint Thomas et l'inspiration des écritures', *Atti del Congresso Internazionale Tommaso d'Aquino*, iii (Naples, 1976), pp. 19–30, esp. p. 21. Those to whom there is no direct revelation have the content on authority: 'principia huius doctrinae per revelationem habentur et sic oportet quod credatur auctoritati eorum quibus revelatio facta est', *ST* I, 1, 8 *ad* 2.

[9] 'ita haec doctrina non argumentatur ad sua principia probanda, quae sunt articuli fidei', *ST* I, 1, 8 *resp.*

[10] 'Nam in doctrina philosophiae . . . prima est consideratio de creaturis et ultima de Deo. In doctrina vero fidei . . . primo est consideratio Dei et postmodum creaturarum. Et

Sacred doctrine is able to start with God. After considering God, it shows how creatures come out from God and how he then brings them back into union with himself. Philosophical reason starts rather with creatures and climbs by a long and difficult ladder to knowledge of God.[11] The order of sacred doctrine determines the order of matters in the tripartite structure of the *Summa Theologiae*. It begins with God and treats him and his creative work in the First Part. The movement in this part is from God's simplicity towards otherness and diversity. There is first God's unity, treated initially as substance, and then as operations. The consideration of substance starts in simplicity and ends in unity, but the self-conscious relation of knowledge dominates the operations. The real relation of God to himself in three persons comes next, and then the work of his power in creation. Creation is treated in three sections. First, by privilege of the likeness of their knowledge and spiritual existence to God's, come the angels, then there is the material creation, and finally, because he unites spiritual and material in himself, is man. Man concludes God's creative work just as he also concluded the last section of this part, the section on God's governance of the world, which has a similar tripartite structure.[12]

The Second Part is the largest of the three. It considers man, the image of God. Man drew together and completed God's work of creation and governance in the First Part; now man's work is considered. Thomas says in the Prologue what he means by treating man as the image of God: 'that is to say, man as a source of his own works because he is free and has power over his own deeds'.[13] This part is organized around the virtues and vices and begins, as one would

sic est perfectior: utpote Dei cognitioni similior', *ScG* II, 4; also *ScG* IV, 1; *In de Trin.* as quoted Endnote 1, p. 162 below. *In Sent.* I, *prol.*, pp. 2 ff.; *epilogus*, p. 1092.

[11] Thomas speaks of the length, difficulty, limited availability, and ultimate inadequacy of the rational way from creatures in a number of places; for example, 'veritas de Deo per rationem investigata, a paucis, et per longum tempus, et cum admixtione multorum errorum homini proveniret', *ST* I, 1, 1 *resp.* See also *ScG* I, chs. 2, 3, 4, and IV, 1; *Comp. Theo.* i, 1.

[12] After three questions on general matters, the treatment of providence proceeds as follows: 'Deinde considerandum est quomodo una creatura moveat aliam. Erit autem haec consideratio tripartita: ut primo consideremus quomodo angeli moveant, qui sunt creaturae pure spirituales; secundo, quomodo corpora moveant; tertio, quomodo homines qui sunt ex spirituali et corporali natura compositi', *ST* I, 106, *prol.*

[13] 'Postquam praedictum est exemplari, scilicet de Deo, et de his quae processerunt ex divina potestate secundum eius voluntatem; restat ut consideremus de eius imagine, id est de homine, secundum quod et ipse est suorum operum principium, quasi liberum arbitrium habens et suorum operum potestatem', *ST* I–II, *prol.* Cf. ch. I above.

expect from the Prologue, with man acting for the sake of an end. Freedom consists in man's capacity to shape his actions in accord with what he regards as his complete fulfilment or happiness.[14]

Man's freedom cannot, however, complete the *Summa Theologiae*. The first article of the first question of the First Part said that sacred doctrine is required just because the ultimate end of man is God, the comprehension of whom exceeds human reason. Consequently the *Summa* requires a Third Part beyond that treating man's freedom, power, and works. This concerns Christ, who, uniting God and man, is our way of actually arriving at God our end. The Third Part thus treats Christ, his sacraments through which we are united to him and attain salvation, and the eternal life at which we arrive through Christ by resurrection.

This is the course then which theology runs, a course determined by its origin in God's revelation of himself from beyond the comprehension of human reason and seeking a union past his natural rational capacity. As we have seen, Thomas refined and clarified this theological structure in important ways, but fundamentally its logic derived from the later Neoplatonists and was set out in systematic form in the Christian west as early as the ninth century by John Scotus Eriugena. The rough use of the *exitus–reditus* pattern by Peter Lombard in his *Sentences*, the theological textbook of the High Middle Ages, assured its influence into modern times. Thomas was content with this basic structure, combining the step-by-step derivation of multiplicity from the divine unity and the gathering in and return of this to God again. Indeed, his alterations of the system, as he received it, have the effect of making the circular form more clearly and completely present. However, if this be granted, the need for proofs of God's existence becomes a problem. If we begin from what we have been told about God and from his inner unity, why does theology need, and how can it have, a proof which rises to God from his sensible effects? How can it have a philosophic proof of God's existence?

To renounce the assistance of philosophy to that theology which is sacred doctrine would mistake theology's strength and weakness. On the one hand, it would violate theology's sovereignty, which uses what is subordinate to it. On the other, it would ignore the necessities of human theological thinking. For, although its beginning is established through God's revelation to faith, yet, because of the frailty of human

---

[14] 'Sed finis est principium in operabilibus ab homine', *ST* I–II, 1, 1 *sed contra*. The title of the first question is 'de ultimo fine hominis'.

reason, theology cannot proceed one step on its immense course without assistance from philosophical reason.[15] St Thomas says: 'Among the inquiries that we must undertake concerning God in Himself, we must set down in the beginning that whereby his existence is demonstrated, as the necessary foundation for the whole work. For if we do not demonstrate that God exists, all consideration of divine things is necessarily destroyed.'[16]

The demonstration of God's existence is the necessary foundation of the whole of theology. This is a surprising statement given the descending logic of theological system for Thomas. What can it mean? Minimally, the proof provides evidence that the subject of theological science exists in contradistinction to knowledge of the nature of the subject. The words of Thomas have been taken in this sense and not without some foundation; for, following Boethius, he does distinguish sharply between the knowledge that a thing exists and the knowledge of what it is, and says that we know properly only that God is.[17] Our human faculties are suited only for the direct knowledge of sensible individuals and even these we know only from the outside, through their sensible accidents, and imperfectly, despite their mode of being corresponding to ours.[18] In them and in us, there is a division between

---

[15] Cf. *ST* I, 1, 5 *ad* 2.

[16] 'Inter ea vero, quae de Deo secundum seipsum consideranda sunt, praemittendum est, quasi totius operis necessarium fundamentum, consideratio qua demonstratur Deum esse. Quo non habito, omnis consideratio de rebus divinis necessario tollitur', *ScG* I, 9.

[17] Thomas's statement at this point is very guarded: 'ex effectibus Dei potest demonstrari Deum esse, licet per eos non perfecte possimus eum cognoscere secundum suam essentiam', *ST* I, 2, 2 *ad* 3. Boethius is cited as an authority for this division. For its Neoplatonic character in Thomas cf. ch. IV n. 42 below. The crucial text in Boethius is *De Hebdomadibus* i, 2, on which Thomas had an important commentary: *Expositio super Boetium de Hebdomadibus*, ed. M. Calcaterra, in *Opuscula Theologica*, ed. R. M. Spiazzi, 2 vols., ii (Turin/Rome, 1954). On the history of the interpretation of this text, cf. P. Hadot, '*Forma Essendi*', pp. 143–56. This must replace M.-D. Roland-Gosselin's views on the relation of Thomas to this text (in his *Le 'De Ente et Essentia' de s. Thomas d'Aquin*, Bibliothèque thomiste 8 (Paris, 1948), p. 186, n. 3), which had dominated Thomistic literature. Pierre Faucon, *Aspects néoplatoniciens*, p. 432, also concludes 'la tradition néoplatonicienne illustrée notamment par Boèce fournit à saint Thomas le couple du *Quod est* et l'*esse* sur lequel va s'ériger au xiii siècle la distinction réelle de l'essence et de l'être', and this takes us beyond any distinction of Aristotle. Dionysius is also a medium of transmission. Throughout the *De Divinis Nominibus* he makes a strong contrast between divine and angelic intellect and human reason.

[18] There is much of this agnosticism in Thomas even in respect to our knowledge of the physical world. For a general treatment of it and why it has been played down in Thomism, cf. Josef Pieper, *The Silence of St. Thomas*, ch. 2, and id., 'The Concept of Createdness and its Implications', *Atti del Congresso Internazionale Tommaso d'Aquino*, v (Naples, 1977), pp. 20–7, where he cites *De Veritate*, 3 vols., *Opera Omnia* (Leonine),

the sensible and intellectual aspects of existence. Yet this agnosticism about the nature of things cannot be pushed too far. Our knowledge from sense means that we have no direct knowledge—vision—of the intellectual, but it does not mean that we have no knowledge at all and this applies also to God. The very simplicity of God, the fact that in him existence—that he is—and essence—what he is—are identical, means that our proof must yield knowledge of his nature.[19] It is then primarily for the sake of making God's revelation thinkable, of making it a science, of allowing a consideration of divine things, that the proof is required.[20] When the five ways in the proof are taken together, they can be immediately seen to produce a considerable knowledge of God. He is the unmoved source of the motion, existence, goodness, and perfection of all else, which is ordered into a unity, because the God who does all this knows.[21]

xxii–xxiv, i (Rome, 1975), 4, 1 ad 8, p. 121; *Sentencia Libri de Anima, Opera Omnia* (Leonine) xlv (Rome, 1984), i, i, p. 7, lines 254–5 and *De Spiritualibus Creaturis*, ed. M. Calcaterra et T. S. Centi, *Quaestiones Disputatae*, 2 vols., ii (Turin/Rome, 1965), i, 11 ad 3, p. 414. For another list of texts cf. A. A. Maurer (trans.), *The Divisions and Methods of the Sciences: Questions V and VI of the Commentary on the De Trinitate* (Toronto, 1963), p. xxxv n. 50. To which one might add as typical: 'Nam cum sensus, unde nostra cognitio incipit, circa exteriora accidentia versetur, quae sunt secundum se sensibilia, ut color, et odor, et huiusmodi; intellectus vix per huiusmodi exteriora potest ad perfectam notitiam inferioris naturae pervenire, etiam illarum rerum quarum accidentia sensu perfecte comprehendit. Multo igitur minus pertingere poterit ad comprehendendum naturas illarum rerum quarum pauca accidentia capimus sensu' etc., *ScG* IV, 1.

[19] 'necesse est uti effectu loco definitionis causae ad probandum causam esse, et hoc maxime contingit in Deo. . . . Nomina autem Dei imponuntur ab effectibus . . .', *ST* I, 2, 2 ad 2. M. Grabmann (*Thomas von Aquin: Eine Einführung in seine Persönlichkeit und seine Gedankenwelt* (Munich, 1920), p. 88) puts it thus: 'Die Erkenntnis des Daseins von etwas birgt schon auch irgendwelche Kenntnis seines Wesens in sich. So schlägt denn auch die Erkenntnis, dass Gott existiert, die Brücke, auf welcher die menschliche Vernunft zur Erkenntnis dessen, was Gott ist, vordringen kann.' É. zum Brunn's exposure of the inadequacies of É. Gilson's 'existentialist' representation of Thomas has also the effect of bringing together the knowledge of God's existence and essence in his thought. Cf. introduction, n. 12, p. 5 above. T. C. O'Brien's criticism of Joseph Owens's 'existential focus' in O'Brien's review of *St Thomas Aquinas on the Existence of God* for *The Thomist*, 46 (1982), 644–53, has the same result.

[20] One manner of putting this is to say that by the ways, God is named. F. van Steenberghen has brought this out in his numerous writings on the proof. Two studies in English also elucidate this well: 'So St. Thomas . . . speaks of the proof that "God is" as among those *praeambula* which are necessary to the *scientia fidei*—i.e. *knowledge* of the faith, not faith itself.' '. . . there is no contradiction at all in saying that our means of proof are effects *and* the *quid significet nomen* of God, for they are one and the same', Victor White, *God the Unknown, and other essays* (London, 1956), pp. 52 and 60. 'There is no separate *theological* question about God's existence: the question about God's existence is only raised at all in connexion with the study of what God is', Edward Sillem, *Ways of Thinking about God*, p. 43; chs. 4, 5, and 6 are all relevant.

[21] We arrive at 'aliquod primum movens . . . aliquam causam efficientem primam, . . .

The proof of God's existence in the *Summa* is primarily a summary of the ways, corresponding to Aristotle's four causes, by which thought moves from the world of sensible creatures to God.[22] So the movement of knowledge coming down from God's self-disclosure mediated to us through Scripture meets the movement of thought rising from the scientific understanding of natural phenomena and reaching up towards God. Theology as sacred doctrine starts in the uniting of these two. 'For our deficient understanding is more easily guided into those things which pass reason and are treated by divine science by passing through the world known by natural reason from which the other sciences proceed.'[23]

In commencing with God, sacred doctrine progresses in the same order as God's own self-knowledge.[24] As sacred theology begins with

aliquid quod sit per se necessarium . . . causa necessitatis aliis . . . causa esse et bonitatis et cuiuslibet perfectionis . . . aliquid intelligens', *ST* I, 2, 3. Cf. for similar positive conclusions about the knowledge gained by the proof: J. H. Walgrave, '*Tertia via*', in *Quinque sunt viae*, ed. L. Elders, Studi tomistici 9 (Vatican City, 1980), pp. 65–74, esp. pp. 73–4 and L. Elders, 'Les cinq voies et leur place dans la philosophie de saint Thomas' in the same collection, pp. 136–46.

[22] Cf. A. Kenny, *The Five Ways: St. Thomas Aquinas' Proofs of God's Existence* (London, 1969), p. 36: '. . . Aquinas has two distinct Ways corresponding to two different aspects of Aristotle's efficient causality. If we take these two Ways together we find that the distinction between the Five Ways reflects the distinction between the Four Causes. This is most obvious in the case of the Fifth Way, which clearly depends on the notion of final causality; but the Third Way, as we shall see, concerns itself initially with material causality, and the Fourth argues from formal causality.' Harold J. Johnson, 'Why Five Ways? A Thesis and some Alternatives', *Arts libéraux et philosophie au moyen âge, Actes du quatrième Congrès international de philosophie mediévale* (Montreal/Paris, 1969), pp. 1143–54: 'the schema underlying the five possible ways by which, according to Thomas, the existence of God can be proved is provided by the four causes of Aristotle. Thomas maintains that all of our natural knowledge of God is derived by causal inference from His empirically known effects. He also specifically asserts that God is first cause of all things *in respect of all four causes*' (p. 1143). Aristotle's own argument against infinite regress in the causes is found in *Metaphysics* α. Cf. also Sillem, *Ways of Thinking about God*, ch. 5, *passim*, and J. Owens, 'Aquinas and the Five Ways', *St. Thomas Aquinas on the Existence of God, Collected Papers of Joseph Owens, C.Ss.R.*, ed. J. R. Catan (Albany, NY, 1980), pp. 132–41.

[23] 'sed propter defectum intellectus nostri; qui ex his quae per naturalem rationem ex qua procedunt aliae scientiae cognoscuntur, facilius manuducitur in ea quae sunt supra rationem, quae in hac scientia traduntur', *ST* I, 1, 5 *ad* 2.

[24] 'In doctrina vero fidei, quae creaturas non nisi in ordine ad Deum considerat, primo est consideratio Dei et postmodum creaturarum. Et sic est perfectior: utpote Dei cognitioni similior, qui seipsum cognoscens, alia intuetur. Unde, secundum hunc ordinem, post ea quae de Deo in se in primo libro sunt dicta, de his quae ab ipso sunt restat prosequendum', *ScG* II, 4. Cf. also *ST* I, 1, 7 and I, 2, *prol.*, and *In de Div. Nom.* VII, iv, 729. G. Lafont, *Structures et méthode*, p. 471, puts it thus: 'La hiérarchie de la connaissance théologique est celle même de la science de Dieu: nous la trouvons au prologue déjà plusieurs fois cité de la question 2: *ipse Deus, Deus ut principium et finis*. Les deux

God and knows all else as coming from him and returning to him, so God knows all things in knowing himself, though, unlike our theology, his is a direct and immediate seeing of everything in his own being. This does not mean that the laborious climb to philosophical or natural theology is solely a human work. Thomas agrees with Aristotle that we can have knowledge of God only because God is not jealous; rather he wishes us to share in his knowledge.[25] Both theologies, theology as philosophy and theology as sacred doctrine, are 'divinely given modes of sharing in the one divine science'.[26] In this sharing, philosophical knowledge is subordinate to the knowledge based on Scripture, just as nature is subordinate to grace but always, indeed eternally, presupposed by it, and present with it.[27] We have come some way in understanding what the proof does, but do we understand sufficiently its necessity?

To get hold of the place of this climb from nature to God in Thomas's theology, and indeed partially the place of nature, human freedom, power, and work in his system, it is necessary to digress a little into the historical background of its inclusion in his system. If the proof is primarily derived from the Aristotelian causes, and is in

aspects sont pratiquement inséparables, mais il faut conserver leur ordre: Dieu en lui-même, c'est-à-dire dans son essence et ses Personnes; Dieu principe et fin, c'est-à-dire origine et terme du créé dans sa nature et son économie—et d'une manière toute spéciale, des créatures spirituelles ordonnées à la possession personelle de Dieu.'

[25] Commenting on *Metaphysics A*, 983ᵃ 5–10, Thomas writes: 'Solus [Deus] quidem habet [hanc scientiam] secundum perfectam comprehensionem. Maxime vero habet, inquantum suo modo etiam ab hominibus habetur licet ab eis non ut possessio habeatur, sed sicut aliquid ab eo mutuatum', *In Meta.* i, iii, 64, p. 19. Cf. R. D. Crouse, *Philosophia Ancilla Theologiae*: Some Texts from Aristotle's *Metaphysics* in the Interpretation of Albertus Magnus', *Actas del V Congreso Internacional de Filosofía Medieval*, 2 vols. (Madrid, 1979), i, pp. 657–61, id., 'St. Thomas, St. Albert, Aristotle: *Philosophia Ancilla Theologiae*', *Atti del Congresso Internazionale Tommaso d'Aquino*, i (Naples, 1975), pp. 181–5. The basis of the argument is that God alone possesses the true knowledge of himself, consequently all true knowledge of him comes from his willingness to share it. This can also be given a more evidently Neoplatonic form as in Dionysius. In commenting on the *Divine Names*, Thomas states: 'Ei [Deo] enim soli competit de se cognoscere quod quid est', i, i, 32. 'Esset enim contra rationem bonitatis divinae, si cognitionem suam sibi retineret quod nulli alteri penitus communicaret, cum de ratione boni sit quod se aliis communicet', i, i, 36. God communicates in different forms but all are revelation: 'studium philosophiae secundum se est licitum et laudabile, propter veritatem quam philosophi perceperunt, Deo illis revelante, ut dicitur *Ad Rom.* I, 19', *ST* I–II, 167 *ad* 3. Cf. J. H. Walgrave, 'The Use of Philosophy in the Theology of Thomas Aquinas', pp. 161–93.

[26] R. D. Crouse, 'St. Thomas, St. Albert, Aristotle', p. 183.

[27] Thus the doctrine of created grace: 'Dicendum quod lumen creatum est necessarium ad vivendum Dei essentiam', *ST* I, 12, 5 *ad* 1.

theology only because of an Aristotelian conception of science which allows God both to be the subject of the investigation and to be established as an object in its course,[28] it follows that it is possible for Thomas to use the ways only because of the third wave, which occurred in his time, of the gradual rediscovery of Aristotle.[29] This third wave was the transmission to the medieval west of the sciences of Aristotle: physics, metaphysics or theology, psychology, politics, and ethics as opposed to the two previous waves of logical works. This is not, however, a sufficient explanation. Just because means are present we are not thereby actually enabled or compelled to use them. Theology is not a salad into which anything edible can be thrown. Because it is the most fundamental science, endeavouring to draw reality together under one principle, the knowledge of how its elements are united is essential to it. With what kind of theological structure will Thomas's proof cohere?

Before St Thomas, Christian theology had often thought that it was unnecessary, inappropriate, or impossible to prove God's existence, or, if it was in fact necessary or useful, that a much more direct method than that employed by him was preferable. In the tradition of pseudo-Dionysius, represented in the west most strongly by Eriugena, God is known first of all as non-being[30] Because all determinate and finite beings come out of his fathomless depths and presuppose them as their horizon, it does not seem necessary, appropriate, or possible to

---

[28] See Endnote 1. Whereas Aristotle, as understood by Thomas, makes being as being and God both subjects of his metaphysics, and Thomas has God as the subject of sacred doctrine and proves his existence, other followers of the Philosopher do not allow the science of first principles both to assume and establish them. This is true of both Avicenna and Averroes; see ch. III pp. 65–9 below.

[29] 'Or l'œuvre d'Aristote fut transmise en trois étapes à la pensée théologique de l'Occident. C'est ce qu'on peut appeler les trois "entrées" d'Aristote. La première entrée est celle de la *Logica vetus*. . . . La deuxième "entrée" d'Aristote apporte, au xiiᵉ siècle, les trois autres livres de l'*Organon*. . . . La troisième "entrée" d'Aristote au début du xiiiᵉ siècle, apporte à la science sacrée un ferment philosophique qui n'est plus purement formel, mais qui concerne l'ordre même des objets et le contenu de la pensée', M. J. Congar, 'Théologie', *Dictionnaire de théologie catholique*, xv (1) (Paris, 1946), p. 359.

[30] For this tradition and its pagan philosophical origins, see the introduction, above; my 'Aquinas' First Principle', pp. 144ff. and J. Macquarrie, *In Search of Deity*, pp. 43ff. Thomas interprets this thinking about the first principle so as to be reconcilable with his more Porphyrian doctrine, but it has its effect. For example, 'Sed Deus non est existens, sed "supra existentia", ut dicit Dionysius. Ergo non est intelligibilis, sed est supra omnem intellectum', *ST* I, 12, 1 *obj.* 3. He interprets this: 'Deus non sic dicitur non existens quasi nullo modo sit existens, sed quia est supra omne existens, inquantum est suum esse' and thus he is known but not comprehended; *ST* I, 12, 1 *ad* 3. On Thomas's alteration of Dionysius' doctrine in a cataphatic direction in his reading of him, cf. J. D. Jones, 'The Ontological Difference', pp. 119–32.

prove his existence.[31] On the other hand, a proof does seem appropriate in an Augustinian perspective where God is thought of more positively as being. But, for the Augustinian spirituality, the most natural motion to him, is inward.[32] Within that perspective, Anselm begins by urging us to turn within ourselves toward God; there our thinking must make contact with the only and divine truth by which all truth is known and touches God. Anselm's ontological argument has such a beginning in coming immediately upon an idea of God which directly leads us to the knowledge of the existence which corresponds to this idea.[33]

For Thomas neither of these approaches was satisfactory. A proof was necessary and possible just because the sensible stands between us and God. Because our minds are not immediately with God, proof is necessary, and because the sensible provides the mediation, it is possible.[34] Without this middle there is no proof and Thomas does not call Anselm's argument a proof.[35] For him, the fact that the fool can say in his heart there is no God compels a proof, and that the invisible things of God are known through created things, as St Paul testifies, enables a proof from sensible effects.[36] Thomas's understanding and

---

[31] Thomas holds to be correct John Damascene's statement that God's name is *Qui est* because 'totum ... in se ipso comprehendens habet ipsum esse velut quoddam pelagus substantiae infinitum et indeterminatum'; for 'quanto aliqua nomina sunt minus determinata, et magis communia et absoluta, tanto magis proprie dicuntur de Deo a nobis', *ST* I, 13, 11 *resp.* (Leonine reading). And he places Damascene's notion that the 'cognitio existendi Deum naturaliter est inserta' at the top of the objections showing that no proof for God's existence is necessary; for, it is '*per se notum*', *ST* I, 2, 1.

[32] The inward movement of Augustine's Plotinian spirituality is treated in W. J. Hankey, 'The Place of the Psychological Image of the Trinity in the Arguments of Augustine's *de Trinitate*, Anselm's *Monologion*, and Aquinas' *Summa Theologiae*', *Dionysius*, 3 (1979), 99–110, and in the chapter on Augustine in A. Louth, *The Origins of the Christian Mystical Tradition*. M.-D. Chenu, *Nature, Man and Society in the Twelfth Century: Essays on New Theological Perspectives in the Latin West*, selected, ed., and trans. J. Taylor and L. K. Little (Chicago/London, 1968), tells us that in contrast to pseudo-Dionysius, Augustine found God 'in the intimate depths of his own mind' (p. 63); his orientation was 'toward an interior life that took external objects as mere occasions for its enrichment' (p. 64). To Augustine's use of ' "signs" corresponded a mysticism of the interior life' (p. 125) as opposed to Dionysius' symbolic theology.

[33] Anselm, *Proslogion, Opera Omnia*, ed. F. S. Schmitt, 6 vols. (Edinburgh, 1946–61), i, 1, p. 97, lines 4–8. Compare Augustine, *De Magistro* xi, 38 (*PL* 32, 1216) and Bonaventure, *Quaestiones Disputatae de scientia Christi, Opera Omnia*, 10 vols. v (Ad Claras Aquas, Quaracchi, 1891), *q.* v, pp. 17ff.

[34] 'Sed quia nos non scimus de Deo quid est, non est nobis per se nota, sed indiget demonstrari per se quae sunt magis nota quoad nos et minus nota quoad naturam, scilicet per effectus', *ST* I, 2, 1 and 'Deum esse ... demonstrabile est per effectus nobis notos', *ST* I, 2, 2.

[35] It is treated under 'utrum Deum esse sit per se notum', *ST* I, 2, 1.

[36] These texts are in the *sed contra* of articles 1 and 2 respectively.

use of this famous text from the Epistle to the Romans to justify the use of Aristotelian arguments from what is evident to sense indicates his turning from the Augustinian perspective.[37] What is the standpoint from which such an enterprise takes place?

To understand this as a theological perspective we need to turn again to the intellectual principles of the tradition of pseudo-Dionysius, Boethius, and the *Liber de Causis*. It is in the direction of this Proclan theological tradition that Thomas's thought is moving. The conventions of the contemporary organization of theological study required Thomas to build his first system as a commentary on the Augustinian *Sentences* of Lombard. But we must recollect that our first autograph from St Thomas is his notes of Albert the Great's lectures on the *Divine Names* of pseudo-Dionysius.[38] St Thomas commented on this work, with its quasi-apostolic authority, on two treatises of Boethius, and on the *Liber de Causis*, the last of which he originally thought Aristotle had written. The movement of St Thomas's thought is indicated by the fact that this last work is his final and most personally revealing commentary. In it he not only tells us a good deal about his own thought—as well as explaining the text of the *Liber de Causis*—but he also reveals that he has read the *Elements*

---

[37] 'Ce qui l'oppose aux partisans de la preuve ontologique, telle que l'a exposée saint Anselme, et en fin de compte à Augustin lui-même, c'est l'epistémologie qu'il choisit pour approfondir la signification du *qui est*. On le voit clairement dans l'interprétation non traditionelle que dès la *Commentaire* (sur les Sentences) saint Thomas donne au fameux verset de *Romains* 1, 20, complémentaire *d'Exode* 3, 14, qui pour les Pères grecs et latins signifiait le retour ou la remontée du monde sensible au monde intelligible. Pour Thomas cette remontée a un tout autre sens: il insiste sur l'impossibilité d'arriver à la connaissance naturelle de Dieu autrement qu'en raisonnant à partir de l'expérience sensible', É. zum Brunn, 'La "métaphysique de l'Exode" selon Thomas d'Aquin', p. 253.

[38] Both Peter Calus, in *Vita S. Thomae Aquinatis auctore Petro Calo*, ed. D. Prümmer, *Fontes Vitae S. Thomae Aquinatis*, Fasc. 1 (Toulouse, 1911), p. 25, and William of Tocco, in *Vita S. Thomae Aquinatis auctore Guillelmo de Tocco*, ed. Prümmer, op. cit., Fasc. 2 (St Maximin, 1924), p. 78, tell us that Thomas attended Albert's lectures on the *Divine Names*; cf. also A. Walz, *Saint Thomas d'Aquin*, adapt. franç. par P. Novarina, Philosophes médiévaux 5 (Louvain/Paris, 1962), p. 68. P. Simon, in his *Prolegomena* to his edition of Albert's lectures—Albert the Great, *Super Dionysium de Divinis Nominibus*, ed. P. Simon, *Opera Omnia*, 37(1) (Cologne, 1972), pp. v–xx—traces the manuscript tradition back to the Codex Neopolitanus, of which he writes: 'Exceptis nonnullis versibus, f. 89r et f. 107vb manu scripturae septentrionalis legibiliter scriptis, totus codex litteris lectu valde difficilibus vel paene illegibilibus seu "inintelligibilibus" scriptus est a scriba Italico, qui Thomas de Aquino iuvenis non temere putatur fuisse. Certe Thomas videtur codicem semper fere secum habuisse' (p. viii). For the influence of Dionysius on Albert cf. F. J. Ruello, *Les 'Noms Divins' et leur 'raisons' selon saint Albert le Grand commentateur du 'De Divinis Nominibus'*, Bibliothèque thomiste 35 (Paris, 1963). Eriugena is also influential through his translation of Dionysius; cf. pp. 72–3 n. 23 and pp. 19–20 n. 37.

of Theology itself.[39] He continues to refer to it in his *De Substantiis Separatis*, which dates from the same period.[40] Thomas must be seen in the context of Albert the Great's enthusiasm for Dionysian theology and his establishment of a tradition which becomes explicitly Proclan in the next generation.[41] Nor are its creative figures found only in the thirteenth century. Meister Eckhart and Nicolaus of Cusa have yet to come. Moreover, though there are exceptions, the later Proclan Neoplatonism tends to overpower and assimilate the more Plotinian Augustinian theology when they come into contact. Boethius credited his trinitarian thought to Augustine when in fact he ordered it within a Proclan schema.[42] Thomas is not likely to have felt the difference between these two traditions. Even when medieval thinkers are sensitive to philosophical and theological divergences, they often reconcile or blend the opposed views—as in Eriugena's conflation of

[39] H.-D. Saffrey, 'L'état actuel des recherches sur le *Liber de Causis*, comme source de la métaphysique au moyen âge', *Die Metaphysik im Mittelalter*, 2 vols., ed. F. Wilpert, Miscellanea Mediaevalia (Berlin, 1963), ii, p. 277: 'On voit que ... le *Liber* est officiellement rattaché à la *Métaphysique* d'Aristote, et dans la charte du 19 mars 1255, qui règle le statut de la faculté des Arts à Paris, nous trouvons inscrit parmi les œuvres d'Aristote comme texte à lire officiellement, le *Liber de Causis*. C'était l'année du *De ente et essentia* de S. Thomas d'Aquin, dans lequel on voit cet auteur s'appuyer trois fois explicitement sur l'autorité du *Liber*.' It was only in his exposition of the work, his last commentary, that he reveals his knowledge of its Arab and Proclan sources: 'in arabico vero invenitur hic liber qui apud Latinos *De causis* dicitur, quem constat de arabico esse translatum et in graeco penitus non haberi: unde videtur ab aliquo philosophorum arabum ex praedicto libro PROCLI [*Elements*] excerptus', *In de Causis, prooemium*, p. 3, lines 5–8. Since this depended on having before him the translation just made by William of Moerbeke of Proclus' *Elements*, the discovery is no doubt actually William's; cf. L. Minio-Paluello, 'La tradition aristotélicienne', p. 171 and Saffrey, art. cit., n. 11, p. 269. Albert the Great did not make the identification before Thomas: Leo Sweeney, SJ, '*Esse Primum Creatum* in Albert the Great's *Liber de Causis et Processu Universitatis*', *The Thomist*, 44 (1980), 603 n. 13. On the date of the *Expositio* (after 1268), cf. Saffrey's edition and article and *De Subs. Sep.*, p. D6. The *Liber de Causis* is printed in *Tijdschrift voor Filosofie*, 28 (1966), 90–203. A new critical edition is now being prepared by Richard Taylor.

[40] '... en effet, le chapitre 20 cite deux propositions de Proclus, les propositions 169 et 196', *De Sub. Sep.*, p. D6.

[41] Berthold of Moosburg, *Expositio in Elementationem Theologicam Procli* is an example. For comments on the history from Albert, see the 'Presentazione' by E. Massa. For connections between Alan of Lille and Boethius, Dionysius, Berthold, and Theodoric of Freiberg, see the articles by J. Châtillon, 'La méthode théologique d'Alain de Lille' and J. Jolivet, 'Remarques sur les *Regulae theologicae* d'Alain de Lille' in *Alain de Lille, Gautier de Châtillon, Jakemart Giélée et leur temps*, textes réunis par H. Roussel et F. Suard (Lille, 1980), pp. 45–60, 83–99.

[42] Cf. my 'The Place of the Psychological Image of the Trinity' and 'The De Trinitate of St. Boethius'.

Augustine and Dionysius.[43] Thomas has little more historical sense than most of his contemporaries.[44]

We have already considered some consequences of the Proclan Neoplatonism for the development and character of Christian systems of theology. Of great importance is his teaching on the soul. Plotinus sees it partly in the world of sense and body, which soul animates, and partly above in the higher realm of pure intellectual life. This higher soul never loses its contemplation of higher things and its direct access to the intellectual world.[45]

Consequently, for Plotinus, as for Augustine and his followers, the movement to God in inward. Proclus, on the other hand, following his predecessor Iamblichus, in accord with their mutual tendency to formalize and to differentiate entities, and with his sense of the weight of the downward movement in reality, and the weakness and evil of our human situation, sees our soul as altogether fallen into the sensible

[43] There is now a large literature on this subject to which one of the latest contributions is B. Stock, 'In Search of Eriugena's Augustine', *Eriugena: Studien zu seinen Quellen, Vorträge des III. Internationalen Eriugena-Colloquiums, Freiburg im Breisgau, 27.—30. August 1979*, ed. W. Beierwaltes (q.v.), Abhandlungen der Heidelberger Akademie der Wissenschaften 1980, 3 (Heidelberg, 1980), pp. 85–104. For further items, cf. nn. 14, 15, and 16 in R. D. Crouse, '*Intentio Moysi*: Bede, Augustine, Eriugena and Plato in the *Hexaemeron* of Honorius Augustodunensis', *Dionysius* 2 (1978), 135–57. Dr Crouse concludes that Eriugena's system is 'by no means a rejection, or a tendentious misinterpretation of Augustine [but] a modification by selection and emphasis' (p. 144). This accords with J. J. O'Meara, 'Eriugena's Use of Augustine in his Teaching on the Return of the Soul and the Vision of God', *Jean Scot Érigène et l'histoire de la philosophie*, Colloques internationaux du CNRS, Laon, 1975 (Paris, 1977), pp. 191–200, and '*Magnorum Virorum Quendam Consensum Velimus Machinari* (804D): Eriugena's Use of Augustine's *de Genesi ad litteram* in the *de divisione naturae*', = *Eriugena: Studien zu seinen Quellen*, pp. 105–16, also for the Third Eriugena Colloquium, and certainly is close to Eriugena's own consciousness. Goulven Madec's piece, 'L'augustinisme de Jean Scot dans le "De praedestinatione"', should be consulted as well.

[44] Considerable claims have often been made for Thomas's historical sense; partly they have been based on the supposition that he discovered the non-Aristotelian character of the *Liber de Causis* and its origins in Proclus. This is no longer held by the best critics; cf. n. 39 above. In fact, Thomas tends to put the best possible interpretation on his sources. An excellent example of this is provided by J. van Banning, 'Saint Thomas et l'*Opus imperfectum in Matthaeum*', *Atti dell'VIII Congresso Tomistico Internazionale*, viii, pp. 73–85. Thomas alters the text of this Arian work in reporting it so as to give it a fully orthodox sense. Delightfully, in one place he reads the author's Arian distinction between Father and Son as anti-Sabellian.

[45] On the division of the soul, see Plotinus, *Enneades, Opera*, ed. P. Henry et H. R. Schwyzer, Museum Lessianum, Series Philosophia 33, 3 vols. (Paris/Brussels, 1951–73), IV, 8, 8, 2–3; V, 1, 10, and C. G. Steel, *The Changing Self: A Study on the Soul in later Neoplatonism: Iamblichus, Damascius and Priscianus* (Brussels, 1978), p. 31 and elsewhere. On the movement inward see *En.* I, 6, 8, 4; I, 6, 9, 1; III, 8, 6, 40; IV, 8, 1, 2; V, 8, 2, 32; V, 8, 11, 11; VI, 9, 7, 17; VI, 9, 11, 38 and A. H. Armstrong, 'Salvation: Plotinian and Christian', *The Downside Review* 75 (1957), 126–39, reprinted in *Plotinian and Christian Studies*.

world.[46] The very last proposition of his *Elements of Theology* is: 'Every particular soul, when it descends into temporal process, descends entire; there is not a part of it which remains above and a part which descends.'[47] Both the content and the position of this statement are important.

The content requires a relation between man and the sensible world. For Proclus, man in his weakened and humbled position requires help from outside. This help takes the form of theurgy.[48] 'Theurgic union is attained only by the perfective operation of unspeakable acts correctly performed, acts which are beyond all understanding, and by the power of unutterable symbols which are intelligible only to the gods.'[49] Thus, although Proclus, in contrast to St Thomas, still holds that the soul knows itself through knowing its higher spiritual causes,[50] an essential move toward exterior sensible reality has been made, both in respect to the soul's return to God, and in its location in the cosmos.

A Christian spirituality moving forward from this position is to be found in pseudo-Dionysius' symbolic theology, which advances to God beginning from symbols 'natural, historical, scriptural or sacramental'.[51] This theology, worked out in Eriugena, forms a foundation

---

[46] 'What Plotinus grasped in one global intuition, will be separated into distinct elements by Iamblichus and, later on, by Proclus. To each logical distinction, there must correspond an ontological differentiation', C. Steel, *The Changing Self*, p. 31. Cf. E. R. Dodds, *Elements*, comment on prop. 211, pp. 309–10. There is an extensive literature on the relation of Plotinus to theurgy: e.g., A. H. Armstrong, 'Was Plotinus a Magician?', *Phronesis*, 1 (1955), 73–9, in *Plotinian and Christian Studies*; E. R. Dodds, *The Greeks and the Irrational*, Sather Classical Lectures 25 (Berkeley and Los Angeles, 1951), and *Pagan and Christian in an Age of Anxiety: Some Aspects of Religious Experience from Marcus Aurelius to Constantine*, Wiles Lectures 1963 (Cambridge, 1965); and J. Trouillard, *La mystagogie de Proclus*, which compares the place of mystical experience for Plotinus and Proclus. A. Smith, *Porphyry's Place in the Neoplatonic Tradition: A Study in Post-Plotinian Neoplatonism* (The Hague, 1974), sees Porphyry as decisive in the move toward philosophical magic because of his desire to find permanent salvation for the whole soul (p. 70).

[47] *Elements*, prop. 211 (Dodds, p. 185).

[48] 'In opposition to Plotinus, Iamblichus contended that the soul could not find salvation without the help and grace of the gods. *Theoretical* contemplation must go together with the performance of holy *acts* and rites which have been instituted by the gods themselves. The philosopher is not only a theologian (one who reveals the divine) but also a theurgist (one who performs divine acts). It is remarkable how closely Iamblichus here approached the criticism which was formulated in some Christian circles against the Platonic doctrine of the soul', C. Steel, *The Changing Self*, pp. 156–7. See also H.-D. Saffrey, 'Quelques aspects de la spiritualité', pp. 172–3.

[49] Iamblichus, *De Mysteriis*, ii, 11 (p. 96, line 17–p. 97, line 2); the translation is from Dodds, *Elements*, p. xx.

[50] *Elements*, prop. 167; cf. Dodds's comments pp. 202–3; for St Thomas, cf. *ST* I, 87, 3.

[51] M.-D. Chenu, *Nature, Man and Society*, p. 125.

for medieval aesthetics, so that Abbot Suger at St Denis structures and adorns his Gothic abbey around the principle that the material light gleaming on silver and gold or in jewel and glass leads the spirit to the immaterial God.[52] The twelfth-century revival of this Dionysian spirituality develops a previously absent sense of the reality of the natural world, a universe functioning by its own second causes through which man comes to God.[53] This movement towards secularization and feeling for the natural world is crucial to Thomas's use of the Aristotelian proofs, and in fact he refers to Dionysius when he wishes to justify the knowledge of God through sensible effects.[54]

One of the characteristics of the later Neoplatonism identified by modern scholarship is its greater acceptance of Aristotle. This also characterizes the Christian thinkers. Whereas Augustine has little use for Aristotle, Boethius thinks that he and Plato have the same teaching, and Boethius is responsible for the first of the three Aristotelian waves to wash the west.[55] Thomas says early in his career that

[52]
>
> Nobile claret opus, sed opus quod nobile claret
> Clarificet mentes, ut eant per lumina vera
> Ad verum lumen, ubi Christus janua vera.

From *Sugerii Abbatis Sancti Dionysii. Liber De Rebus in Administratione Sua Gestis*, xxvii, in E. Panofsky, *Abbot Suger* (2nd edn.; Princeton, 1979), pp. 46–8. Again, 'Unde, cum ex dilectione decoris domus Dei aliquando multicolor, gemmarum speciositas ab exintrinsecis me curis devocaret, sanctarum etiam diversitatem virtutum de materialibus ad immaterialia transferendo, ... videor videre me quasi sub aliqua extranea orbis terrarum plaga, quae nec tota sit in terrarum faece nec tota in coeli puritate, demorari, ab hac etiam inferiori ad illam superiorem anagogico more Deo donante posse transferri', ibid., xxxiii, pp. 62–4. Cf. W. Beierwaltes, '*Negati Affirmatio*'.

[53] M.-D. Chenu, *Nature, Man and Society*; the majority of the essays in this volume touch on this question, the most important being perhaps 'The Platonisms of the Twelfth Century', pp. 49–98. On the idea that the world constituted a whole, see p. 67. Cf. also R. D. Crouse, '*Intentio Moysi*', pp. 153–5 on Honorius and the Platonists of Chartres, their sense of cosmos, and openness to the world. Eriugena's influence is of great importance; for him 'matter was no longer that independent and opposing principle which it had so readily appeared to be for earlier Christian interpreters of the *Timaeus*, nor was it that "nearly nothing" but yet something which troubled Augustine's striving for a philosophically consistent cosmology' (p. 142).

[54] See *ST* I, 1, 9 and n. 57 just below. This identification is not unique to Thomas; cf. M.-D. Chenu, *Nature, Man and Society*, p. 135: 'pseudo-Dionysius himself, thanks to his religious sense, so deflected Platonic idealism toward a keener subjection to sensible realities that, later, he was occasionally bracketed with Aristotle in concordances or "harmonies" of "the authorities" (*concordia auctoritatum*)'.

[55] Boethius and Porphyry, as opposed to Plotinus, try to reconcile Plato and Aristotle; cf. on Boethius, *De interpretatione*, ed. C. Meiser (2nd edn.; Leipzig, 1880), p. 79, on Porphyry and later Neoplatonism, R. T. Wallis, *Neoplatonism* (London, 1972), pp. 24ff. On the Christians: André Tuilier, 'La tradition aristotélicienne à Byzance des origines au VIIᵉ siècle. La formation de la scolastique byzantine', *Actes du Congrès de Lyon 1958*, *Association Guillaume Budé* (Paris, 1960), pp. 186–97. Christian Neoplatonists in this

Dionysius follows Aristotle,[56] and, while he later comes to understand the Platonic character of Dionysius' thought, he continues to see what is usually regarded as the Aristotelian ascent to God through knowledge of the sensible world in Dionysian terms.[57] To Dionysius he credits the following: 'Men reach the knowledge of intelligible truth from proceeding from one thing to another.' 'The intellectual soul then ... holds the last place among intellectual substances ... it must gather its knowledge from divisible things by way of sense.' 'The human mind cannot rise to the immaterial contemplation of the celestial hierarchies unless it uses the guidance of material things.' 'Divine things cannot be manifested to men except under sensible likenesses.' 'Men receive the divine illuminations under the likeness of sensible things.'[58] (It is worth noting the necessity of the turn to the sensible expressed here and that it is precisely this which divides Thomas from Bonaventure, who is also less Aristotelian than Thomas. Bonaventure certainly uses the sensible way in his theology but he regards it as only one way. The soul may also take the Augustinian, more directly inward route.)[59] Thus, the context of this turning to the sensible in which an Aristotelian proof eventually becomes necessary and intelligible is originally religious, in the most cultic and mystical signification of that term. It is the subsequent development of what has been called a more 'secular' feeling for the natural world,[60] and the discovery of the sciences of such a world, which actually brings us to the proof itself.

The place of man and the position of the statement about his place

tradition are comparatively more accepting of Aristotle than their pagan predecessors; because of their 'belief that as long as God's transcendence is preserved the difference between various levels of creation diminishes in importance' (p. 205), they have a 'tendency to apply Aristotelian principles at all levels of the created world in contrast to the pagan approach in which such doctrines were confined in their application to the realm of sense', pp. 235–6, S. E. Gersh, *From Iamblichus to Eriugena*. On the congeniality of Dionysius' turn to the sensible and an Aristotelian perspective, cf. M.-D. Chenu, *Nature, Man and Society*, p. 135. R. D. Crouse, '*Semina Rationum*' speaks of the 'ecumenical' position of Boethius (p. 77).

[56] 'Dionysius autem fere ubique sequitur Aristotelem, ut patet diligenter inspicienti libros ejus', *In II Sent. d.* 14, *q.* 1, *a.* 2, p. 350.

[57] 'plerumque utitur stilo et modo loquendi quo utebantur platonici', *In de Div. Nom.*, proem.

[58] *ST* I, 79, 8; I, 76, 5; I, 88, 2 *obj.* 1; I–II, 99, 3 *ad* 3; I, 108, 1. The list is from A. C. Pegis, Index of Authors, *The Basic Writings of Saint Thomas Aquinas*, 2 vols., ii (New York, 1945), p. 1168.

[59] E. H. Cousins (ed.), *Bonaventure: The Soul's Journey into God, The Tree of Life, The Life of St Francis*, The Classics of Western Spirituality (London, 1978), p. 23.

[60] M.-D. Chenu, *Nature, Man and Society*, pp. 45 ff., and id., 'S. Thomas innovateur'.

in the *Elements of Theology* is really part of this content. His soul descends into the temporal process and all of it is there. In Proclus, this is the final statement in his systematized theology. Although St Thomas's view of man is exactly of this kind, for him and for the first western Christian systematic theologian, Eriugena, this is not the end of theology. Man is rather the pivot-point, the hinge or crux, on which the cosmos turns. For these thinkers, man's reason is distinguished from intuition or *intellectus* by reason's divided or discursive nature. In Eriugena, Gen. 2: 20, associating man with the naming of the beasts, means that the sensible world comes into particularized sensible being through man and his form of divided knowing, and is restored to its heavenly and intellectual unity in the redemption of man in Christ.[61] We have seen how man, uniting the material and spiritual creation through his unity of body and soul and, as free agent in the world, forms the structural centre of the *Summa Theologiae*.

Neoplatonic theology, Christian or pagan, by no means universally applauds this anthropocentrism, which is not to be identified with the very general conception that man is a microcosm, uniting in himself the elements of spiritual and material reality.[62] We have referred

---

[61] 'in homine . . . universaliter creatae sunt', *De Divisione Naturae* iv, 8 (PL 122, 774A). 'Quoniam substantiarum divisio quae a deo sumpsit exordium et gradatim descendens in divisione hominis in masculum et feminam finem constituit, iterum earundem substantiarum adunatio ab homine debuit inchoare et per eosdem gradus usque ad ipsum deum ascendere in quo . . . non est divisio quoniam in eo omnia unum sunt', *De Div. Nat.* ii, 6 (532A), p. 20. Cf. É. Jeauneau, 'La division des sexes chez Grégoire de Nysse et chez Jean Scot Érigène', *Eriugena: Studien zu seinen Quellen*, ed. W. Beierwaltes, pp. 33–54; B. Stock, 'The Philosophical Anthropology of Johannes Scottus Eriugena', *Studi medievali*, 8 (1967), 1–57, and R. D. Crouse, '*Intentio Moysi*', especially pp. 142–4 and D. F. Duclow, 'Dialectic and Christology in Eriugena's *Periphyseon*', *Dionysius*, 4 (1980), 99–118. I. P. Sheldon-Williams, 'Eriugena's Greek Sources', The Mind of *Eriugena*', ed. O. O'Meara and L. Bieler (Dublin, 1973), pp. 1–15, notes that Dionysius has no extended anthropology and that Eriugena must leap over him to the Greek fathers and to Augustine for this element of his thought. He sums up the central role of man in Eriugena nicely: 'This is the process of creation and the constitution of nature, the *datum optimum*. The process culminates in man and is thus contained in man, and it is from man that the return takes its inception. Since this is the same process in reverse, the hierarchies are disposed in man in the reverse order, and since time is created with the universe and man therefore in his present state is a creature of time, they succeed one another in time, and are the three stages of human history, past, present, and future' (p. 12).

[62] Thus the term microcosm is not used in Eriugena except in one unfavourable context: 'La raison en est à chercher dans le *De hominis opificio* de Grégoire de Nysse. Au chapitre 16 de cet ouvrage (PG 44, 177D—185D) Grégoire critique violemment la théorie philosophique de l'homme-microcosme. Loin d'exalter la nature humaine, pense-t-il, cette théorie la dégrade et l'avilit, puisqu'en insistant sur le fait que l'homme est composé des quatre éléments, elle lui fait gloire d'une propriété qui lui est commune

already to the ridicule of the notion by Plotinus[63] and, while the Proclan psychology provides philosophical means by which Christian theology can develop its humanism, this was not its original purpose or meaning. The doctrine that every particular soul is totally descended into the realm of becoming has its origin in Iamblichus' reflection that the Plotinian view is inconsistent with the facts of human sin and misery.[64] Proclus' *Elements* presents the degradation of man. As H.-D. Saffrey puts it: 'le malheur de l'homme c'est d'être un individu, et tout l'effort du philosophe consiste à se hausser de nouveau à l'universel et au Tout'.[65] We have seen that Augustine, Gregory the Great, Boethius, Anselm, and Peter Lombard all hold a view which seems incompatible with the anthropocentrism of Eriugena and Aquinas, viz. that man makes up the number of the angels who fell with Satan.

The much more positive view of man in Eriugena, his twelfth-century followers like Honorius Augustodunensis and St Thomas, emphasizes rather his relation to the sensible creation and his freedom. Significantly, for both Eriugena and Thomas the dominant influence at this point is that of the Greek Fathers. Man's place at the bottom of the ladder of spiritual creatures is seen positively in Thomas, because, as in Eriugena, his knowing is the source of the begin of sensible creatures, and his redemption is the basis of their return to God. In Thomas, man's knowing is also suited to the sensible world so that his body becomes essential, not only to his communication with all other reality, but even for his knowledge of himself.[66] We have suggested how the Proclan–Dionysian Neoplatonism is at work

avec les moucherons et les rats', É. Jeauneau, *Jean Scot, Homélie sur le Prologue de Jean*, Sources chrétiennes 151 (Paris, 1969), appendix vii, p. 337. '... within the Christian tradition ... —as among Platonists— ... there will necessarily be a certain tension between the understanding of man as being, as it were, in the image of the material creation, and the idea that man was created in the image and likeness of God; the latter view implying, as it does, a super-human destiny, which could not be fulfilled within the function of a microcosm related primarily to the empirical world as macrocosm', Lars Thunberg, *Microcosm and Mediator: the Theological Anthropology of Maximus the Confessor*, Acta Seminarii Neotestamentici Upsaliensis 25 (Lund, 1965), p. 142. As the following quotations from Plotinus show, this is only part of the problem.

[63] *En.* II, 9, 5, 1–11; also II, 9, 9, 46–56 and A. H. Armstrong, 'Man in the Cosmos: A Study of Some Differences between Pagan Neoplatonism and Christianity', *Romanitas et Christianitas*, ed. W. den Boer *et al.* (Amsterdam/London, 1973), pp. 5–14, reprinted in *Plotinian and Christian Studies*.

[64] Cf. Dodds, *Elements*, p. 309.

[65] H.-D. Saffrey, 'Théologie et anthropologie', p. 208, where he is summarizing the doctrine of *In Remp.* i (Festugière, p. 52, lines 6–24).

[66] 'seipsum intelligat intellectus noster secundum quod fit actu per species a sensibilibus abstractas per lumen intellectus agentis', *ST* I, 87, 1.

in this development. But further, the sensible world provides the sphere in which man shows his freedom. As its governor, he stands to it as God stands to the whole of creation, and so he is seen as image of God.[67] It is for him. On this account, the eternal raising up of the sensible world is also related to man. 'Because the bodily creation is finally ordered to be in accord with the state of man ... it will be necessary for it to have a participation in the light of his glory.'[68] The sensible world has become something separate from man, but their interrelation requires resurrection of sensible creation with him.

The proof of God's existence is necessitated by the position of man descended into the temporal, sensible world and turning toward it in order to rise out of it. Theology evidently needs this rise in order to make its beginning intelligible to man, for it starts with God, and is addressed to this humble creature separated from the intelligible world. But it is not because theology is human science that man has a crucial place in it. Man's place and role are objectively given. Because theology is primarily the knowledge of God and those who have the vision of him, man's crucial role is determined by the structure of reality. The movement from both God and man which determines the rhythm and structure of the *Summa Theologiae* is a reflection of the inner rhythm and structure of being. Not only is the whole a movement from God to material creation and back through man, but this pulse of going out and return runs through the individual parts of the work.

The Neoplatonists gave this form to the Aristotelian notion of activity or pure act,[69] by which Thomas understands God,[70] and he

---

[67] See *ST* I–II, *prol.*, and *ScG* III, 1: 'Quaedam namque sic a Deo producta sunt ut, intellectum habentia, ejus similitudinem gerant et imaginem repraesentent: unde et ipsa non solum sunt directa, sed et seipsa dirigentia secundum proprias actiones in debitum finem.' The difference between the freedom and ruling power of God and of man is indicated structurally in the *Summa Theologiae* by placing the treatment of man's nature in the *de deo* under creation while his operations go into the second part. God's nature and operations are treated together.

[68] The full text is: 'Quia vero omnia corporalia sunt quodammodo propter hominem ... tunc etiam totius creaturae corporeae conveniens est ut status immutetur, ut congruat statui hominum qui tunc erunt.... Quia igitur creatura corporalis finaliter disponetur per congruentiam ad hominis statum; homines autem non solum a corruptione liberabuntur, sed etiam gloria induentur ... oportebit quod etiam creatura corporalis quandam claritatis gloriam suo modo consequatur', *ScG* IV, 97. Cf. also *Comp. Theo.* i, 69–70.

[69] 'According to Proclus' general principles, we should expect it to be possible to identify motions described as processions and reversions with motions described as activities, for the strictest definition of activity is "the combination of procession and reversion in a single cyclic process"', S. E. Gersh, *ΚΙΝΗΣΙΣ*, p. 131. Cf. also p. 4.

[70] 'primum ens oportet esse purum actum', ST I, 9, 1.

and they both regard this activity as a kind of motion.[71] This motion-less motion structures the five ways of the proof, which allows us some understanding of God's being, just as it orders the proof that he is the first cause in each of the four senses of cause, with which the treatment of creatures begins.[72] In both cases the causes are arranged in a way never used by Aristotle.[73] Thomas starts with the source of motion and concludes with the final cause, so that there is a return to the motion-less beginning.[74] Between these two opposed causes are placed, first the material cause, and then the formal. The reduction of the material cause to God shows that there is no barrier to his efficacy. The formal is linked to the final, since the moving end is the good as known and perfected in form, here the divine essence itself.[75] Thus, the being which God is may be said to return to itself.[76]

---

[71] 'actus perfecti ... hoc igitur modo quo intelligere est motus, id quod se intelligit, dicitur se movere', *ST* I, 18, 3 *ad* 1. Cf. also *ScG* I, 13; *ST* I, 9, 1 *ad* 1 and *ad* 2; I, 19, 1 *ad* 3; and ch. III below.

[72] *ST* I, 44.   [73] See ch. VII below.

[74] The doctrine that God remains in himself when he moves upon himself in love and knowledge is found in Dionysius. Cf. *In de Div. Nom.* IV, vii, 369; IV, viii, 390; IV, x, 439; IV, xi, 444. It is worked out systematically in the relation of the first and fourth divisions of nature in Eriugena, i.e. 'quae creat et non creatur' and 'quae nec creat nec creatur'; *De Div. Nat.*, i, 1 (PL 122, 441), p. 36. 'Prima nanque et quarta unum sunt, quoniam de Deo solum modo intelliguntur; est enim principium omnium, quae a se condita sunt, et finis omnium quae eum appetunt, ut in eo aeternaliter immutabiliterque quiescant', ibid., ii, 2 (PL 122, 526), p. 8. The passage just following, which contains the same doctrine, was in the *Corpus Dionysianum* used by Thomas; cf. H. F. Dondaine, *Le Corpus Dionysien de l'Université de Paris au XIIIe siècle* (Rome, 1953), p. 137. Thomas probably has the doctrine from Dionysius, but he might also know this portion of the *De Divisione Naturae*.

[75] 'Quia igitur mundus ... est factus a Deo per intellectum agentem ... necesse est quod in mente sit forma, ad similitudinem cuius mundus est factus. Et in hoc consistit ratio ideae', *ST* I, 15, 1. The ideas are the divine essence 'secundum quod ad alia comparatur', *ST* I, 15, *ad* 2. The essence is also his end and good: 'nihil aliud a Deo sit finis Dei ... ipsemet est finis respectu omnium quae ab eo fiunt. Et hoc per suam essentiam, cum per suam essentiam sit bonus ... finis enim habet rationem boni', *ST* I, 19, 1 *ad* 1. It is because he is the object of his own knowing and willing that he is spoken of as moving: 'obiectum divinae voluntatis est bonitas sua, quae est eius essentia. Unde cum voluntas Dei sit eius essentia, non movetur ab alio a se sed a se tantum, eo modo loquendi quo intelligere et velle dicitur motus', *ST* I, 19, 1 *ad* 2.

[76] 'redire ad essentiam suam nihil aliud est quam rem subsistere in seipsa', *ST* I, 14, 2 *ad* 1. Cf. K. Rahner: 'The beingness (*Seiendheit*), the intensity of being (*Seinsmächtigkeit*) of the being of an existent is determined for Thomas by the *reditio super seipsum*, the intensity of being is determined by the degree of possibility to be able to be present to itself', *Spirit in the World*, trans. from the 2nd German edition by W. Dych (London, 1968), p. 69. P.-C. Courtès, 'L'être et le non-être selon saint Thomas d'Aquin', *Revue thomiste* 67 (1967), 389–90: 'Là, dès le départ, la métaphysique de l'être se lie à la *conversio ad seipsam*, qui est la loi de la substance spirituelle pour saint Thomas comme pour l'auteur du "*de Causis*". Ce n'est donc pas une métaphysique du sens commun, purement et simplement. La métaphysique ne se constitue pas comme un discours sur l'être

The five ways provide, as has often been claimed, the philosophic rationality through which the subsequent argument of the *de deo* becomes intelligible. There are many ways of establishing this connection. Some to which we will not attend in detail are different from but are compatible with the path we shall follow.[77] The return of being upon itself, or motionless motion, is a conception which is capable of giving divine intelligibility to a theology which unifies motions from above and from below. What we will attempt to show in what follows is how this form, which unifies the five ways into a single proof and makes their presence and position in Thomas's *Summa* understandable, exhibits the idea which links the levels of divine, spiritual, and corporeal life internally and to each other. The motion and multiplicity within the divine spiritual life is the intelligible pattern and basis of the motion and multiplicity at the lower levels.[78] The whole is constructed out of circular activities uniting two contrary motions. The proof is crucial in Thomas because the five ways initiate that movement from below, from man to God, which is essential to theology. The proof stands at the beginning but it is not a ladder which is then pushed away. It remains present in the content and structure of what follows. The way toward understanding the unity in Aquinas of form and content, of natural and revealed theology, of God and his creation, is indicated by this epigrammatic formula: 'Quia vero naturalis ratio per creaturas in Dei cognitionem ascendit, fidei vero cognitio a Deo in nos e converso divina relevatione descendit; est autem eadem via ascensus et descensus' (*ScG* IV, 1).

---

en soi; elle s'élabore dans la conscience de la jonction de l'être et de l'esprit.' And F. M. Genuyt, *Vérité de l'être et affirmation de Dieu: essai sur la philosophie de saint Thomas*, Bibliothèque thomiste 42 (Paris, 1974), ch. vii, pp. 139 ff., discusses the *redire ad essentiam suam*: 'L'être en soi est donc Réflexion sur soi' (p. 150).

[77] e.g. Leo Elders, SVD, 'L'ordre des attributs divins dans la *Somme théologique*', *Divus Thomas*, 82 (1979), 225–32; id., 'Le problème de l'existence de Dieu dans les écrits de s. Thomas d'Aquin (A propos du livre de F. van Steenberghen)', *Divus Thomas*, 86 (1983), 171–87; and id., 'Les cinq voies'.

[78] This is a way of relating the divine and creation which is central to Proclan Neoplatonism; cf. S. E. Gersh, *ΚΙΝΗΣΙΣ*, p. 2.

III

Rediens ad seipsum: Questions 3 to 11[1]

THE matter of questions 3 to 11 is the attributes of God's unity of essence—how he is, or better, is not.[2] Thomas begins by showing us how and why God is called simple, and he concludes the series with the name one. Only part of what is ascribed to the divine unity falls into this first section. Here Thomas treats what belongs to God's substance as opposed to his operations. The difference between them is that the substantial predicates do not depend directly upon self-consciousness, but this is the foundation of the operations. For example, under substance God is recognized as good; the corresponding operation is will.[3] God's will is just his possession of his own good as the object of desire.[4]

The sources of some principles by which this material is structured, and which situate it in the *Summa Theologiae*, are already before us. A Proclan logic, which separates the simple from the complex and so also substance from activities, makes it intelligible why, in treating God, unity should be divided from the distinct persons and substance from operations. Within this Neoplatonic thinking, it is evident how and why theology should begin with God and with him as one or simple and good. We have found a Christian model for this treatise: an exemplar which Thomas thought about carefully and for a long time, written by a man who had great authority for him. Moreover, the *De Divinis Nominibus* of Dionysius also treats the names belonging to the unity of the divine persons, and, beginning with unity, draws the naming of God back to the simplicity from which it started. None of these principles or sources would, however, allow us to suppose that

---

[1] A shorter version of this chapter was presented to the Sixth International Congress for Mediaeval Philosophy in Bonn in 1977 and is published as 'The Structure of Aristotle's Logic and the Knowledge of God in the *Pars Prima* of the *Summa Theologiae* of Thomas Aquinas', *Sprache und Erkenntnis im Mittelalter*, Miscellanea Mediaevalia 13/2, ed. A. Zimmermann (Berlin/New York, 1981), pp. 961–8.

[2] 'Sed quia de Deo scire non possumus quid sit, sed quid non sit, non possumus considerare de Deo quomodo sit, sed potius quomodo non sit', *ST* I, 3, *prol.*

[3] *Q.* 6, 'de bonitate Dei' and *q.* 19, 'de voluntate Dei'.

[4] 'Sed objectum divinae voluntatis est bonitas sua, quae est eius essentia', *ST* I, 19, 1 *ad* 3.

affirmative predications could properly be made of God. A tradition originating in Porphyry has been discerned in which it becomes comprehensible how being can have a priority in theology and thus such predications might be ascribed to God, but Porphyry himself did not draw this conclusion.[5] Identifying operative principles and sources helps define our questions, but it is not the same as discerning the logic by which the argument of Aquinas proceeds.

Understanding Thomas's own peculiar synthesis of the diverse theological logics which he inherited has enabled us to recognize why the nine questions which first name God were preceded by a proof for God's existence. Further, we have some hold on why the proof starts with the moving sensible. Discovering how Thomas's ordering of the five ways differs from the sequences of the four causes in Aristotle's various lists points us to the notion of motionless motion. This idea suggests a means of uniting being and essence and also unifying knowledge of the finite and knowledge of God. If motionless motion describes the logic of a circle by which God's name simple is joined to his name one after he is extended to infinity and seen to exist in things (*qq.* 7–8), then we may well have found what unites God's being and his activities, and what enables affirmative predication of him. Our task is to see how the circle which is the return of being to itself provides the means of understanding the structure of questions 3 to 11. But further, we must understand how Thomas uses this result of Proclus' fusion of Plato and Aristotle so as to arrive in questions 12 and 13 at a more positive account of how we name God than that given by Proclus or any of his followers prior to St Thomas himself. Bringing out what is more positive in Thomas's use in theology of the circular form requires us to begin by going over again some previously covered ground. We commence by looking once more at question 1 and the structure of the five ways in the proof of God's existence.

The first question, 'de sacra doctrina, qualis sit et ad quae se extendat', starts with an article asking whether it is necessary to have another knowledge beyond what natural reason can attain in the philosophical disciplines: 'utrum sit necessarium praeter philosophicas disciplinas aliam doctrinam haberi'. Such a knowledge, namely *sacra doctrina*, is compelled by the ordination of man to an end exceeding reason's comprehension: 'quia homo ordinatur ad Deum sicut ad quendam finem qui comprehensionem rationis excedit'. The imme-

---

[5] While Porphyry's position as identified by P. Hadot is a negative theology of being, it does make proper predication comprehensible or at least was used to this end.

diately subsequent articles continue to place this knowledge beyond
the categories of the humanly achieved arts and sciences. It transcends
the distinction of *scientia* and *sapientia*,[6] namely the difference between
the intellectual intuitive wisdom which knows the first principles and
the rationative activity which applies this knowledge to the various
objects of the sciences.[7] It is primarily speculative, but it comprehends
the practical within itself, thus passing beyond the distinction of
human sciences into theoretical and practical.[8] Moreover, it has no
place in the mutually certifying structure of scientific knowledge—the
hypothetical rise from science to wisdom and the deduction from wisdom to science. Plato established this as the dialectic through which
knowledge attained whatever certainty belongs to it. Finding such a
unifying dialectic is the problem Aristotle set himself in his *Metaphysics*, first philosophy, or theology.[9] The transcendence of the
categories of human knowledge is necessary because of the incapacity
of man for his principle. The weakness of his intelligence, adapted to
the knowledge of sensible particulars, makes him presently unfit for
the splendid vision of pure intellectual substance. Man cannot raise
himself to the knowledge of God: God must reveal himself. On the
other hand, it is the character of God, the object of this knowledge,

[6] Cf. *ST* I, 1, 2 'uturm sacra doctrina sit scientia' and article 6 'uturm haec doctrina sit
sapientia'.

[7] Wisdom is knowledge of the principles: 'sapiens dicitur in unoquoque genere, qui
considerat causam altissimam illius generis.... Ille igitur qui considerat simpliciter
altissimam causam totius universi, quae Deus est, maxime sapiens dicitur: unde et
sapientia dicitur esse divinorum cognitio', *ST* I, 1, 6. Science applies the principles:
'ratio scientiae consistat in hoc quod ex aliquibus notis alia necessario concludantur', *In
de Trin.* ii, 2, p. 86, lines 22–3; 'principia cuiuslibet scientiae vel sunt nota per se, vel
reducuntur ad notitiam superioris scientiae', *ST* I, 1, 2 *ad* 1. These notions of science
and wisdom come from Aristotle; cf. *Post. Analytics* i, 2; *Metaphysics A*, 2; *Nic. Eth.* vi.

[8] 'Unde licet in scientiis philosophicis alia sit speculativa et alia practica, sacra
tamen doctrina comprehendit sub se utramque, sicut et Deus eadem scientia se cognoscit, et ea quae facit. Magis tamen est speculativa quam practica, quia principalius
agit de rebus divinis quam de actibus humanis . . .', *ST* I, 1, 4. 'Cum ista scientia quantum ad aliquid sit speculativa, et quantum ad aliquid sit practica, omnes alias transcen-
dit tam speculativas quam practicas', *ST* I, 1, 5. See also *ST* I, 14, 16.

[9] Plato, *Republic* vii, 13–14; Aristotle, *Metaphysics*, especially *B*. Sacred theology does
not have its principles provided by any of the philosophical sciences—'non enim accipit
sua principia ab aliis scientiis, sed immediate a Deo per revelationem' (*ST* I, 1, 5 *ad* 2)—
nor does it provide their principles: 'Propria autem huius scientiae cognitio est quae est
per revelationem, non autem quae est per naturalem rationem. Et ideo non pertinet ad
eam probare principia aliarum scientiarum, sed solum iudicare de eis', *ST* I, 1, 6 *ad* 2.
As D. J. M. Bradley puts it, 'The philosopher cannot allow and the theologian should
not demand that theology be placed at the apex of a philosophically constructed
hierarchy of the sciences', 'Aristotelian Science and the Science of Thomistic
Theology', 170. Cf. Endnote 1, p. 162 below.

which enables this transcendence. 'Dicendum quod Deus sit subiectum scientiae' (I, 1, 7).

He reveals its principles, the articles of faith.[10] Sacred doctrine is wisdom and science, when it knows both God in himself, and all else in relation to him. It is theoretical, because it knows the God who possesses all things by seeing them in his own essence, and it is subordinately practical, because this God makes all things in his vision of them. This is possible because theology's subject, God, stands above these human divisions and is the absolutely free self-sufficient source and end of everything. God's own science is the only ground of all theology.

On account of the dependence of human knowledge in this life upon sense, neither the metaphysical theology, which crowns the natural and moral sciences as they seek their principle, nor revealed theology is capable of *propter quid* demonstration, that is deduction of the content from intuitive vision of the divine essence. Metaphysical theology can give a demonstration *quia* about divine things, proceeding from the natural creation as an effect. For sacred doctrine, faith provides the knowledge of the principles, and the demonstrations in sacred theology are of the consequences of these presupposed principles. Since both theologies depend upon a knowledge, God's own, which in this world neither kind of theologian possesses in its proper form, both are subalternate to God's science of himself and of all else in himself. In this subordinate relation, revealed and natural theology become two sides of a circle moving up toward God and descending from him. God unites the arcs and alone enables the movement of theological reasoning. Just how man is drawn into this motion appears in articles 8, 9, and 10.

After the transcendence of sacred doctrine is established in repect of the twofold relation—natural and gracious—of man to his principle, the argument turns. The modes of human rationality, against which sacred doctrine was originally set in contrast, are now restored to it. The sovereignty of its object places all at its disposal: 'Since grace does not destroy nature but perfects it, it is necessary that natural reason should serve faith, just as the natural inclination of the will follows love. Hence also the Apostle says, 2 Cor. 10: 5: "Bringing every thought into captivity for the service of Christ".'[11] Thus the three

---

[10] 'Quod etiam manifestum fit ex principiis huius scientiae, quae sunt articuli fidei, quae est de Deo', *ST* I, 1, 7.

[11] 'Cum igitur gratia non tollat naturam, sed perficiat, oportet quod naturalis ratio

articles which follow article 7, 'utrum Deus sit subjectum huius scientiae', show that sacred doctrine is 'argumentativa', that Sacred Scripture uses metaphors and has one literal sense. That the science is argumentative establishes its use of the modes of discursive human reason despite its superiority. The very superiority, which enables this free use, compels it, for, as we discovered in article 5, the raising of the mind through the discipline of its sciences is necessary for the better adaptation of its weakness to this supra-rational knowing. The employment of metaphor by Scripture involves the same free condescension of the divine superiority to our weakness. The reason for this condescension is learned from the pseudo-Dionysius:

For God provides for everything in accord with what is proper to its nature. It is however natural to man that he come through sensible things to intellectual, because all our cognition has its beginning in sense. So properly in Sacred Scripture spiritual things are handed on to us under corporal metaphors. And this is what Dionysius says, I cap. *De Cael. Hier.*: 'It is impossible for the divine ray to shine on us except wrapped up in different sacred veils.'[12]

Because Scripture has spiritual things under material images, it cannot communicate its highest teaching directly and it has many senses. The three spiritual senses—'allegoricus', 'moralis', and 'anagogicus'—are more appropriate to the higher forms of theological discourse, those which show us the kind of life we should imitate, and which take us to speculative contemplations of the eternal glory. But divine concession to the limits of our reason tied to sensation, and the consequent constraint on what will persuade mankind, founds theological discourse, and reveals what all men must know to be saved, in a primary sense which is historical and literal.[13] The sense human reason is best fitted to understand. So the last articles of question 1 restore a subordinated human reason

subserviat fidei, sicut et naturalis inclinatio voluntatis obsequitur caritati. Unde et Apostolus dicit, II *ad Cor*. X[5]: "In captivitatem redigentes omnem intellectum in obsequium Christi"', *ST* I, 1, 8 *ad* 2. Cf. I, 5 *ad* 2 on the ancillary character of other sciences and R. D. Crouse, 'St. Thomas, St. Albert, Aristotle', on the source in Aristotle of this image.

[12] 'Deus enim omnibus providet secundum quod competit eorum naturae. Est autem naturale homini ut per sensibilia ad intelligibilia veniat, quia omnis nostra cognitio a sensu initium habet. Unde convenienter in Sacra Scriptura traduntur nobis spiritualia sub metaphoris corporalium. Et hoc est quod dicit Dionysius, I cap. *De Cael. Hier.*: "Impossibile est nobis aliter lucere divinam radium, nisi varietate sacrorum velaminum circumvelatum"', *ST* I, 1, 9.

[13] *ST* I, 1, 10; cf., for this interpretation, M. D. Jordan, 'The Modes of Thomistic Discourse', 95 ff.

which the first article had found incapable of reaching man's true good.[14]

The first question is then a dialectical circle in form, suggestive of the Neoplatonic structures we have previously identified in the content and ordering of Thomas's theology. This is present for St Thomas's own understanding in terms of the meeting of the movement of God's self-revelation coming down from him and of the human philosophical endeavour to rise from creatures toward God—the latter enterprise archetypically displayed in the work of Aristotle, the Philosopher. The logic of sacred doctrine is revealed by identifying what Aristotle's science cannot reach. It uses his categories to point at what escapes them, and then it incorporates within the sovereign sufficiency of sacred doctrine the Aristotelian argumentative *ratio*, by which the necessity of principles is discovered, and the Aristotelian rise through the sensible to the spiritual, the latter significantly given authority by Dionysius. Thomas identifies the movement downward from the principle as sacred doctrine's peculiar privilege. We, however, know it to belong to Neoplatonism and to have been made explicit as the origin of theological system by Proclus. Dionysius communicates the theurgic side of Proclus to Aquinas; using it, suitably transformed, Thomas is able to give a theological justification to Aristotle's logic. None the less, the deficiency of Aristotle's philosophical science is the same for Thomas and Proclus.

Prop. 12 follows *Rep.* 509B in identifying the efficient with the final cause of the universe: the ἀρχὴ τῆς προόδου is also the τέλος τῆς ἐπιστροφῆς. It is Pr.'s prime quarrel with Aristotle that on this cardinal point he lapsed from the Platonic teaching: the Aristotelian system affirms the upward tension towards

---

[14] All these elements—Aristotle's psychology, *ratio* in theology, the primacy of the literal sense of scripture—are wonderfully unified by Beryl Smalley: 'The Aristotelian held that substance could only be known through its sensible manifestations. In adapting Aristotle to Christianity, St. Thomas united soul and body much more closely than the Augustinians had done.... Transferring his view of body and soul to "letter and spirit", the Aristotelian would perceive the "spirit" of Scripture as something not hidden behind or added on to, but expressed by the text.... Under the influence of the Aristotelian concept of science, theologians brought themselves to admit in theory what they had long recognized in the practical organization of teaching. Theology is a "speculative science"; it proceeds to new conclusions from the premises of revelation just as each of the inferior sciences starts from its own agreed assumptions. Its method is argumentative, not exegetical. At last theologians felt sufficiently sure of themselves to drop the fiction that all their work was a mere training for the allegorical interpretation. They formally freed theology from exegesis, and hence exegesis from theology', B. Smalley, *The Study of the Bible in the Middle Ages* (2nd edn.; Oxford, 1952), pp. 292–4.

a God who κινεῖ ὡς ἐρώμενον without tracing the downward chain of causal
dependence. Pr. urges that the conception of deity as goal of desire is unintel-
ligible when divorced from its counterpart, the conception of deity as source
of being. . . .[15]

The initial question also involves another union of Aristotle and
Proclus.

Historians are correct in identifying a relation to Aristotle in
Thomas's notion that theology is a science with God as its subject.[16]
Thomas is quite explicit that God, as principle of being, is the subject
of the Aristotelian metaphysics, in fact this is what makes it theology.[17]
God in himself is one of the topics treated in sacred doctrine and the
Summa Theologiae begins with a treatise *de deo*. Its form resembles the
treatise *de divinis nominibus* established by Proclus more than anything
found in Aristotle, but certain features mark it as Aristotelian. First,
Thomas's treatise on the names of God is about the absolutely first
principle. It is not about inferior gods and it makes proper predications about the first. It is probably because Thomas was also an heir of
the Neoplatonic tradition stemming from Porphyry that one of the
characteristics given to the first is *esse*. What, however, most definitely
marks Thomas's theology as neither Porphyrian nor Proclan is his
description of the nature of sacred doctrine corresponding to his con-
fidence that positive predications are properly made of the absolutely
first principle. That is, that theology is called by Thomas a *scientia*
having *deus* as its *subiectum*. Such a statement, implying the validity of
epistemic knowledge in respect of the principle itself, would be impossible for a Neoplatonist.[18] It is not a Dionysian conception; for the

[15] Dodds, *Elements*, p. 198.

[16] M.-D. Chenu is the special historian of scientific theology in the High Middle
Ages; his article 'La théologie comme science au XIIIe siècle', *Arch. hist. doct. lit. du moyen
âge*, 2 (1927), 31–71, shows how Thomas as theologian 'travaille selon toutes les
exigences et les lois de la *demonstratio* aristotélicienne' (p. 33). Cf. also his *La théologie
comme science au XIIIe siècle*, 3rd edn. revised, Bibliothèque thomist le 33 (Paris, 1957), *La
théologie au douzième siècle, S. Thomas d'Aquin et la théologie*, and *Toward Understanding Saint
Thomas*.

[17] Cf. ch. I pp. 23–5 above.

[18] Thus *obj.* 1 *art.* 7 depends upon the statement of John of Damascus: 'In Deo quid
est, dicere impossibile est.' Cf. S. Lilla, 'The Notion of Infinitude in Ps. Dionysius
Areopagita', *Jour. of Theo. Studies*, 31 (1980), 93–103, which brings out the unknowability
of God resulting from his infinity both as this derives from Dionysius' Neoplatonic
sources and from the influence of Gregory of Nyssa's Aristotelian argument. This
essential unknowability prevents science of the highest principle. Stated just in this
way, there is no contradiction with H.-D. Saffrey's assertion that Iamblichus and his
followers 'sont les fondateurs de la "théologie comme science"', 'Quelques aspects',
p. 169.

pseudo-Areopagite, the names are not proper predicates of God. Proclus is explicit that the soul must altogether pass beyond ἐπιστήμη to rise to God. For Plotinus, union with the One is perfectly achieved neither in νόησις, nor certainly in science, but only when the soul has gone beyond that self-knowledge by which it turned back toward its source, and discovered a more profound identity than knowledge gives.[19] Their views on predications complement what moderns call their epistemologies.[20]

It is not only the Neoplatonic tradition which is incomplete from Thomas's standpoint, owing to what its negative theology of the One excludes, but Aristotle and his followers have also a conception of theology which lacks the breadth of *sacra doctrina*. The relation of the various objects of such a theology is considered within Aristotle's tradition in the form of the question as to whether being as being or separate substance is the subject of metaphysics. Thomas interprets Aristotle as teaching that the highest science has both subjects: being because of its inclusiveness, and separate substance because it is principle. The subject of metaphysics, being as being, is given in the most immediate and confused human apprehension of reality.[21] As such it is assumed. What primarily interests wisdom as the most intelligible being (thus the highest fulfilment of knowledge and the appropriate object of the highest science) and as the most real being (thus the principle of the subject, being as being) is God, who is himself the

---

[19] *En.* VI, 9 endeavours at many points to describe the union beyond the duality of νοῦς, the vision beyond the distinction of subject and object: τάχα δε οὐδὲ "ὄψεται" λεκτέον "τὸ δὲ ὀφθέν", εἴπερ δεῖ δύο ταῦτα λέγειν, τό τε ὁρῶν καὶ τὸ ὁρώμενον, ἀλλὰ μὴ ἓν ἄμφω · τολμηρὸς μὲν ὁ λόγος. (VI, 9, 10, lines 11-14.) Plotinus searches for another language than that of thinking or seeing: τὸ δὲ ἴσως ἦν οὐ θέαμα, ἀλλὰ ἄλλος τρόπος τοῦ ἰδεῖν, ἔκστασις καὶ ἅπλωσις καὶ ἐπίδοσις αὐτοῦ καὶ ἔφεσις πρὸς ἁφὴν καὶ στάσις (VI, 9, 11, lines 22-5). As beyond νοῦς, the final union is above the discursive reasonings in the soul which are, for Plotinus, the sciences. Νόησις is beyond these and union is still higher (*En.* VI, 9, 5). The doctrine of Proclus at *In Timaeum*, 92 C, i, p. 301, 23 ff., seems fundamentally the same. The noetic activity which is the prelude to union is beyond ἐπιστήμη. Indeed, it will call these reasonings stories: ὅτε καὶ τοὺς ἐπιστημονικοὺς λόγους μύθους ἡγήσεται συνοῦσα τῷ πατρὶ καὶ συνεστιωμένη τὴν ἀλήθειαν τοῦ ὄντος (92 D, i, p. 302, lines 4-6).

[20] Cf. P. Hadot, 'Apophatisme et théologie négative'.

[21] *In Meta.* I, ii, 46, pp. 13-14; IV, vi, 605, pp. 167-8. It is impossible here to go into the great question which divides the realist and the transcendental Thomists, namely how *esse* is known, whether there is an intuition of being as being; compare J. Maritain, *Challenges and Renewals: Selected Readings*, ed. J. W. Evans and L. R. Ward (London, 1966), p. 121 and É. Gilson, *Réalisme thomiste et critique de la connaissance* (Paris, 1939), p. 215, with K. Rahner, *Spirit in the World*, pp. 25-9, esp. p. 25 n. 8 and the introduction by J. Metz, pp. xliii-xlv; E. Coreth, *Metaphysics*, ed. and trans. J. Donceel (New York, 1968), pp. 34-5; B. Lonergan, 'Metaphysics as Horizon' in Coreth's *Metaphysics*, pp. 207-9.

object of demonstration.[22] On the basis of this understanding of Aristotle, Thomas is able to think how philosophical theology, rising from sense knowledge, and scriptural theology, descending from the self-revelation of spiritual substance, are able to meet. Aristotle's unification of ontology and theology is thus crucial for Thomas's conception of sacred doctrine. Yet metaphysics, first philosophy or theology, remains a distinct science among others for Aristotle, and the inclusion of the whole scope of articulated reality in theology as the only knowledge is not directly the work of Aristotle.[23] But it is at the point where Aristotle's onto-theo-logy is necessary for Aquinas that his followers fail Thomas.

Avicenna's *De Philosophia Prima* or *Metaphysica* or *Scientia Divina*[24] forms a part of a larger work *Kitāb al-shifā'* (The Healing).[25] The larger whole contains logic, physics, and mathematics as well as this metaphysics and so it resembles a Neoplatonic system. Moreover, the metaphysical part, although having elements corresponding to the content of Aristotle's *Metaphysics*, comprehends as well moral and political sciences and a psychology through which transition is made from intellect to will. The treatise, consequently, concludes with the contracts which constitute the family and the state. In this way, Avicenna's system is moving, under the obvious influences, in the direction which Thomas's sacred doctrine assumes. On the other hand, Avicenna is determined that our knowledge of God has an independence of the sensible which is appropriate to the absolute being of God himself and desires that a certain basis for all science be provided. Metaphysics cannot then receive its object as something given to it and established by physics but must prove its existence; the proof must not be from sensible existences, hence its special metaphysical or ontological character. However, Avicenna also accepts that a science cannot prove its own subject. Where, then, would it start? In

[22] *In Meta.*, *prooemium*, p. 1: 'oportet illa esse maxime intelligibilia, quae sunt maxime a materia separata'; cf. also *ST* I, 12, 1. *In de Trin.* v, 4, p. 194: 'quod est principium essendi omnibus, oportet esse maxime ens'.

[23] What there is in Thomas beyond Aristotle is put nicely by J. Owens, 'Existence and the Subject of Metaphysics', p. 256: 'the subject of sacred theology includes many things besides God. Correspondingly, the subject of metaphysics includes God as well as all other things.'

[24] References are to Avicenna Latinus, *Liber de Philosophia Prima sive Scientia Divina*, i–iv, ed. S. van Riet (Louvain/Leiden, 1977). The Venice edition of 1495 gives the title as *Metaphysica sive Prima Philosophia*; I am dependent upon it for what lies outside the critical edition.

[25] Cf. the 'introduction doctrinale' entitled 'Le statut de la métaphysique' by G. Verbeke, pp. 1*ff.

consequence, although God or separate substance is among its objects as principle of its subject, he is not its subject. Because 'the subject of every science is something the existence of which is conceded',[26] the subject of this science must be being as being. God is 'himself one of those things sought in this science'.[27] Indeed 'divine sciences do not inquire about anything else except things separate from matter both in definition and existence'.[28] Yet it is only as united with other beings under a common conception that God is in the science. 'If, however, one considers the causes inasmuch as they possess being and considers all that belongs to them so considered, it will be necessary that the subject be being as being.'[29] This position is not without likenesses to that of Thomas, but it is unable to hold together the extremities as Thomas does. That theology could both call God the *subiectum*, and prove his existence from sensible things, would be unthinkable within Avicenna's categories. Similarly, the elements of the Thomistic synthesis fall apart in Averroes.

Agreeing with Avicenna that a science cannot demonstrate its own object, but differing on the nature of physics and metaphysics and their relation, Averroes drives the sides apart in another way. He does not begin with being precedent to matter but with physical reality; the proof for God's existence belongs to physics. Metaphysics receives its subject from physics and is dependent upon it.

Physics studies material forms and secondly it studies simple forms separate from matter, and it is the science which considers being taken simply. But it ought to be noted that this kind of being, being which is separate from matter,

---

[26] 'subiectum omnis scientiae est res quae conceditur esse', Avicenna i, 1, p. 4, line 62. He also teaches 'Nulla enim scientiarum debet stabilire esse suum subiectum', ibid., p. 5, line 85.

[27] 'ipse unum de his quae quaeruntur in hac scientia', ibid., p. 4, line 60.

[28] 'divinae scientiae non inquirunt nisi res separatas a materia secundum existentiam et definitionem', ibid., p. 2, lines 28–30.

[29] 'Si autem consideratio de causis fuerit inquantum habent esse et de omni eo quod accidit eis secundum hunc modum, oportebit tunc ut ens, inquantum est ens, sit subiectum', ibid., i, 2, p. 8, lines 49–51. This is the penultimate sentence of the first chapter. Commencing with being as being enables a demonstration of God without dependence on physical reality, for being as being is prior to matter: 'quia ens, inquantum est ens, et principia eius et accidentalia eius inquantum sunt, sicut iam patuit, nullum eorum est nisi praecedens materiam nec pendet esse eius ex esse illius', i, 2, p. 16, lines 97–9. This self-sufficient science provides the certitude of the lower sciences: 'Contingit igitur ut in hac scientia monstrentur principia singularium scientiarum quae inquirunt dispositiones uniuscuiusque esse', i, 2, p. 15, lines 77–9. God will then be named 'certitudo veritatis', i, 2, p. 16, line 93. Thomas is not likely to have regarded Avicenna's enterprise as a proper demonstration but rather it would seem, like Anselm's argument, an attempt to treat God's existence as self-evident; on this see further below.

is not demonstrated except in this natural science, and whosoever says that first philosophy is necessary to demonstrate the existence of separate beings errs. For these separate beings are the subjects of first philosophy, and it is shown in the *Posterior Analytics* that it is impossible that any science demonstrate the existence of its own subject, but rather it concedes its existence. This is either because its existence is self-evident, or because it is demonstrated in another science. Here Avicenna made a great error when he said that the metaphysician demonstrates the existence of the first principle, and when he proceeded to do this in his own book about the divine science, through the way he thought necessary and essential in that science.[30]

Averroes' position establishes a more immediate relation between physics and metaphysics than Avicenna's does, but it deprives theology of the independence and absolute character, its judgemental freedom, the movement from above, which belongs to theology as sacred doctrine in Thomas. Further, in the end, metaphysics, as the investigation of one kind of being, becomes an isolated special science. Neither of these Aristotelian solutions has the breadth of the sapiential science of Thomas.

In his *Summa Theologiae*, the five ways demonstrate an object already given for faith. And analogously, like Avicenna and Aristotle, Thomas permits the subject of metaphysical theology both to be given and to be demonstrated. But for Aquinas, the ontological arguments provided by Avicenna or Anselm are not real demonstrations of God's existence because they are not adequately grounded in the sensible, where human knowledge of God must begin. So Thomas turns to Averroes to correct Avicenna. The proof must begin with the sensible physical. On the other hand, the opposing demand for a recognition of the freedom of theology is conceded by drawing the physical into theology.

Thomas's movement beyond Aristotle and those self-consciously following him is comprehensible only through his own way of taking

---

[30] 'Naturalis considerat de formis materialibus, secunda autem de formis simplicibus abstractis a materia, et est illa scientia, quae considerat de ente simpliciter. Sed notandum est, quod istud genus entium, esse, secundum separatum a materia, non declaratur nisi in hac scientia naturali. Et qui dicit quod prima Philosophia nititur declarare entia separabilia esse, peccat. Haec enim entia sunt subiecta prima Philosophiae et declaratum est in Posterioribus Analyticis quod impossibile est aliquam scientiam declarare suum subiectum esse, sed concedit ipsum esse, aut quia manifestatum per se, aut quia est demonstratum in alia scientia. Unde Avicenna peccavit maxime, cum dixit quod primus Philosophus demonstrat primum principium esse, et processit in hoc in suo libro De Scientia Divina, per viam quam existimavit esse necessariam et essentialem in illa scientia', Averroes, *Commentaria in I Physicorum*, in Aristotle, *Opera*, iv (Venice, 1574), pp. 47ʳF8–47ᵛH. For a summary of Averroes' doctrine and further references, cf. E. Gilson, *History*, p. 644 n. 21.

up the Neoplatonic and especially Proclan theology. The theology of
Proclus, as opposed to that of Aristotle, is not directly a knowledge of
the first principle but rather a knowing of it only as manifest in all else
and of all else as unified into one reality through relation to the unknown
One. The development of this unified systematic knowledge occurs
together with a strongly negative theology; there is a determination to
set the first beyond all science, predication, and being. The negative
element is certainly present in Thomas and modifies his science of God
in himself; his *Summa Theologiae* is a wonderfully ordered and comprehensive treatment of all else as it comes from and returns to God. After
question 1 is concluded wherein theology appeared as the science
which treats God and all else *sub ratione Dei*, Thomas sets out in the prologue of question 2, 'de Deo, an Deus sit', his plan for the whole work.
There, Aristotle is present when he speaks of sacred doctrine as cognition of God 'secundum quod in se est', but Proclus makes his influence
felt when Thomas goes on to say that he will also treat God in this
science 'secundum quod est principium rerum et finis earum'. It is a
Christian understanding of sacred doctrine involving a positive revelation of the divine nature, and a humanity raised to receive this through
its reasonings about physical things, which is able to unite as never
before these two aspects of divinity and these two opposed theologies in
one science under a most comprehensive conception of the *ratio Dei*.

Earlier we attempted to show that the five ways in the proof of
God's existence, though they correspond to the four causes of Aristotle, are given an order never used by Aristotle when listing his
causes. Rather they constitute in Thomas's ordering a Neoplatonic
circle. This merging of Aristotle and Neoplatonic logic was also
represented as appearing in Thomas's use of Dionysius to provide
theological authority for his emphasis on the rise of man to spiritual
things through the sensible, which ascent is also typified for him in the
structure of the sciences of Aristotle. The unification of these Hellenic
and Hellenistic approaches is readily enough seen. What is not so
clear is their import and balance. We propose now to restate the circle
described by the ways in order to bring out its significance for
Thomas's restoration of the finite, namely sense and discursive reason
and their objects, and the affirmation of positive predication in the
knowledge of God in the *Summa Theologiae*.[31]

[31] As also L. Elders, 'L'ordre des attributs', p. 229, who shows 'la présence massive
des cinq voies dans les questions concernant les attributs divins et montre comment la
voie négative et la voie affirmative se complètent mutuellement'.

The order of the five ways not only demonstrates once more that the separation of the divine from the finite and their subsequent unification is the characteristic logical structure of these questions, but also clarifies its theological point. The first way identifies God as first in a series of movers. The second, from efficient causality, distinguishes the first and what follows on it as belonging to different orders of being. Efficient cause is separated from moving cause by its capacity to produce a new substantial being, rather than a modification of an existing being. The third way emphasizes the gulf between the first principle and all else. For it deals with the contrast between the generated and corrupted and what is not subject to these changes in the form of the distinction between the possible and the necessary. 'It proceeds from the connatural material composition of the beings of experience that is an intrinsic "possibility" to existence and non-existence, i.e. to come into being and to pass away.'[32] This is the way most satisfactory to thinkers like Avicenna and John Duns Scotus. They endeavour to move to the necessary being from the possible in order to have a proof for God which reflects his own independence of actual finite existents. For these thinkers the first two ways cannot be transformed so as to free them from their beginning in sense experience. Thomas is not following Avicenna on the meaning of 'possibilia esse et non esse', but the form in which he adverts to the materiality of things so as to raise the mind to God passes beyond the sense matter has in physics and we find ourselves 'sur le plan plus [*sic*] profond de la considération métaphysique'.[33] This way seems then to represent the furthest distance in the movement from sense experience and it is the turning-point. Thomas explicitly includes here a return to creatures in the denomination of God at the end of the way. He is 'causa necessitatis aliis'. The fourth carries this further. God is in all things as 'causa esse et bonitatis et cuius perfectionis'. Finally, reflecting upon the perfection of nature in that it has a purpose and end operative in it rather than considering its incompleteness as moved or contingent or corruptible, God is named positively. This is not only because he is immanent in things, being that 'a quo omnes res naturales ordinantur ad finem', but also because he is himself 'intelligens'. The argument has come full circle. For in thought, the return of being upon itself becomes explicit and it can be known how beginning and end are joined in a motionless motion. The first principle thinks and, through this thinking, by which the divine orders to itself

---

[32] T. C. O'Brien, review of Owens, 647.   [33] See Endnote 2, p. 163.

as end its goodness, being, and perfection dispersed as finite existence, there is a return to the motionless beginning, 'primum movens quod a nullo movetur'.[34] What has itself as end and is moved by nothing outside it fully possesses itself in all it does. The form here displayed in which Thomas both distinguishes the first and what comes from it and unites them involves the development of the conception of God in the direction of all-inclusive self-relation and provides a plan for the questions which follow.

Thomas certainly regards unmoving motion, in the sense of 'actus perfecti', as a valid way of speaking about God, showing that he has brought together Plato and Aristotle, in a way Stephen Gersh has shown to be characteristic of the later Neoplatonists.[35] In applying their conceptions to the absolutely first, Thomas would shock these Hellenistic thinkers. Still, since at this point in the *Summa Theologiae*, it has not been said that intellection is this return upon self, some evidence is required to make clear that the logic which we ascribe to Thomas's treatment of our knowledge of God from creatures in the context of sacred doctrine is not an extraneous invention.

Thomas set it out himself when he described how men know God in this life (question 12, article 12).[36] We know first that he is the cause of all, 'omnium est causa'. Secondly, we grasp the difference between him and them, that he is not any of the things which he causes, 'differentiam creaturarum ab ipso, quod scilicet ipse non est aliquid eorum quae ab eo causantur'. Thirdly, we understand that this difference is not because anything good is excluded from him, that he is defective or lacking. Rather, he superexceeds everything; 'haec non removentur ab eo propter eius defectum, sed quia superexcedit'. This is a description of the logic ordering questions 2 to 11. Question 2 establishes that God is *causa omnium*. Thomas states that question 3 'concerns his simplicity, through which composition is removed from him', 'de simplicitate ipsius, per quam removetur ab eo compositio'. But he also adds that this negation must be overcome by the subsequent questions on God's perfection, goodness, infinity, and existence in things. Because we know God from creatures, we may confuse his simplicity with theirs. Simple corporal things are imperfect; they are

---

[34] See *ST* I, 19, 1 *ad* 3 and ch. II n. 74, above and ch. VII below.

[35] See ch. II n. 54 above, and Gersh, *KINHΣIΣ*, p. 4 and p. 131. Thomas confronts the difficulty at *ST* I, 19, 1 *ad* 3, and at *ScG* I, 13. E. R. Dodds gives some Neoplatonic endeavours to reconcile them at *Elements*, p. 207.

[36] 'Utrum per rationem naturalem Deum in hac vita cognoscere possimus', but compare *ST* I, 13, 1.

only parts of larger complex wholes. Their simplicity is incompleteness; 'simplicia in rebus corporalibus sunt imperfecta et partes'.[37] We will consider questions 3 to 11 in detail, but before this we must consider another change by Thomas in the ordering of what he takes from his sources. He has altered the order of the process of knowing, which has just been described, from its source in Dionysius.

If Aquinas reforms Aristotle using a Neoplatonic logic, he also restructures his most authoritative and most apophatic late Neoplatonist source so as to restore the validity of finite knowledge. M.-D. Chenu reports:

About the knowledge we can have of God, Dionysius says (*De div. nom.*, c. 7 . . .): '. . . we rise [to God] by removing from Him all else, by attributing to Him all else in an eminent degree, by making of Him the cause of all else'; Saint Thomas, however, restates these three operations in an inverted order: '[Dionysius] says that from creatures we arrive at God in three ways, namely: by way of causality, of removal, of eminence' (*In I Sent.*, *d.* 3, div. textus). De facto, the entire Dionysian doctrine is thus reversed.[38]

[37] Simplicity in creatures has the opposite significance of God's; *ST* I, 3, *prol.*: 'simplicia in rebus corporalibus sunt imperfecta et partes'. Creatures cannot represent God's simplicity adequately. 'Effectus Dei imitatur ipsum non perfecte . . . id quod est simplex et unum, non representari nisi per multa', *ST* I, 3, 3 *ad* 2. Cf. also *ST* I, 88, 2. On distinction, cf. *ST* I, 32. 1.

[38] Chenu, *Toward Understanding St. Thomas*, pp. 228–9 n. 51. Besides *ST* I, 12, 12, the texts mentioned are: εἰς τὸ ἐπέκεινα πάντων ὁδῷ καὶ τάξει κατὰ δύναμιν ἄνιμεν ἐν τῇ πάντων ἀφαιρέσει καὶ ὑπεροχῇ, καὶ ἐν τῇ πάντων αἰτίᾳ, *De Div. Nom.* viii, 3 (PG 3, 869 D–871 A). 'Sic ergo ex ordine universi, sicut quadam via et ordine, ascendimus per intellectum, secundum nostram virtutem ad Deum, qui est super omnia et hoc tribus modis: primo quidem et principaliter in omnium ablatione, inquantum scilicet nihil horum quae in creaturarum ordine inspicimus, Deum aestimamus aut Deo conveniens; secundario vero per excessum: non enim creaturarum perfectiones ut vitam, sapientiam et huiusmodi, Deo auferimus propter defectum Dei, sed propter hoc quod omnem perfectionem creaturae excedit . . . ; tertio, secundum causalitatem omnium dum consideramus quod quidquid est in creaturis a Deo procedit sicut a Causa', *In de Div. Nom.* VII, iv, 729. Thomas is proposing to make Dionysius' transformed logic the basis of his own theological order in the *Commentary on the Sentences*, where he writes: 'Dicit enim quod ex creaturis tribus modis devenimus in Deum: scilicet per causalitatem, per remotionem, per eminentiam', *In Sent.*, I, iii *div. textus*, p. 88. While beginning with causality, the list at *Summa Theologiae* I, 13, 1 does not end positively: 'Deus in hac vita . . . cognoscitur a nobis ex creaturis secundum habitudinem principii, et per modum excellentiae et remotionis.' What Thomas is doing to Dionysius certainly goes beyond the letter, but may be faithful to the direction of his theology when he is compared to his pagan forebears; cf. S. Gersh, 'Ideas and Energies in Pseudo-Dionysius the Areopagite', *Studia Patristica*, xv, ed. E. A. Livingstone, Texte und Untersuchungen 128 (Berlin, 1984), pp. 297–300; C. Andresen, 'The Integration of Platonism', pp. 404–5; G. Lafont, 'Le *Parménide* de Platon'.

The three ways have an earlier history. E. R. Dodds, *Pagan and Christian in an Age of Anxiety*, p. 87, writes of Plotinus that he 'relies on the three traditional approaches to the

Thomas maintains Dionysius' order when he comments on this passage in his exposition of the *Divine Names*. When, on the other hand, he is setting it out as a basis for the structure of his own theological work, as in the *Commentary on the Sentences*, or when the order affects the content of his argument, as in *Summa Theologiae* I, 12, 12, he changes the arrangement of the Dionysian steps. There is no reference to Dionysius in this article, but the language is so like that in the commentaries on the *Divine Names* and the *Sentences* that he must have had Dionysius in mind. So Aristotle is restructured to conform to Dionysius and Dionysius is reordered to admit Aristotle.

The simplicity of God is that by which he is separated from creatures and what prevents our knowledge of him through them. The imperfect representation of God by his effects stems from their multiplicity in contrast to his simplicity: 'hoc ad defectum imitationis pertinet, quod id quod est simplex et unum, non potest repraesentari nisi per multa' (I, 3, 3 *ad* 2). This multiplicity also affects our speech:

It ought to be said that we are not able to speak about simple things except through the mode of composition, by which we receive our knowledge. And therefore speaking about God we use concrete words in order to indicate the subsistence of a thing because with us things do not subsist except in composition; and we use abstract words to indicate their simplicity.[39]

However, the division this implies between thought and the object of thought does not belong to intellectual things themselves but to our manner of thinking and speaking about them. Thomas is fully aware of the negative implications of God's simplicity for our knowledge; he is explicit that God's simplicity removes him from all else. What must surprise the reader is that in this question, set at the head of his theology and formally giving God his first name, Thomas moves unalterably forward in the determination of God as infinite self-relation.

knowledge of God which were already listed by Albinus a century earlier—the way of negation (perhaps originally Pythagorean), the way of analogy (based on Plato's analogy of the sun and the Good), and the way of eminence (based on the ascent to absolute Beauty in Plato's *Symposium*).' On p. 92, Dodds adds: 'It seems to have been in fact the Platonists of Justin's time who elaborated the doctrine of the Three Ways to the knowledge of God ... the doctrine that was taken over into the philosophy of medieval Christendom.'

[39] 'Dicendum quod de rebus simplicibus loqui non possumus, nisi per modum compositorum, a quibus cognitionem accipimus. Et ideo de Deo loquentes utimur nominibus concretis, ut significemus eius subsistentiam, quia apud nos non subsistunt nisi composita; et utimur nominibus abstractis, ut significemus eius simplicitatem', *ST* I, 3, 3 *ad* 1. The doctrine here is repeated at *ST* I, 13, 1 *ad* 2. The division in our concepts and speech reflects a division in our faculties of knowing, i.e. sense and intellect; see *ST* I, 14, 11, and this follows from our existence as rational beings in sensible matter.

For there is developed, in the very process of separating God from the finite, an ever fuller statement of his own nature.

The principle of this argumentation is the conception of God reached in the five ways and it must consequently be conceded that they do more than indicate that he is, they involve insight into the divine essence. The first reference to the demonstration of God's existence simply designates him as 'primus movens immobile', but immediately thereafter the first being is said to be 'esse in actu et nullo modo in potentia' (I, 3, 1). It may not be directly seen how these descriptions involve self-relation; indeed this is drawn out only in the second article. Yet it is of the greatest significance that the first article in which they occur shows God has no body. This leads to the demonstration, in the second, of his utter immateriality: 'impossibile est in Deo esse materiam . . . materia est id quod est in potentia. Ostensum est autem quod Deus est purus actus.' What is immaterial has complete return upon itself—a Proclan principle communicated to Thomas in the *Liber de Causis* and used by Aquinas to connect the questions on God as one to his knowledge and its consequent attributes.[40] So, in this second article, it appears first that God is 'bonum per essentiam' and 'per essentiam suam forma'; indeed, form which is 'per se subsistens ex hoc ipso individuatur' is God (I, 3, 2 *ad* 3). These forms are 'supposita subsistentia' and this substance is able to be predicated of God (I, 3, 3). 'Substantia vero convenit Deo secundum quod significat existere per se' (I, 29, 3 *ad* 4). It is only inasmuch as substance also means other than 'quod est per se esse' that this predication is impossible.[41] It is in terms of this self-related activity, 'eius est primo et per se agere' (I, 3, 8), like the self-subsistence of substance, that what has been taken as the defining statement of Thomistic metaphysics, 'sua . . . essentia est suum esse' (I, 3, 4), is to be understood. God's existence is actuality of this kind. The intention is

---

[40] 'Omnis sciens scit essentiam suam, ergo est rediens ad essentiam suam reditione completa', *In de Caus.*, prop. 15 (Saffrey, p. 88), Thomas identifies as derived from Proclus, *Elements*, prop. 16: 'All that is capable of reverting upon itself has an existence separable from all body' (Dodds, *Elements*, p. 19), although he uses no less than five propositions from the *Elements* to explain this one proposition from the *Liber de Causis*. Proposition 15 of *de Causis* is essential for explaining propositions 7 and 25 on the undivided nature of intelligence as well as on the nature of the angels, and Thomas regards it as implying that intellection involves a circular motion (Saffrey, p. 90, line 14–p. 91, line 1). It is to prop. 15 that Thomas is referring at *ST* I, 14, 2 *ad* 1. Cf. ch. II n. 75 above and M. L. Carreker, '*Motus in Deo*: Motionless Motion and its Relation to the Doctrine of the Trinity of St. Thomas Aquinas', unpublished MA thesis, Department of Classics, Dalhousie University, Halifax, 1983, pp. 51–3.

[41] *ST* I, 3, 5 *ad* 1.

that knowledge of his existence should be the beginning of the unfolding for us of his nature, not that we should be left knocking our heads vainly against the blank wall of this *esse*.

If the consideration 'de Dei simplicitate' separates God from all else and raises difficulties about the possibility of knowing him in the forms belonging to human cognition and which it gives to language, 'de Dei perfectione' moves in the opposite direction. The distance of God from all else appears as the problem; his simplicity, or what is implied by it, constitutes half the objections in this question, for example: 'God is simple as has been shown. But the perfections of things are multiple and diverse. Therefore all the perfections of things are not in God.'[42] The requirement is to bring the two sides together in so far as the perfections of all things are in God and his creatures are like him. Crucially for our argument, it is the positive conception of God developed in considering his simplicity that now enables the apparent limitations of that simplicity to be overcome. It is the actuality of God and the other forms of being which allows both to be called perfect; 'a thing is said to be perfect, according as it is actual, for perfection is an attribute of that to which nothing is lacking which is proper to its kind of perfection'.[43] Because God is 'ipsum esse per se subsistens, ex quo oportet quod totam perfectionem essendi in se contineat' (I, 4, 2). There is a likeness between God and all else: 'ipsum esse est commune omnibus' (I, 4, 3). The *analogia entis* based on the likeness and difference between his perfection or being and that of all else is the principle of all community between them and him.

The double-mindedness of Thomas in respect to the opposition between Aristotle and the Neoplatonists comes out in the questions on goodness in general and God's goodness. For Neoplatonists, being belongs to νοῦς and is subsequent to the One or the Good. Thomas determines the order both ways: in the *respondeo* of question 5 article 2, being is made prior to good because of the priority of knowledge to desire, 'ens secundum rationem est prius quam bonum'. In the response to the first objection, good is said to be prior from the perspective of causation, and also within this Platonic–Dionysian view, when the extension of God's activity beyond the existent is

---

[42] 'Deus enim simplex est, ut ostensum est. Sed perfectiones rerum sunt multae et diversae. Ergo in Deo non sunt omnes perfectiones rerum', *ST* I, 4, 2 *obj.* 1. Piana does not give the 'non' but it is reported as an alternative reading and is required by the sense and context. See also I, 4, 1 *obj.* 3; I, 4, 2 *objj.* 1 and 3; I, 4, 3 *objj.* 2 and 3.

[43] 'Secundum hoc enim dicitur aliquid esse perfectum, secundum quod est actu, nam perfectum dicitur, cui nihil deest secundum modum suae perfectionis', *ST* I, 4, 1.

considered.[44] If the priority of either being or goodness depends upon your vantage-point, goodness will not ultimately be able to be kept apart from intellectual or, in general, self-related activity, as it is in Proclus for example.[45] Despite Thomas's balancing of the Platonic and Aristotelian sides, the argument moves forward in the direction which we have already discerned. For emanation is referred to final cause, 'bonum dicitur diffusivum sui esse, eo modo quo finis dicitur movere'. It is thus given the character Aristotle claims it lacks in Plato, though such a conception of it is for Proclus the deficiency of Aristotle.[46] Progressing further toward Aristotle, the good is brought within self-consciousness when final causality is subjected to will, 'Voluntas autem respicit finem ut objectum proprium.'[47] Still, the placing of the divine perfection and goodness just after the simplicity of God, and before intellect, shows Aquinas has not sacrificed the causal priority of goodness.

The questions on goodness have internally the logical structure already identified. After showing that God's perfection implies his goodness, Thomas distinguishes this goodness from that of other things and in such a way as to remove it from any genus or order of things. So God is 'summum bonum simpliciter' (I, 6, 2) and 'per suam essentiam' (I, 6, 3). But this is just what enables him to contain all perfection and to inhere in every good thing so as to be that by which they are called good. 'Therefore from the first essential being and goodness, everything is able to be called good and existent, inasmuch as it participates in the character of the first by a certain assimilation, though remotely and deficiently. . . . So therefore a thing is called good by the divine goodness.'[48] The superiority of the divine goodness

---

[44] Cf. introduction, nn. 7 and 8. That God is named good because he is first cause is also affirmed at *ST* I, 6, 1; the reference to Dionysius at this point is significant: 'Cum ergo Deus sit prima causa effectiva omnium, manifestum est quod sibi competit ratio boni et appetibilis. Unde Dionysius, in libro *De Div. Nom.* attribuit bonum Deo sicut primae causae efficienti, dicens "quod bonus dicitur Deus, sicut ex quo omnia subsistunt".' This directly repeats the doctrine of *ST* I, 5, 2 *ad* 1 and makes doubtful the general contention that there he is reporting an opinion he rejects.

[45] Proclus, *Elements*, prop. 10.

[46] *ST* I, 5, 4 *ad* 2, and cf. J. Peghaire, 'L'axiome "Bonum est diffusivum sui" dans le néo-platonisme et l'thomisme', *Revue de l'Université d'Ottawa*, 1 (1932), section spéciale, pp. 5*–30*. Aristotle, *Metaphysics A*, 7, 988^{b}8–16; for Proclus, see Dodds, *Elements*, p. 198.

[47] *ST* I, 5, 4 *ad* 3; see also I, 6, 1.

[48] 'A primo igitur per suam essentiam ente et bono, unumquodque potest dici bonum et ens, inquantum participat ipsum per modum cuiusdam assimilationis, licet remote et deficienter. . . . Sic ergo unumquodque dicitur bonum bonitate divina', *ST* I, 6, 4 *ad* 1.

is not exclusive, 'Et sic est bonitas una omnium; et etiam multae boni-
tates' (I, 6, 4 *ad* 1).

The next two questions are a development of these concluding
words of the 'de bonitate Dei'. 'De infinitate Dei' and 'de existentia
Dei in rebus' evidently explore how God is in things and includes all
that is. The dialectical structure of this consideration comes out when
the two questions are taken together, as Thomas directs; 'for God's
ubiquity and presence in all things is attributed to him in so far as he is
uncircumscribed and infinite'.[49] Infinity appears first as exclusive self-
relation. Infinity is a perfection in form apart from matter. Because
'maxime formale omnium est ipsum esse' and because 'esse divinum
non sit esse receptum in aliquo, sed ipse sit suum esse subsistens' (I, 7,
1), God is infinite. He is unlimited because there is no matter to
receive and limit the pure form which he is. It belongs to the very
notion of this formality that it is exclusive, self-related, self-subsistent.
God is distinguished 'ab omnibus aliis et alia removentur ab eo' (I, 7, 1
ad 3). The remaining articles in this question sharpen and complete
this separation, not only by showing that infinity belongs essentially to
God, but also by demonstrating that nothing else can actually be infinite. The argument is then primarily negative and it remains for the
next question to accomplish the reunion of the infinite and finite.
Hence, 'because it seems to belong to the infinite to be everywhere
and in all things',[50] we treat the existence of God in things.

That God is existent through his own essence is once again the
turning-point. Just as earlier this notion of self-sufficient actuality has
served both to distinguish God from his creation and unite him to it,
so it reappears here. 'Cum autem Deus sit ipsum esse per suam essentiam oportet quod esse creatum sit proprius effectus eius' (I, 8, 1).
Because God is cause and cause of the very being of things, he is intimately present to all by his own essence: 'Deus dicitur esse in omnibus
per essentiam, non quidem rerum, quasi sit de essentia earum; sed per
essentiam suam, quia substantia sua adest omnibus ut causa essendi'
(I, 8, 3 *ad* 1). Indeed, he is wholly everywhere: 'secundum se totum est
ubique' (I, 8, 4).

The next two questions 'de Dei immutabilitate' and 'de Dei aeternitate' are also connected: 'the notion of eternity is consequent on that

---

[49] 'attribuitur enim Deo quod sit ubique et in omnibus rebus, inquantum est incir-
cumscriptibilis et infinitus', *ST* I, 7, *prol.*

[50] 'Quia vero infinito convenire videtur quod ubique et in omnibus sit . . .', *ST* I, 8,
prol.

of immutability as the definition of time is upon motion'.[51] É. zum Brunn has pointed out Thomas's reversal, after his *Sentences* commentary, of Augustine's placing of immutability after eternity.[52] She shows that this change is owing to Thomas's ascent to God from the way of motion; a way of demonstration common to him, Aristotle, and Proclus. At this point in the *Summa Theologiae*, Thomas's argument is dependent on Aristotle's definition of time, which he gives as 'numerus motus secundum prius et posterius' (*ST* I, 10, 2).

The connection of this inversion with the origins of the whole treatise in the five ways, beginning as they do at the demonstrations 'ex parte motus', is perhaps hinted in the affirmation 'quod Deus movet seipsum' found in the first article of the pair. Further, as eternal, life belongs to God and so the second question is the more positive of the two. But in general, these questions are negative when compared with those immediately preceding them. They deny motion and time of God. Since these belong to the very finitude and corruptibility of the world in which we found him entirely and everywhere present according to his own essence, the negation of them relative to God would seem necessary to protect his mode of being from confusion with that of his creation. So the possession of all things which has already been affirmed of God is understood negatively by its qualification as 'interminabilis', in the definition of eternity Thomas adopts from Boethius.[53] Thomas is explicit about this. This negativity follows from the necessity of our cognition of the simple through the composite:

As we must arrive at the cognition of simple things through the composite, so we arrive at the cognition of eternity through time.... Simples must be defined by negation, e.g. the point is that of which there is no part. But this is not because negation belongs to their essence, but because our intellect, which first knows composites, is not able to come to the understanding of simples except by passing beyond composition.[54]

---

[51] 'ratio aeternitatis consequitur immutabilitatem, sicut ratio temporis consequitur motum', *ST* I, 10, 2.

[52] Cf. ch. I n. 42 above; Aristotle's definition of time is given at *Physics* iv, 11 (220^{a}25); for Proclus, cf. *Plat. Theo.* i, 14 ff.

[53] 'definitio aeternitatis, quam Boëthius ponit in *De Consol.* dicens quod "aeternitas est interminabilis vitae tota simul et perfecta possessio"', *ST* I, 10, 1.

[54] 'sicut in cognitionem simplicium oportet nos venire per composita, ita in cognitionem aeternitatis oportet nos venire per tempus ... simplicia consueverunt per negationem definiri, sicut punctus est cuius pars non est. Quod non ideo est, quod negatio sit de essentia eorum, sed quia intellectus noster, qui primo apprehendit composita, in cognitionem simplicium pervenire non potest, nisi per remotionem compositionis', *ST* I, 10, 1 *resp.* et *ad* 1.

This negation provides a starting-point for the last question of this part of the treatise *de deo uno*.

This last question is 'de unitate Dei'. It represents a return to the point from which the predications of God began, that is his simplicity. The argument has run full circle. This is made explicit by Thomas not only in subsequently turning to the questions on how God is known and named by us as a reflection on a completed series of names, but also by his conclusion of the last article. We are referred back to the starting-point. 'He is moreover most undivided, in so far as he is neither divided actually or potentially according to any mode of division whatever, since he is simple in every way, as has been shown above. Hence it is clear that God is maximally one.'[55] But as the structure demands this return into unity as the absolutely undivided, simple first principle, so it also determines the form this unity must have. This is not the Plotinian unity above substance, life, and being; these have been attributed to God in the course of these questions. Rather, the unity here genuinely predicated of God is the unity which he has 'per suam substantiam' (I, 11, 1 *ad* 1).

This is said in the first two articles where unity is first shown to be convertible with being, and so the problem arises 'whether one and many are opposed'.[56] Not having accepted the Neoplatonic separation of unity from being, Thomas is confronted with the question of how his earlier division between God and all else in terms of the difference between simplicity and composition can hold. Since everything has unity to the degree it has being, God and creation seem to compose a single continuity. The second objection of article 2 puts the problem thus: 'Nothing opposed to something else is constituted out of its opposite. But unity constitutes the many. Therefore it is not opposed to the many.'[57] Thomas's balanced solution to the contrary difficulties

---

[55] 'Est autem maxime indivisum, in quantum neque dividitur actu neque potentia, secundum quemcunque modum divisionis, cum sit omnibus modis simplex, ut supra ostensum est. Unde manifestum est quod Deus est maxime unus', *ST* I, 11, 4.

[56] The first article is 'utrum unum addat aliquid supra ens', the second 'utrum unum et multa opponantur'. It is interesting that Dionysius is the authority for the convertibility of unity and being. From the last chapter of the *Divine Names*, Thomas quotes: 'Nihil est existentium non participans uno' and 'non est multitudo non participans uno' (I, ii, 1 *sed contra* et *ad* 2). The second is virtually the same as prop. 1 of the *Elements of Theology*: πᾶν πλῆθος μετέχει πῃ τοῦ ἑνός and the other is the doctrine of propositions 3, 11, and 12. They could be interpreted in the very opposite way from the one Thomas chooses. On the ambiguity of the position of Dionysius, see my 'Aquinas' First Principle', p. 145 n. 62 and p. 167 n. 188.

[57] 'Nullum oppositum constituitur ex suo opposito. Sed unum constituit multitudinem. Ergo non opponitur multitudini', *ST* I, 11, 2 *obj.* 2.

represented by the first two articles is best captured in the *respondeo* of the third article which recapitulates the whole logical movement to his conception of the divine unity.

The *respondeo* consists of three proofs of God's unity. Like the five ways to God's existence, they are not redundant repetitions but the three moments of a movement by which the divine unity is understood and explicated. The first way is 'ex eius simplicitate'. This was the beginning of the whole argument. God is the singularity of his own nature, 'idem est Deus, et hic Deus'; hence, by his own essence, there is only one God. But this obviously constitutes him as totally outside all else; he would be negatively self-limited if he were one in this sense alone. Consequently, the second and mediating way is 'ex infinitate eius perfectionis'. 'God comprehends in himself the whole perfection of being.'[58] He does not just exclude but also includes everything. This is the same logical movement from negative simplicity to positive perfection which Thomas set out in his plan for these questions. God's inclusive infinity makes him exist in all things. Therefore, the third way to the divine unity does not start with a name of God at all but rather with his unity communicated. It begins 'ab unitate mundi'. God is the *per se* one which is the cause of unity. And so God is 'maxime unus' because he is 'maxime ens et maxime indivisum'. So little is this the Plotinian unity into which the Neoplatonic return has taken place that the *sed contra* of the final article designates it as the Trinity.[59]

The aim of this structural analysis of questions 3 to 11 has been to show that there is in them a positive knowledge of God, to display how it occurs and how it is qualified and conditioned by the form through which it appears. They originate in a Neoplatonic descent from the first principle, understood as the peculiar logic of Christian revelation, and in a rise from the sensible, through which Aristotelian science human knowing acquires the concepts with which revelation can be grasped. The questions themselves unite in a number of ways these two contrary movements so that their characteristic form is a dialectical circle beginning in the rational and sensible, which is negated as adequate to the apprehension of God, but to which a return is finally made. Expressed in a word, the result is that reason gives knowledge of God only if its mode is denied as belonging to its divine

[58] 'Deus comprehendit in se totam perfectionem essendi', *ST* I, 11, 3.

[59] 'Sed contra est quod dicit Boëthius, quod "inter omnia quae unum dicuntur arcem tenet unitas divinae Trinitatis"', *ST* I, 11, 4. On the priority given to unity in the medieval interpretation of Boethius, see my 'The *De Trinitate* of St. Boethius', p. 370 n. 25.

object. Whether such a conclusion is either the real final result of what Thomas has done, or whether it is in fact a genuinely thinkable notion must occupy us later. What is now required is to confirm these statements about what the structure conveys by demonstrating that Thomas himself draws them in those questions, meant as a reflection on what questions 3 to 11 attain.

IV

Intellectus sunt rerum similitudines: Questions 12 and 13

THE structural purpose and justification of questions 12 and 13 are to separate the treatment of the essence from the operations. This accords with a general Neoplatonic logic which understands activities as belonging to a different level of reality because operations are more divided than substance. In Aristotle the distinction between first and second act, which is how he distinguishes them in *De Anima*, cannot be so sharply drawn. But the greater Neoplatonic separation explains why these two questions occur where they are rather than at the end of the operations, or even after the Trinity has been considered.[1] After all, both these sections also involve knowing and naming God. But why do 12 and 13 not occur before predications have in fact been made? Why do we not have swimming lessons before we are thrown into the water? The answer to this question is from Aristotle. Thomas's views on how we know our own psychic capacity are dependent on Aristotle's determination that the soul's acts are known through its objects, and its powers from its acts.[2] When this is combined with the Philosopher's theory of language, the relation of 12 and 13 to the earlier questions and to each other is manifest.

It ought to be said that according to the Philosopher, words are signs of concepts and concepts are likenesses of things. And so it is clear that words refer to things signified by means of an intellectual conception. And therefore according as something is able to be known by our intellect, it is able to be named by us.[3]

---

[1] Cf. introduction, n. 42, p. 12 above, and my 'Aquinas' First Principle', pp. 162–5, and 'The *De Trinitate*', pp. 373–4.

[2] 'quod primo cognoscitur ab intellectu humano, est huiusmodi objectum; et secundario cognoscitur ipse actus quo cognoscitur objectum; et per actum cognoscitur ipse intellectus, cuius est perfectio ipsum intelligere', *ST* I, 87, 3 and cf. J. Gervais, 'La place et le sens des questions 12 et 13 dans la *Prima Pars* de la *Somme Théologique*', *Revue de l'Univ. d'Ottawa* 19 (1949), sect. spéc., pp. 80*–4*. And cf. Aristotle, *De Anima* ii, 4 and iii, 4.

[3] 'Dicendum quod, secundum Philosophum, voces sunt signa intellectuum, et intellectus sunt rerum similitudines. Et sic patet quod voces referuntur ad res significandas

Thomas is absolutely explicit that predication is dependent on know-ledge and knowledge on being. The structure of God's being and the structure through which it is known ought then to be reflected in—indeed determinative of—what is said of him. Consider the prologues of questions 12 and 13:

Because in the above we have considered how God is in himself, it remains to consider how he is in our knowledge, that is how he is known from creatures.... Having considered what pertains to knowledge of God, we ought to proceed to the treatment of the divine names; for everything is named by us as we know it.[4]

The names belong to God as part of his perfection. They follow on the twelfth question rather than coming directly after the eleventh because intellect links the thing and its sign. Question 12 has the structural logic we found in its predecessors and the doctrine of ques-tions 12 and 13 reflects what precedes them.

The dialectic of question 12 is subtle and beautiful; it is also impor-tant because it enables the most radical preservation by Thomas of human nature in the face of the absolute knowledge of God. This is the doctrine of created grace. The general structure is clear enough. The thirteen articles of the question begin by affirming that by nature and grace the knowledge of God is necessary to the fulfilment of man and that this knowledge must be the seeing of God's very essence, since he cannot be adequately known through any likeness. The argu-ment then takes a more negative direction, at least in respect to man as we now find him in the body, knowing by his natural powers through sense. It is made clear that this vision is not for bodily eyes: it is by the assistance of grace and it is not comprehensive. Man cannot have the proper vision of God in this life and he never knows either all that God knows or just as God knows. After this the descent takes place. The last three articles all concern knowledge 'in statu huius vitae', 'in hac vita', 'in praesenti vita'. Here is set out that positive development of

mediante conceptione intellectus. Secundum igitur quod aliquid a nobis intellectu cog-nosci potest, sic a nobis nominari', *ST* I, 13, 1.

    [4] 'Quia in superioribus consideravimus qualiter Deus sit secundum seipsum, restat considerandum qualiter sit in cognitione nostra, id est quomodo cognoscatur a creaturis', *ST* I, 12, *prol.* 'Consideratis his quae ad divinam perfectionem pertinent, procedendum est ad considerationem divinorum nominum; unumquodque enim nomi-natur a nobis, secundum quod ipsum cognoscimus', *ST* I, 13, *prol.* Note that the names belong to God as part of his perfection; they follow on the twelfth question rather than directly on the eleventh because intellect links the thing and its sign. See also *ST* I, 14, 8 *ad* 3, 'res naturales sunt mediae inter scientiam Dei et scientiam nostram', etc.

Dionysius's dialectic to which we have already referred and which provides the basis for the positive doctrine of predication of God found in question 13. What makes question 12 worth exploring in detail is the marvellous way in which the integrity of human nature is preserved in the middle articles, while the modes of our present human life are denied as adequate to full knowledge of God.

The first article, 'whether a created intellect is able to see God through his essence',[5] involves an affirmation set against Dionysian Neoplatonic objections. Against vision of the divine essence is placed Dionysius's view that of God there is 'neither sense, nor image, nor opinion, nor reason, nor science', that God is unknown because infinite, because he is not, and because there is an infinite distance between him and creatures.[6] But the denial of such sight is contrary to both faith and reason, which are distinguished here and in the last article of the question. Faith would be nullified because its basis is the actuality of man's beatitude in God. 'Since the final happiness of man consists in his highest activity, which is that of reason, if no created intellect could see God, either it would never achieve happiness or its happiness would consist in something other than God. This is foreign to faith.'[7] Reason would be denied. Its fulfilment is in knowledge of the principles and causes; this frustrated, man's natural desire would be vain. So both faith and reason demand that 'the blessed see the essence of God'.[8] At this point it also comes out that there is indeed a

---

[5] 'Utrum aliquis intellectus creatus possit Deum videre per essentiam', *ST* I, 12, 1.

[6] 'Dionysius etiam, I cap. *De Div. Nom.*, loquens de Deo, dicit: "Neque sensus est eius, neque phantasia, neque opinio, nec ratio, nec scientia"', *ST* I, 12, 1 *obj.* 1. 'Omne infinitum, inquantum huiusmodi, est ignotum', ibid., *obj.* 2. 'Sed Deus non est existens, sed "supra existentia" ut dicit Dionysius', ibid., *obj.* 3. 'Sed nulla est proportio intellectus creati ad Deum, quia in infinitum distant', ibid., *obj.* 4.

[7] 'Cum enim ultima hominis beatitudo in altissima eius operatione consistat, quae est operatio intellectus, si numquam essentiam Dei videre potest intellectus creatus, vel numquam beatitudinem obtinebit, vel in alio eius beatitudo consistet quam in Deo. Quod et alienum a fide', *ST* I, 12, *resp.*

[8] 'Unde simpliciter concedendum est quod beati Dei essentiam videant', *ST* I, 12, 1. The 'simpliciter' strengthens the affirmation. There is an immense literature on the question of whether there is natural desire and capacity of man for beatitude in Aquinas. Because the structure of the *Summa contra Gentiles* demands that the nature of desire be treated extensively in separation from grace and faith, this is largely a problem for those trying to work out the logic of that *Summa*. The crucial material is referred to by A. Pegis in the introduction to his translation of the *Summa contra Gentiles* and is discussed at considerable length by A. Gauthier in his introduction to the recent French translation of the work, cf. ch. I n. 41, above. The *Summa Theologiae* does not so sharply divide nature's desire and faith's hope but it does distinguish them here, at *ST* I, 1, 1, and elsewhere. That the attempt of nature to seek God should be recognized by Thomas is consistent with his whole theology as interpreted in this thesis. The denial of it stems

proportion between the creatures and God. 'And so it is possible for there to be a proportion of the creature to God, in so far as it is related to him as effect to cause, and as potential to act. And in this way, created intellect is able to be proportionate to the knowledge of God.'[9] The negative side appears later when it is shown that the relation is not in God but in creatures, a doctrine of Proclus.

The words just quoted conclude the reply to objection 4 of article 1 and the whole article. The second article brings out the disproportion between God and created intellect; the created knows either through external likenesses (in the case of the human knowing adapted to sense) or internal ones (in the case of angels), but neither of these are adequate to the knowledge of God because of the inequality of all effects to their cause. This reason E. R. Dodds singles out as 'the principle on which the whole structure of Neoplatonism is really founded'.[10]

It is just at this point that the argument takes a very remarkable turn. Instead of inferring that the created never knows God's essence, Thomas concludes rather that it must be known directly, without a similitude. What both nature and grace require is not to be frustrated. Instead, created intellect is 'a certain participated likeness of first intellect'[11] and demands that its vision be perfected. It will be raised up and strengthened to know directly God's essence. The adaptation of nature will take place on the subjective rather than the objective side. Yet the integrity of the subject must then be respected and so the basis of the doctrine of created grace is developed.

To say that God is seen through a likeness is to say that the divine essence is not seen which is erroneous. Therefore it must be said that for the seeing of the essence of God some likeness is required on the side of the power of seeing, namely the light of divine glory strengthening the intellect for seeing God, of whom is said in the Psalm 'in your light we will see light'. Not,

largely from contemporary despair about human reason or the determination that it should not have any rights against theology. The contemporary controversy is illuminated by an examination of the disputes about the relations between philosophy and theology in neo-Thomism.

[9] 'Et sic potest esse proportio creaturae ad Deum, inquantum se habet ad ipsum ut effectus ad causam, et ut potentia ad actum. Et secundum hoc, intellectus creatus proportionatus esse potest ad cognoscendum Deum', *ST* I, 12, 1 *ad* 4.

[10] There are three 'modes' showing this in I, 12, 2. The first is drawn from Dionysius: 'per similitudines inferioris ordinis rerum nullo modo superiora possunt cognosci'. For Dodds see his *Elements*, p. 193.

[11] 'aliqua participata similitudo ipsius, qui est primus intellectus', *ST* I, 12, 2.

however, through any created likeness is the essence of God able to be seen, which would represent the very divine essence as it is in itself.[12]

The sublime excellence of the final end of created intellect also assures, however, that a strong contrast must be drawn between knowledge deriving from sense and its ultimate hope. So the reply to the second objection distinguishes between knowledge of God *in via* and the vision of which Thomas has just spoken. Article 3 therefore asks 'whether the essence of God is able to be seen by bodily eyes'.[13] The response is of course negative. Article 4, 'whether any created intellect is able to see the divine essence through its own nature',[14] is primarily about the angels, as the objections make clear. It continues the negation of nature inasmuch as a natural inadequacy is found in the angels as well as in men and the absolute necessity of grace is brought out. 'Knowing subsistent being itself is natural to the divine intellect alone. . . . It is not therefore possible for created intellect to see God except in so far as God by his own grace joins himself to the created intellect so as to be understood by it.'[15] Yet the negation of nature here is not total. Neither the human nor the angelic forms of knowledge are the same as God's; they are not of the same nature, 'connaturale', but, because they are elevated above the material, they have the capacity to be raised by grace. And while humans do not know intellectual forms directly, they do know them by abstraction. 'And therefore, since the created intellect is made to naturally apprehend individualized form and concrete being abstractly by means of a certain power to separate out, it is able through grace to be raised so that it can know subsisting separated substance and separated subsisting being.'[16]

[12] 'Unde dicere Deum per similitudinem videri, est dicere divinam essentiam non videri; quod est erroneum. Dicendum ergo quod ad videndum Dei essentiam requiritur aliqua similitudo ex parte visivae potentiae, scilicet lumen divinae gloriae confortans intellectum ad videndum Deum: de quo dicitur in Psalmo: "In lumine tuo videbimus lumen." Non autem per aliquam similitudinem creatam Dei essentia videri potest, quae ipsam divinam essentiam repraesentet ut in se est', *ST* I, 12, 2.

[13] 'Utrum essentia Dei videri possit oculis corporalibis', *ST* I, 12, 3.

[14] 'Utrum aliquis intellectus creatus per sua naturalia divinam essentiam videre possit', *ST* I, 12, 4.

[15] 'cognoscere ipsum esse subsistens sit connaturale soli intellectui divino. . . . Non igitur potest intellectus creatus Deum per essentiam videre, nisi inquantum Deus per suam gratiam se intellectui creato coniungit, ut intelligibile ab ipso', ibid.

[16] 'Et ideo cum intellectus creatus per suam naturam natus sit apprehendere formam concretam et esse concretum in abstractione per modum resolutionis cuiusdam, potest per gratiam elevari ut cognoscat substantiam separatam subsistentem, et esse separatum subsistens', ibid., *ad* 3.

Thus, through these most negative questions, we are prepared for the explicit teaching of created grace in article 5. In it the immediate vision of God is affirmed through a light which makes the rational creature 'deiformis' (I, 12, 5 *ad* 3). To preserve his nature in the vision, the light must actually become a power possessed by the creature; the grace must be created. To be raised above its created nature, 'it must be disposed by some disposition above its own nature'—'oportet quod disponatur aliqua dispositione, quae sit supra suam naturam'. 'Hence it is necessary that some disposition supernatural to it be superadded to it so that it is elevated into such sublimity.' 'Unde oportet quod aliqua dispositio supernaturalis ei superaddatur ad hoc quod elevetur in tantam sublimitatem' (I, 12, 5).

What succeeds maintains the integrity of the created, not only its difference from God, but also the differences between one creature and another. Thus, despite the gracious character of the power of vision by which God is seen, some see him more perfectly than others. The differences between individuals become differences in charity or desire; 'and desire in a certain way makes the desirer apt and ready for receiving the desired object. Hence, who has more charity, will more perfectly see God and will be happier.'[17] This is the point of article 6. The next three articles define how God is known and what is known in him.

Although the blessed are perfectly fulfilled and nature is in no way frustrated, we cannot comprehend God. This would just exactly do away with the difference between the created and the creator. He is infinite and, as formally, not materially, infinite, he is perfectly known to himself. In contrast, the created does not know the infinite infinitely; this would destroy the finite. 'Since therefore the created light of glory, received in whatever created intellect, is not able to be infinite, it is impossible that any created intellect should know God infinitely.'[18] It is most important to notice that, in contrast to his Neoplatonic sources, Thomas does not deduce that God is unknown from his infinity. Because God's infinity is purely formal (*ST* I, 7, 1) it is both the only actually existing infinity (*ST* I, 7, articles 2, 3 and 4) and is the complete self-return which distinguishes the spiritual from

[17] 'et desiderium quodammodo facit desiderantem aptum et paratum ad susceptionem desiderati. Unde qui plus habebit de caritate, perfectius Deum videbit, et beatior erit', *ST* I, 12, 6.

[18] 'Cum igitur lumen gloriae creatum, in quocumque intellectu creato receptum, non possit esse infinitum, impossibile est quod aliquis intellectus creatus Deum infinite cognoscat', *ST* I, 12, 7.

the material (*ST* I, 3, 2 and I, 14, 2 *ad* 2). This complete self-return is knowing. These ideas are brought together in question 12 in order to equate God's knowability and his infinity.

Dicendum quod infinitum quod se tenet ex parte materiae non perfectae per formam, ignotum est secundum se; quia omnis cognitio est per formam. Sed infinitum quod se tenet ex parte formae non limitatae per materiam, est secundum se maxime notum. Sic autem Deus est infinitus, et non primo modo ... (I, 12, 1 *ad* 2).

Unumquodque enim sic cognoscibile est, secundum quod est ens actu. Deus igitur, cuius esse est infinitum, ut supra ostensum est, infinite cognoscibilis est. (I, 12, 7.)

God's infinity makes him absolutely known to himself and knowable by others in so far as they are receptive of his life. The opposing teaching of Dionysius is treated by S. Lilla.[19]

In the course of replying to the objections of the seventh article, Thomas states what applies both to our knowledge *in patria* and *in via*: 'the mode of the object is not the mode of the knower'.[20] This determines what is positive and negative in articles 8, 9, and 10. Positively, they maintain that what we know in God we know through the vision of his essence, not through exterior likenesses, and all at once, not successively. This is also how God knows what is outside him: 'omnia per unam essentiam Dei' (I, 12, 10). Negatively, we will not know all that God knows. Created intellect will not know what God was capable of doing but has not done.[21] This would be to grasp his essence infinitely and comprehensively, as he himself possesses it. Further, the differences between the blessed, already established in principle, will consist in knowing more or less of his effects through his essence.[22]

The remaining articles return us to this world and human knowing now. Here as well, even for our knowledge of God, Thomas is concerned to hold to the especial character of the human as he understands it. Thus, when he denies in article 11 that anyone in this life is able to see God through his essence, the objections are primarily drawn from Augustinian illuminationist epistemology, which would seem to deny the necessity of proceeding to God through sensible effects and to assert in its place an immediate grasp of the forms in the

---

[19] S. Lilla, 'The Notion of Infinitude' cf. ch. III n. 18, above.
[20] 'modus obiecti non est modus cognoscentis', *ST* I, 12, 7 *ad* 3.
[21] 'Nullus igitur intellectus creatus, videndo Deum, potest cognoscere omnia quae Deus facit vel potest facere; hoc enim esset comprehendere eius virtutem', *ST* I, 12, 8.
[22] 'pauciora et plura cognoscantur in eo', *ST* I, 12, 8 *ad* 3; cf. also *ad* 4.

divine truth.[23] This appears to Thomas to amount to that knowledge of things in the divine essence, which he has just affirmed of our knowing *in patria*, and to forget the contrasting movement from sensible effects, which Thomas takes as the defining feature of human cognition. This explains why the doctrine of article 12, which shows what knowledge we can in fact have of God in this life, uses the teaching of Dionysius, in contrast to Augustine, though transformed, in the way set out in chapter III, into a more positive dialectic. The anthropology determinative at this point is the same which compells Thomas to regard Anselm's argument as a statement that the existence of God is self-evident and to move him instead to demonstrate God's existence from sensible effects.

The final article makes it comprehensible how the predications of God in the *de deo uno* can be drawn together with those of the *de deo trino*. The question is 'whether through grace a higher knowledge of God is possessed than that which is had by natural reason'.[24] The answer is affirmative and so, by revelation in this life, we are able to reach what the natural reason cannot attain, 'ut Deum esse trinum et unum' (I, 12, 13 *ad* 1). But this knowledge does not destroy the characteristic human mode of knowing. The knowledge is 'ex phanthasmatibus, vel a sensu acceptis secundum naturalem ordinem, vel divinitus in imaginatione formatis'.[25] It is still tied to image and sense. However, the light of grace enables more to be seen in these than the natural light grasps. 'For the natural intellectual light is strengthened by the infusion of the light of grace.'[26] The principle is the same as that governing the raising of the created intellect to see the divine essence—a natural power is not destroyed but strengthened.

The logic of question 12 is reflected in the doctrine of 13, though the tensions of the system come out very strongly. Partly, question 13 has to do only with the concluding articles of 12; it is about naming God from creatures, naming according to our knowledge *in via*.[27] But the perfect knowability of God in himself and our heavenly vision of his essence are not forgotten. Only this can explain how Thomas, holding

---

[23] He draws on the *Confessiones*, *De Vera Religione*, *De Trinitate*, and *Super Genesim ad Litteram*.

[24] 'Utrum per gratiam habeatur altior cognitio Dei quam ea quae habetur per rationem naturalem', *ST* I, 12, 13.

[25] *ST* I, 12, 13 *ad* 2. The ultimate basis of revelation is the vision of God's essence. This was given to Moses and Paul. But it is not the general means; cf. ch. II n. 8.

[26] 'Nam et lumen naturale intellectus confortatur per infusionem luminis gratuiti', *ST* I, 12, 13.

[27] 'Sic igitur potest nominari a nobis ex creaturis', *ST* I, 13, 1.

to a conformity of being, knowing and naming, can both maintain
steadfastly the form of human *ratio*, subject and predicate logic, on
the one hand, and assert, on the other, that the simple divine nature
is able to be affirmatively named through it. God can be named from
creatures and substantially.[28] The names signify him properly;
indeed, 'they more properly belong to God than to creatures'.[29] They
are not mere synonyms; their variety and plurality make them more
adequate for speaking of him than the contrary.[30] They are not stated
of him univocally but analogically, in the way a principle is related to
inferior causes;[31] thus, 'as far as what is signified through the name is
concerned they are more primarily predicates of God than of
creatures'.[32] God is not really related to creatures but rather they to
him.[33] This, however, does not prevent using language of him which
implies a temporal relation to creatures. His name 'Deus' is the
name of his nature and is thus incommunicable. He has a most
proper name, 'Qui est', and affirmative propositions are able to be
formed of God.[34] All of this is possible, because, in doing it, we can
affirm the content of the predication while denying its mode.

Abstract and proper nouns are both necessary in naming God
'although both kinds of noun are defective in respect to his own
proper mode, as our intellect is not able in this life to know him as
he is'.[35] 'Creatures imperfectly represent him.'[36] The human 'modus

[28] 'Sic igitur praedicta nomina divinam substantiam significant, imperfecte tamen',
ST I, 13, 2.

[29] 'nomina, proprie competunt Deo, et magis proprie quam ipsis creaturis, et per
prius dicuntur de eo', *ST* I, 13, 3.

[30] 'nomina Deo attributa, licet significent unam rem, tamen, quia significant eam sub
rationibus multis et diversis, non sunt synonyma', *ST* I, 13, 4.

[31] *ST* I, 13, 5 and 10. Those discussing the source and nature of Thomas's doctrine of
analogical predication take insufficient notice of its Neoplatonic context. Analogy is
necessary when one is conscious of the difference between the simplicity of God and the
mode of creatures. 'The transference of Aristotelian concepts primarily applicable to
the sensible world *per analogiam* to the intelligible sphere is a favourite philosophical
method among later Neoplatonists', Gersh, *From Iamblichus*, p. 58 n. 147. There is now
an excellent study of analogy in this context: Pierre Aubenque, 'Les origines néoplatoniciennes de la doctrine de l'analogie de l'être', *Néoplatonisme: mélanges offerts à Jean
Trouillard*, pp. 63–76.

[32] 'quantum ad rem significatam per nomen per prius dicuntur de Deo quam de
creaturis', *ST* I, 13, 6.

[33] 'Deus sit extra totum ordinem creaturae, et omnes creaturae ordinentur ad ipsum
et non e converso', *ST* I, 13, 7.   [34] see *articuli* 8, 9, 11, and 12.

[35] 'quamvis utraque nomina deficiant a modo ipsius, sicut intellectus noster non
cognoscit eum ut est, secundum hanc vitam', *ST* I, 13, 1 *ad* 2.

[36] 'creaturae imperfecte eam representant', *ST* I, 13, 2. This is because they are composite, see *ST* I, 3, 3 *ad* 2.

significandi' is inadequate to God; it is for representing creatures.[37] The problem is that the composition in human knowledge and naming is untrue to this 'unity entirely simple'.[38] But the very division, plurality, and variety are necessary to our speech about God. Nothing created reveals God perfectly, rather 'the simple principle is represented through the divine perfections of creatures variously and in plurality'.[39] The relation of division and unity in a sentence becomes a mirror of how both are necessary to express our knowledge of God as adequately as we can.

To this diversity which belongs to reason, there corresponds the plurality of predicate and subject; the intellect signifies the identity of the thing through the very fact of uniting them (*per ipsam compositionem*). However, God considered in himself is entirely one and simple; but our intellect knows him by differing concepts; this is because it is not able to see him as he is in himself. Yet, although it understands him under diverse conceptions, it actually knows that to all these notions there corresponds one and the same object simply. This plurality, therefore, which is according to reason, it represents through the plurality of predicate and subject; the unity however intellect manifests by composing them into unity.[40]

Man's understanding is on both sides of the relation of God and creation.[41] It reasons about composite sensibles, and thus attempts to

---

[37] 'Quantum vero ad modum significandi, non proprie dicuntur de Deo; habent enim modum significandi qui creaturis competit', *ST* I, 13, 3.

[38] 'unum omnino simplex', *ST* I, 13, 4.

[39] 'Sicut igitur diversis perfectionibus creaturarum respondet unum simplex principium, repraesentatum per diversas perfectiones creaturarum varie et multipliciter', ibid. The ontological basis of this is that the procession of God *ad extra*, i.e. creation, is distinguished from the internal processions by the fact that outside the essence the divine being can only be represented 'multitudine', 'distinctione', 'inaequalitate', *ST* I, 47, 1 and 2.

[40] 'Huic vero diversitati quae est secundum rationem, respondet pluralitas praedicati et subiecti; identitatem vero rei significat intellectus per ipsam compositionem. Deus autem in se consideratus est omnino unus et simplex; sed tamen intellectus noster secundum diversas conceptiones ipsum cognoscit, eo quod non potest ipsum ut in seipso est, videre. Sed tamen, quamvis intelligat ipsum sub diversis conceptionibus, cognoscit tamen quod omnibus suis conceptionibus respondet una et eadem res simpliciter. Hanc ergo pluralitatem, quae est secundum rationem, repraesentat per pluralitatem praedicati et subiecti; unitatem vero representat intellectus per compositionem', *ST* I, 13, 12. There is considerable controversy over just how, for Thomas, logic reflects things, but our purpose does not require a judgement as to whether the correspondence is isomorphic or hardly more than metaphorical. H. Veatch, 'St. Thomas' Doctrine of Subject and Predicate', *Commemorative Studies*, ed. A. A. Maurer, ii, pp. 401–22, opts for the latter while J. E. Brush, *Language and Verification in Thomas Aquinas: A Contribution to Fundamental Theology* (Zurich, 1984), takes the first alternative. It is necessary only that the unity be composed (*per compositionem*).

[41] When we use the name 'wisdom' of God, there is 'a signifying which is, so to speak,

rise to God, but participating, through the mediation of the angels, in the prime intellect, it looks down and judges the inadequacy of the composed and the *ratio* appropriate to it for knowing God as he is.[42] Though it can name God only from creatures in accord with a cognitive power suited to sensible things, man also knows that he is made for the direct vision of God's essence without the intermediation of created likenesses. The origin of theology in revelation gives him already a participation in that vision now enjoyed by the blessed. Thus, he can affirm the content of his rationative knowledge and predications, because he judges how their form is inadequate to the thing they describe. Neoplatonic descent and Aristotelian ascent, Aristotle's science of God and Proclus' theological knowledge of all else, meet in the affirmation of content and the denial of mode. But this only states the profound difficulties of the position of Thomas. Form and content are not ultimately separable.

There is a fundamental conformity between what is maintained about the being (or non-being), knowledge and predication of the first principle in the traditions upon which Thomas draws. Yet they say exactly opposed things. Further, although efforts have been made to resolve the difficulty by suggesting the contrary, Thomas believes there is a coherence between ontology, knowing, and naming.[43] Clearly there is a unity on the subjective side. How we name God from creatures follows from how he is known through them and this is a result of their composed unity. In all three there is a division and unity. On the other side, the divine side, God is fully known to himself

conscious of its own imperfection' (p. 25). 'The eye of the mind must move, as it were, from bounded to unbounded *in the ratio*, the meaning, of the divine names' (p. 30): Lawrence Dewan, OP, 'St. Thomas and the Divine Names', *Science et esprit* 32 (1980), 19–33. Fr Dewan is helpful on the use of both concrete and abstract names (as in n. 39 above): 'They are not merely excess baggage in the task of naming God, but have a communicative role' (p. 31).

[42] See Endnote 3, p. 165 below.

[43] Fr Herbert McCabe thinks Thomas maintains a difference between knowing 'how to use our words' about God and knowing 'what they mean', see his Appendix 3, 'Signifying Imperfectly', St. Thomas Aquinas, *Summa Theologiae*, 60 vols., iii (Blackfriars, 1964), pp. 104–5. This allows Fr McCabe to be more strongly and unambiguously negative about our knowledge of God than St Thomas is at this point and at the same time to assert Thomas's positive teaching about our capacity to name God. This results in at least one misleading translation. Fr McCabe translates 'quod cognitio Dei per quamcumque similitudinem creatam non est visio essentiae ipsius' as 'that any knowledge of God that we have through a created likeness is not a knowledge of his essence', ibid., pp. 38 and 39. Fr McCabe's position seems to resemble that of Plotinus as described by P. Hadot, 'Apophatisme et théologie', p. 189. Professor Hadot compares Plotinus and Wittgenstein, which is suggestive (pp. 192–3).

because his immaterial simple being is a complete return upon itself and his names belong to his perfection. The subjective and objective are connected in our heavenly knowledge of God directly through his essence. Incoherence occurs because our knowledge *in via* is not this direct essential knowledge. Yet Thomas's teaching about naming God is remarkably positive. Can this be justified without dissolving the unity of ontology, psychology, and logic?

For Aristotle, the first principle is one of the separate substances. The divine is the activity of thought; it is not a capacity which might reveal its hidden nature in the form of noetic activity. Rather the divine element is the active possession of the object. Aristotle's psychology of knowledge is similar. The power of the soul is known through its acts which its objects reveal. What soul is is known only in reflection on the activities by which it is one with its objects. Soul knows itself to be separable when it has found an object separable from matter, and it is thinkable in exactly the same way as its objects are. Because the unified activity of subject and object in thought is the highest metaphysical and psychological truth, the Aristotelian subject–predicate logic is not untrue to what is and how it is known but rather reveals its structure. Logic has its justification in a doctrine of what primarily is, the self-thinking activity. The *Categories* simultaneously teach what is, and how statements are made. The logic set out there remains valid when Aristotle reaches the heights of divinity and he shows no hesitation in making predications of the first. It is noetic activity, it is eternal, it is life, and it is happy.[44]

With Plotinus, there is a similar unity of all the elements, ontological, psychological, and logical, but the whole concatenation has the opposite import. Above noetic activity there is the One. Nothing beneath the One reveals it as it is, though all else is nought except the

---

[44] This is a summary of Aristotle's doctrine drawn from several places. See *Metaphysics* Λ for the treatment of the first principle as one of the separate substances, and chs. 7, 9, and 10 for the noetic nature of the first, his self-knowledge and for the predications made of him. That the divine is theoretical activity, and some of the predicates of this life, also come out in *Nic. Eth.* K, 7 and 8. *De Anima* ii, 4 teaches the order of knowing in respect to soul; iii, 4 maintains the theoretical soul to be formed through its objects and known by reflection on its objective acts; iii, 5 teaches the same doctrine of the nature of the first as *Metaphysics* Λ, 7, and brings psychology and theology together. *Categories* 5 is perhaps best in showing the doctrine of being which goes with Aristotle's logic but the whole treatise assumes the unity of the two. H. B. Veatch maintains in *Aristotle* (Bloomington, 1974) and *Two Logics* (Evanston, 1969) that Aristotle's logic is purposely limited because its role is to bring out the nature of being and not just to formalize relations. See also P. F. Strawson, 'Semantics, Logic and Ontology', *Semantik und Ontologie, Neue Hefte für Philosophie*, 8 (1975), 1–13.

revelation of it. Noesis is the highest and first revelation but thought and vision are also untrue to it for they make its absolute simplicity dual. The structure of soul corresponds to that of reality. The divine hypostases are known when the soul returns upon itself and seeks to know its origins and nature. Soul has levels of existence—immersion in the sensible, the government of the sensible, noetic activity, and union with the first above the noetic—which mirror the levels of what is and what is not. The divided activity which is noesis ultimately fails; soul seeks a union which is beyond it and which language cannot express. So too the subject–predicate logic of our speech is incapable of the ultimate truth and the first cannot be named. Calling it the One is not to designate it as it is, but only to locate it for us. 'The One is' is not a statement of the One in itself; this is already the second hypostasis.[45]

The ineffability of God is even more strongly developed in some at least of the subsequent Neoplatonists.[46] They refuse to link him to the structure of what is beneath him even through the notion of activity. Although, beginning already with Porphyry, the Aristotelian logic is regarded more positively again, it is only a logic of the finite. It is impossible without severing ontology, psychology, and logic to make proper predications of the absolutely simple. Dionysius and Eriugena are in grave difficulties as the Neoplatonic separation of the hypostases starts to disappear in their systems but neither of them would assert unambiguously with Thomas that proper affirmative predication can be made of God.[47] There is not in Thomas a complete and

[45] This is a precis of Plotinus' teaching taken from several places. A good part can be found in *En.* VI, 9 and some of the doctrine there is given in ch. III n. 19 above. V, 1, 7 speaks of the noetic as revelation of the One. V, 6 teaches that the intellect is dual and that the first must be beyond this. Something has been said of the Plotinian doctrine about the soul above, ch. II pp. 48–9. VI, 1 makes clear that knowing the hypostases comes through knowing the origin and true nature of the soul. II, 9. 1, 8–9 says that calling the first 'one' is not a proper predication but only locates it for us. A. H. Armstrong writes of Plotinus: '[his] demonstrations that intellect cannot be the first principle (or conversely that the One is not intellect and does not think as in VI, 7, 40–1) always take the form of showing the insufficient simplicity of the Aristotelian self-thinking intellect', 'The Background of the Doctrine "That the Intelligibles are not Outside the Intellect"', *Les Sources de Plotin*, Entretiens Hardt 5 (Vandœuvres/Geneva, 1960), p. 409 = *Plotinian and Christian Studies*, p. 409. The soul seeking salvation is seeking simplicity; cf. A. Louth, *The Origins of the Christian Mystical Tradition*, pp. 42–4.

[46] See introduction, n. 38.

[47] Thomas is generally aware of the historical process by which hypostases become predicates: '... Platonici, quos multum in hoc opere Dionysius imitatur, ante omnia participantia compositionem, posuerunt separata per se existentia.... Haec autem separata principia ponebant ab invicem diversa a primo principio quod nominabant per

direct contradiction between the doctrine of God's being, on the one hand, and his teaching about knowledge of it and predications about God, on the other, but neither can there be a total consistency.

Contradiction is apparent if one sets sharply against each other his statements on the divine simplicity and those on predication. On the one hand, he teaches that God is entirely simple, without any composition, that what he is is consequently unknowable through the composed. He gives the simplicity, goodness, and unity of God structural priority in his system and divides sharply the *de deo uno* and *de deo trino*, because, from the unity, the three cannot be known and that God is one and three is inconceivable; it is for faith only, not for reason. On the other hand, he teaches that God's proper nature is signified in affirmative propositions. But there is more yet to Thomas.

If one takes that aspect of his theology which we have described as drawing the Neoplatonic *exitus–reditus* structure of the finite into the first principle, then a mediation between these two contradictory poles appears. Then, we explore the implications of Thomas's conceiving the entirely simple as pure act—the self-revelation of subsistent substance—and of his teaching that the good is the self-possession of absolute will. Aristotle is transformed through his use by the Neoplatonists, and we see how Thomas, by such means, develops a positive dialectic. By it, the nature of God is even more fully manifested in ever more complete forms of self-relation, so that the theological movement from unity through operations to Trinity and creation becomes thinkable as one continuity. This mediating dialectic overcomes the contradiction between God's simple being and our knowing and naming him. However, by such a solution, God's simplicity is no longer absolute and it would be wrong to deny absolutely the mode of our predication when speaking of God. Its justification would no longer be simply in the subjective necessities belonging

se bonum et per se unum. Dionysius autem in aliquo eis consentit et in aliquo dissentit: consentit quidem cum eis in hoc quod ponit vitam separatam per se existentem et similiter sapientiam et esse et alia huiusmodi; dissentit autem ab eis in hoc quod ista principia separata non dicit esse diversa, sed unum principium, quod est Deus . . .', *In de Div. Nom.* v, i, 634. His commentary on the *Liber de Causis* is full of reflections on the matter also. Cf. E. Corsini, *Il trattato*; S. Gersh, *From Iamblichus*, p. 11 and *passim*; id., 'Ideas and Energies in Pseudo-Dionysius'; C. Andresen, 'The Integration of Platonism'; and G. Lafont, 'Le *Parménide* de Platon'. Cf. ch. III n. 38 above. On the metaphorical character of names for Eriugena, see *De Div. Nat.* i, 15 (PL 463B–C), Sheldon-Williams, i, p. 86, 1–6. For Dionysius, attributions from creatures belong to God because he is immanent cause, thus they are not proper: *De Div. Nom.* v, 2–3 (PG 816D); vii, 2–4 (PG 868B–873A). Thomas is conscious of this as we may judge from the objections to *ST* I, 13 articles 6, 11, and 12.

to our form of cognition. Rather, as in Aristotle, the subject–predicate logic would reveal something about how God is in himself.

This statement of the implications of the analysis being attempted here will perhaps suffice for this point of the discussion. No doubt some hint of the relation of these questions to the controversies of contemporary Thomism will have suggested themselves. Further treatment of these must wait for the concluding chapter. What remains is to continue the exploration of how the logic of infinite self-relation can tie together the parts of the treatise on God and some of the ways in which the opposing Aristotelian and Neoplatonic onto-logical, psychic, and logical structures are modified in their unifica-tion within Thomas's argument.

V

Intelligere est motus: the Divine Operations

QUESTIONS 14 to 26 treat the operations, or activities, of God. As already suggested, Thomas strongly separates the operations from the being, or substance, of God and gives priority to the divine substance. The reasoning involved was initially known to him from Dionysius and the *Liber de Causis*, but ultimately Thomas found and recognized it in *The Elements of Theology* of Proclus.[1] Something has been said already of Thomas's originality in placing the operations before the Trinity, rather than between the considerations of God as one and three and of his creatures. Indeed, the fundamental division necessary to the plan of the whole *Summa Theologiae* makes its appearance here; for the immanent operations produce the Trinity, and the operation *ad extra* is the very power of creation. But it will be more comprehensible to look at the continuity of the divine operations with what follows them after their consequences have been presented. So this, and some doctrinal matters concerning the activities, which are primarily important to illuminate these connections (and distinctions), will be treated in the next chapters. The work of this chapter is a more detailed analysis of these thirteen questions.

Beginning in God's knowledge, the movement of the questions is outward through will and love, and those activities, like providence and predestination, which combine them, to the operation *ad extra* of power and back to God's knowing self-enjoyment in beatitude. Within the parts of this general *exitus–reditus* pattern, there are a number of movements of the same type. It would be prolix to detail them all but some substantiation of the argument is no doubt required.

The first question of the group 'de scientia Dei' has the familiar order.[2] Thomas begins by asserting that God knows. A millennium

---

[1] Cf. introduction, n. 42.

[2] A useful treatment of the early transmission of some of the problematic of this question is Luca Obertello, 'Proclus, Ammonius and Boethius on Divine Knowledge', *Dionysius*, 5 (1981), 127–64. An examination of the sources and structure of it which is close to the one offered here is R. T. Wallis, 'Divine Omniscience in Plotinus, Proclus

and a half of controversy since Aristotle agrees that this entails some identification of God and creatures. Formally this identity requires the self-relation and motion that knowing involves. Article 1 of question 14 concludes by deducing his knowing from his immateriality: 'Unde cum Deus sit in summo immaterialitatis . . . sequitur quod ipse sit in summo cognitionis.' Article 2 moves from immateriality to absence of potentiality, and from this to God as pure act, from which it follows that he must be the object of his own understanding. 'Et sic seipsum per seipsum intelligit.' The objections bring out the circular self-relation involved in this. In the reply to objection 1, the *Liber de Causis* is quoted to the effect that 'sciens essentiam suam redit ad essentiam suam'. The reply to objection 2 brings out that 'intelligere est motus' as 'actus perfecti existens in ipso agente'. The third and fourth articles absolutely assimilate this self-related activity to God as his self-comprehension and his very substance.[3] The drawing together of God and creatures which knowledge entails becomes most explicit and problematic in article 5 which asks, 'utrum Deus cognoscat alia a se'. The answer here and at 6, 'utrum Deus cognoscat alia a se propria cognitione', is affirmative. In order to prevent a complete dissolution of the mode of the divine into the mode of the finite, it is determined that 'he sees things other than himself not in themselves but in himself, in so far as his essence contains a likeness of things other than himself'.[4] This creates the problem of article 6, as the first objection makes explicit.[5] For how is something known properly if it is known as it is in the knower rather than as it is in itself? The only solution to this is that the thing must exist more perfectly in God than in itself. 'Sic igitur dicendum est quod Deus non solum cognoscit res esse in seipso; sed per id quod in seipso continet res, cognoscit eas in propria natura; et tanto perfectius, quanto perfectius est unumquodque in ipso.'[6]

and Aquinas', *Neoplatonism and Early Christian Thought: Essays in honour of A. H. Armstrong*, ed. H. J. Blumenthal and R. A. Markus (London, 1981), pp. 223–35.

[3] 'seipsum perfecte comprehendit', *ST* I, 14, 3; 'ipsum eius intelligere sit eius essentia et eius esse', *ST* I, 14, 4.

[4] 'Alia autem a se videt non in ipsis sed in seipso, inquantum essentia sua continet similitudinem aliorum ab ipso', *ST* I, 14, 5.

[5] 'Sic enim cognoscit alia a se, ut dictum est, secundum quod alia ab ipso in eo sunt. Sed alia ab eo sunt in ipso sicut in prima causa communi et universali. . . . Ergo Deus cognoscit alia a se in universali, et non secundum propriam cognitionem', *ST* I, 14, 6 *obj*. 1.

[6] *ST* I, 14, 6 *ad* 1; that they are more perfectly in God causes Plotinus to deny that God would want to know things other than as they are in him; see Wallis, 'Divine Omniscience', p. 225.

Things are so much the more perfectly known by God as they are so much the more perfectly existent in him. The essence of creatures is compared to God's essence as imperfect to perfect. This determines the complete knowability of creatures by God but the inadequacy of our knowledge of him from creatures.[7] The strong sense of the eminence of the being of effects in their causes is Neoplatonic, and comes out forcefully in the *Liber de Causis*, which begins with the material on causation from the *Elements of Theology*.[8] It is in such a framework that the divine ideas enter Thomas's theology with question 15. The ideas are the exemplars and the truth of all that is other than God, the standard by which it is judged.[9]

Fr L. B. Geiger has shown that they enable Thomas both to identify the object of the divine thinking with the act of God's knowing, thus making his knowing and self-conscious act causative, and yet to keep God free from the finitude of the world which he makes.[10] This is fully worked out in the questions following that on the divine knowledge, but the problems are present already in 14.

Immediately after Thomas has most radically assimilated the caused object of thought and its causal subject, by insisting that in their own proper nature particular existents are more perfectly in God than in themselves, he is forced to turn to the negative aspect of causation so as to protect God's simplicity. Aquinas denies that God's knowledge is discursive and this is just because he knows things in himself as their cause. 'Unde, cum Deus effectus suos in seipso videat sicut in causa, eius cognitio non est discursiva.'[11] The next article, 8, has a curious, though crucial, dialectical role. Its objections bring out the opposed sides of the dilemma whose solution lies in a partial

[7] 'essentia creaturae comparatur ad essentiam Dei, ut actus imperfectus ad perfectum. Et ideo essentia creaturae non sufficienter ducit in cognitionem essentiae divinae, sed e converso', *ST* I, 14, 6 *ad* 2.

[8] Consider *Elements*, props. 7, 18, 30, 103. Dodds's comments on 7 and 103 are particularly important (pp. 193–4 and 217–18). This doctrine results primarily from understanding causation through participation. The first proposition of the *Liber de Causis* is 'omnis causa primaria plus est influens super suum causatum quam causa secunda universalis', *In de causis*, prop. 1, p. 4. Thomas in his commentary refers correctly to *Elements*, props. 56 and 57. At prop. 12 of *In de Causis*, Thomas discusses extensively prop. 103 of the *Elements*, 'All things are in all things, but each according to its proper nature . . . in Intelligence, being and life . . .'; cf. pp. 78–9 of *In de Causis* and p. 93 of the *Elements*.

[9] 'in mente divina sit forma, ad similitudinem cuius mundus est factus. Et in hoc consistit ratio ideae', *ST* I, 15, 1. See also *ST* I, 16, 1.

[10] 'Les idées divines dans l'œuvre de s. Thomas', *Commemorative Studies*, ed. A. A. Maurer, i, pp. 175–209.

[11] *ST* I, 14, 7; see also the replies to objj. 2 and 3.

distinction between God's knowing and his causing. Objection 1 pro-
poses that God cannot be the cause of the future as future because he
always is, that is, he is eternal. If causing the future threatens to lower
God, the second objection fears his causation may remove the difference between God and his world: 'scientia Dei est aeterna. Si ergo
scientia Dei est causa rerum creaturarum, videtur quod creaturae sint
ab aeterno.' In his reply, Thomas answers affirmatively; God's knowledge is cause. But between his self-knowledge and things something
else, a different relation to things than knowledge must intervene.
Forms do not produce without an 'inclinatio ad effectum', knowledge
does not cause 'nisi adiungatur ei inclinatio ad effectum, quae est per
voluntatem. . . . Unde necesse est quod sua scientia [Dei] sit causa
rerum, secundum quod habet voluntatem coniunctam.' So the solution of objection 1 is the addition of will to knowledge, and of 2, the
distinction between the mode of cause and that of effects.[12] Thomas
has now the foundation to give God knowledge of that to which he is
opposed.

As cause of being, he has knowledge of non-being,[13] as cause of
good, evil.[14] As cause, he knows singulars and quantitative infinity in
the unity of his being, future contingents and the temporally variable
in his eternal being, and propositions, with their inherent division, in
his simple being. Because knowing is not simply causing, and
because the cause has a higher mode of being than the effect, he is
able to know reality without the non-being, evil, multiplicity, potentiality, change, and division which belong to it.[15] None the less,

---

[12] *ST* I, 14, 8 *ad* 1 and *ad* 2.

[13] This comes out in its most general form if causation is expressed as participation;
'Deus sit ipsum esse, intantum unumquodque est, inquantum participat de Dei
similitudine. . . . Sic et ea quae sunt in potentia, etiam si non sunt in actu, cognoscuntur
a Deo', *ST* I, 14, 9 *ad* 2. The knowledge of non-being is a knowledge of the potentiality
of what is—ultimately God's own essence.

[14] 'Dicendum quod scientia Dei non est causa mali, sed est causa boni, per quod
cognoscitur malum', *ST* I, 14, 10 *ad* 2.

[15] 'cum Deus sit causa rerum per suam scientiam . . . intantum se extendit scientia
Dei, inquantum se extendit eius causalitas. Unde, cum virtus activa Dei se extendat . . .
usque ad materiam . . . necesse est quod scientia Dei usque ad singularia se extendat,
quae per materiam individuantur', *ST* I, 14, 11. 'Deus autem non sic cognoscit infinitum
vel infinita, quasi enumerando partem post partem; cum cognoscat omnia simul non
successive', *ST* I, 14, 12 *ad* 1. '. . . aeternitas autem, tota simul existens, ambit totum
tempus. . . . Unde omnia quae sunt in tempore, sunt Deo ab aeterno praesentia', *ST* I,
14, 13. The following articles are argued according to the same principle. In each case
what is fundamental is that God knows his essence as the power in which all else is
implicit. Even *in patria* created intellect does not know the infinite potentiality of God.
Further, God knows what is in his essence in accordance with the mode of his being

finally, a reconciliation between the two sides is achieved. Their separation depends upon a distinction between the practical and speculative in God. This difference is preserved in the sixteenth and last article. 'Deus de seipso habet scientiam speculativam tantum; ipse enim operabilis non est. De omnibus vero aliis habet scientiam et speculativam et practicam.' But as already seen in the first question of the *Summa*, Thomas does not hold to any final division between speculative and practical in theology. The concluding words of question 14 close the gap: 'quia [Deus] omnia alia a se videt in seipso, seipsum autem speculative cognoscit; et sic in speculativa sui ipsius scientia, habet cognitionem et speculativam et practicam omnium aliorum.' Significantly, this is a reply not to the initial objections but to the *sed contra* and is intended to correct Aristotle's view that speculative science is more noble than practical.

The questions which immediately follow 14, on the divine ideas, truth, falsity, and life, are still a consideration 'eorum quae ad divinam scientiam pertinent'.[16] Their effect is to develop the self-relation belonging to the divine knowing as it is presented by Thomas from the very beginning. By this means the transition to will is made.

Question 15, 'de ideis', despite the evident Platonism, has not been included by Thomas by external necessity, 'ou par respect à l'égard l'autorité de S. Augustin (Gilson)', but because it has 'une nécessité intelligible dans sa synthèse théologique'. They allow Thomas 'éviter la contradiction entre la thèse de la simplicité divine et la nécessité d'affirmer la connaissance distincte, par Dieu, d'une multiplicité d'*objets* de sa connaissance'.[17] These ideas are not just imitable by things, as in Thomas's *Commentary on the Sentences*, where 'Hoc nomen "idea" nominat essentiam divinam secundum quod est exemplar imitatum a creatura'.[18] But crucial to Thomas's argument in the

rather than its own. This distinction of modes has already been compromised at I, 14, 9 and Thomas will not be able to maintain it absolutely. The principle that 'each faculty's mode of knowledge depends on the nature of that faculty, not of the object known' Wallis finds in Proclus where it is 'ascribed to Iamblichus'; see 'Divine Omniscience', p. 226.

[16] *ST* I, 19, *prol.*

[17] Geiger, 'Les idées divines', p. 179.

[18] *In I Sent.*, *d.* 36, *q.* 2, *a.* 2 *sol.*; p. 842 quoted by Geiger, 'Les idées Divines', p. 188, n. 33. Eriugena identifies the ideas with his second division 'quae creatur et creat'. These are the primordial causes which the Father 'in verbo suo, unigenito videlicet filio ... praeformavit', *De Div. Nat.* ii, 2 (PL 122, 529), p. 14, lines 20–4. I. P. Sheldon-Williams notes: 'Since the Forms were, from the time of Plotinus at least, held by pagan and Christian alike to reside in the Mind of God, Henry of Ostia held it as one of the three principal errors of Eriugena that he taught that they were created', *Periphyseon II*,

Summa contra Gentiles and *Summa Theologiae* is a 'distinction entre l'essence divine imitable et l'essence connue comme imitable'.[19] The ideas do not fall outside the divine knowledge, but, as in the Neoplatonists, they are within it. The multiplicity of the ideas express their difference from the essence of God and the fact that they are this essence as turned toward creatures and productive of their manifold existence. But God's knowledge also reaches around the ideas and knows them as the truth of creatures, it knows the relation of the ideas to creatures:

Sic igitur inquantum Deus cognoscit suam essentiam ut sic imitabilem a tali creatura, cognoscit eam ut propriam rationem et ideam huius creaturae.... Deus autem non solum intelligit multas res per essentiam suam, sed etiam intelligit se intelligere multa per essentiam suam. Sed hoc est intelligere plures rationes rerum; vel, plures ideas esse in intellectu eius ut intellectas.... Dicendum quod huiusmodi respectus, quibus multiplicantur ideae, non causantur a rebus, sed ab intellectu divino, comparante essentiam suam ad res.[20]

The ideas prevent the divine simplicity being directly divided in causing the proper diversity of things; still, so that it remains

n. 29, p. 216. Modern commentators have followed Henry of Ostia in this criticism; see É. Gilson, *History*, p. 118, and *Being and Some Philosophers*, p. 37. Professor Gilson thought that Aquinas and Eriugena were sharply distinguished on this matter (see also Geiger, 'Les idées divines', p. 179) but in fact Thomas goes some way toward John the Scot in differentiating the essence and ideas of God and uses Eriugena's language when at *ST* I, 41, 3 *ad* 4 he speaks of the second person as 'Sapientia' both 'genita' and 'creata' (see also *ST* I, 34, 3). Thomas's position has its own difficulties and Eriugena holds more closely to something like a pagan Neoplatonic separation of the hypostases. D. F. Duclow, 'Dialectic and Christology in Eriugena's *Periphyseon*' is a sympathetic exposition of Eriugena's doctrine. F. J. Kovach, 'Divine Art in Saint Thomas Aquinas', *Arts libéraux et philosophie au moyen âge*, pp. 663–71, shows, with Geiger, that Thomas, treating divine art, unites Plato and Aristotle, makes knowing the basis of art, and turns the divine essence toward creatures as exemplar.

[19] Geiger, 'Les idées divines', p. 188.

[20] *ST* I, 15, 2 *resp.*, *ad* 2 and *ad* 3. That God reaches around the mode of his knowledge to compare it with the created thing, itself within God's knowledge, is also obscurely suggested in Thomas's attempt to express how the temporal is known in God's eternity. God does not just know future things in their causes—this is also possible for finite thinking—'sed eius intuitus fertur ab aeterno supra omnia, prout sunt in sua praesentialitate'. It is done without leaving God's eternity because eternity contains time, as God contains a relation to creatures in his self-relation; cf. *ST* I, 14, 13. '... the most important modification of Plotinus' system to be found in Proclus [is] that the gods or Henads ... know individuals', Wallis, 'Divine Omniscience', p. 226. 'Aquinas' claim that, since divine power extends to individuals as well as universals, divine knowledge must also embrace them both, is likewise an echo of Proclus, whose views are no less influential on Aquinas' discussion whether God knows what is infinite' (p. 229).

ultimately the cause of multiplicity, it must develop self-relation. Significantly, in the reply to the last objection of article 2, Thomas is
forced to distinguish this relation and the real relations which are the
persons of the Trinity.[21]

The circle of self-knowledge by which God knows his relation to
things becomes more explicit in question 16 'de veritate'. It is well
known that Thomas rejects in this question more Platonic notions of
truth, which place truth in the ideas as separate beings. Rather truth is
in the intellect: 'verum sit in intellectu secundum quod conformatur
rei intellectae'. It is only secondarily in things. 'Sic ergo veritas principaliter est in intellectu; secundario vero in rebus, secundum quod
comparantur ad intellectum ut ad principium' (I, 16, 1). A relation or
comparison is essential to truth either in intellect or in things; for truth
proper, the comparison must fall within the intellectual act. Truth is
'in intellectu componente et dividente'. Truth is not in the intuitive
identity of sense or of intellect with their respective objects; 'non
autem ut cognitum in cognoscente, quod importat nomen veri; perfectio enim intellectus est verum ut cognitum' (I, 16, 2).

For truth proper, intellect must know its conformity with its
object. God is 'summa et prima veritas' (I, 16, 5). All 'compositio et
divisio' is denied of his intellect as truth (*ad* 1). Yet it is not enough
to say, as Thomas does, that 'est conforme suo intellectui, sed etiam
est ipsum esse intelligere; et suum intelligere est mensura et causa
omnis alterius esse, et omnis alterius intellectus' (I, 16, 5). God
knows this conformity; therefore he is truth. Because his being perfectly returns on itself, it is called *intelligere* as well as *esse*. Because
he knows the relation between his essence as ideal exemplars and
what is caused, he is the truth of them. 'Res naturales dicuntur esse
verae, secundum quod assequuntur similitudinem specierum quae
sunt in mente divina' (I, 16, 1). It is now clear not only why 'de ideis'
follows 'de scientia Dei', but also why it intervenes between God's
knowledge and 'de veritate'. 'De falsitate' is dependent on 'de veritate' as its negative contrary.[22]

There are many considerations deriving from his precedecessors
which might incline Thomas to place and treat 'de vita Dei' dif-

---

[21] *ST* I, 15, 2 *ad* 4.

[22] 'verum et falsum opponuntur ut contraria', *ST* I, 17, 4. Yet neither the false nor the
evil 'fundatur in . . . sibi contrario', but rather in the being of which they are predicated.
Because true and false are convertible with being, 'unde sicut omnis privatio fundatur
in subiecto quod est ens, ita omne malum fundatur in aliquo bono, et omne falsum in
aliquo vero', ibid., *ad* 2.

ferently.[23] Yet Thomas is perfectly explicit that life is predicated of God because he is intellectual: 'intelligere quoddam vivere est' (I, 14, *prol.*), 'intelligere viventium est' (I, 18, *prol.*), 'vivere Dei est eius intelligere' (I, 18, 4). He also states that he is following Aristotle in this.[24] Two features of the question allow it to be understood as a summary of what precedes and a transition to what follows. The first is the positive treatment of self-motion in God which would seem to follow from the reasoning about the reflective character of divine knowing as truth. The second nearly concludes the question and, in opposition to question 14, brings out the sense in which material things are more truly in their existence external to the divine ideas than in God's intellect.

It is not possible for Thomas to affirm life of God unless he find some sense in which motion belongs to the divine. For he defines life in terms of self-movement, though importantly Thomas returns to a distinction between the motion which is the act of the imperfect and that which is the act of the perfect:

It is clear that those beings are properly living, which move themselves according to some form of motion; either what is taken as motion proper, then motion is called the act of the imperfect, that is the act of a thing existing in potentiality, or motion taken more generally, as when it is said of the act of the

---

[23] Life might precede intelligence because it is more generic and more simple—it is not necessarily divided by self-conscious thought. Or it might come after will, as in the *Summa contra Gentiles*, being associated with the third hypostasis, soul, and the descent into material non-thinking existence. Thomas is explicitly following Aristotle in his treatment of life in the Summa Theologiae and these other reasonings belong to the more Platonic side of later Neoplatonism. Thomas is explicit: 'Unde Philosophus in XII *Metaph.* ostenso quod Deus sit intelligens, concludit quod habeat vitam perfectissimam et sempiternam', *ST* I, 18, 3. By a similar reasoning, Plotinus places life within νοῦς; cf. A. H. Armstrong, 'Eternity, Life, and Movement in Plotinus' Accounts of Νοῦς', *Plotinian and Christian Studies*, xv. In Proclan teaching, as more generic, life precedes intelligence; cf. *Elements*, props. 101–3, Dodds's comments, pp. 252–3, the order of *caput* VI, *de Vita*, relative to *caput* VII, *de Sapientia*, etc., in the *Divine Names* of Dionysius and S. Gersh, *From Iamblichus*, pp. 83, 87, 113, 115, etc. For the problems in Proclus' logic associated with this ordering, cf. Lowry, *Logical Principles*, ch. v. By ordering providence under intellect and will, Thomas clearly rejects Proclus' doctrine in *Elements*, prop. 120. Yet Thomas does hold to prop. 122—that God acts without relation to what he acts upon—*In de Caus.*, prop. 20, *ST* I, 13, 7, and I, 45, 3 *ad* 1. Thus, Aquinas maintains the point of Proclus' placing of providence above intelligence—that it is in virtue of their being τῷ εἶναι (prop. 120) and without themselves being moved or affected, ἀσχέτως ποιεῖ (prop. 122) that the gods act—but does not accept Proclus' structure ἡ πρὸ νοῦ ἐνέργεια (prop. 120) and diminution of intellect. On Plotinus, cf. Armstrong, 'Eternity', and Dodds, *Elements*, p. 263.

[24] *ST* I, 18, 3.

perfect, namely when understanding and sensing are called motions, as is said in *De Anima* iii.[25]

In the second sense 'vita maxime proprie in Deo est'. Those living things which 'operantur ex seipsis, et non quasi ab aliis mota' (I, 18, 3) possess highest life. God's knowing is such a motion.[26] Other forms of life are compared unfavourably to intellection. Further, the thinking activity of all except the first is found to be dependent upon given first principles. Only God has himself both as principle and object of his thinking—this, incidentally, is why he must be the subject of the ultimate science which participates his knowing, namely sacred doctrine—'sua natura est ipsum eius intelligere'. Thus Thomas concludes with Aristotle that life most perfect and eternal belongs to God 'quia intellectus eius est perfectissimus et semper in actu' (I, 18, 3). But the argument here is as much Platonic as Aristotelian.

In article 2 Aquinas identifies life and activity, 'operatio', because he defined life in terms of self-movement in the first article. And so, in the third, Plato and Aristotle are explicitly assimilated. This is a typically Neoplatonic equation. For the intellectual God of whom Aristotle predicates life in *Metaphysics* is complete activity, but is the *unmoved* mover. And, in *De Anima*, i, 3, Aristotle is at pains to show, against Plato and others, that soul is not self-moving. Thomas is quite clear about the reason for this when he comments on the text at 406ᵃ30: 'appetere et velle et huiusmodi non sunt motus anime, sed operationes, motus autem et operatio differunt quia motus est actus inperfecti, operatio vero est actus perfecti.'[27] At *De Anima* iii, 7 Aristotle states that, because the faculty is not itself changed into its contrary, the passive affection of sense in knowing is not motion ($\kappa\iota\nu\eta\sigma\iota\varsigma$), though it is $\dot{\epsilon}\nu\acute{\epsilon}\rho\gamma\epsilon\iota\alpha$. Thomas's text seems to have translated $\delta\iota\grave{o}$ $\ddot{\alpha}\lambda\lambda o$ $\epsilon\hat{i}\delta o\varsigma$ $\tauο\hat{υ}\tauο$ $\kappa\iota\nu\acute{\eta}\sigma\epsilon\omega\varsigma$ (431ᵃ6), as 'unde alia hec species motus'. Taking a comparative as a partitive genitive, he interprets the first sentences of the chapter as follows:

Set iste motus est actus *perfecti* (est enim operatio sensus iam facti in actu per suam speciem, non enim sentire convenit sensui nisi actu existenti) et ideo est motus simpliciter alter a motu phisico. Et huiusmodi motus dicitur proprie

---

[25] 'Ex quo patet quod illa proprie sunt viventia, quae seipsa secundum aliquam speciem motus movent; sive accipiatur motus proprie, sicut motus dicitur actus imperfecti, idest existentis in potentia; sive motus accipiatur communiter, prout motus dicitur actus perfecti, prout intelligere et sentire dicitur moveri, ut dicitur in III *De An.*', *ST* I, 18, 1.

[26] *ST* I, 18, 3 *ad* 1.

[27] *Sentencia libri de Anima* I, vi, p. 30, lines 219–22; cf. also I, x, p. 51, lines 207–10.

operatio, ut sentire, intelligere et velle, et secundum hunc motum anima movet se ipsam secundum Platonem, in quantum cognoscit et amat se ipsam.[28]

Moreover the self-moving Platonic soul is assimilated, by this argument, to the unmoved mover in the arguments for God's existence in the *Summa contra Gentiles*.

Sciendum autem quod Plato, qui posuit omne movens moveri, communius accepit nomen *motus* quam Aristoteles. Aristoteles enim proprie accepit motum, secundum quod est actus existentis in potentia secundum quod huiusmodi: qualiter non est nisi divisibilium et corporum, ut probatur in VI *Physic*. Secundum Platonem autem movens seipsum non est corpus: accipiebat enim motum pro qualibet operatione, ita quod intelligere et opinari sit quoddam moveri; quem etiam modum loquendi Aristoteles tangit in III *de Anima*. Secundum hoc ergo dicebat primum movens seipsum movere quod intelligit se et vult vel amat se. Quod in aliquo non repugnat rationibus Aristotelis: nihil enim differt devenire ad aliquod primum quod moveat se, secundum Platonem; et devenire ad primum quod omnino sit immobile, secundum Aristotelem.[29]

Thus, in the *ad primum* of article 3 of the question 'de vita Dei', Thomas unites Plato and Aristotle, by finding a way of regarding the complete activity of God's intellect as both life and motion. One recollects that this is a common enterprise of later Neoplatonists and yet that Thomas divides himself sharply from them by applying this motion to the absolutely first principle. After referring to *De Anima* iii, 7, he says: 'Hoc igitur modo quo intelligere est motus, id quod se intelligit, dicitur se movere. Et per hunc modum etiam Plato posuit quod Deus movet seipsum, non eo modo quo motus est actus imperfecti.'

The fourth and last article of question 18, 'utrum omnia sunt vita in Deo', reunites the life and motion of what is other than God, 'actus imperfecti', with the eternal and absolutely complete life, 'actus perfecti', from which it had been distinguished in article 3. That 'omnia in

---

[28] *Sentencia libri de Anima* III, vi, p. 230, lines 29–36. The editors note that Thomas gives the same reading as Albert the Great: 'oportet quod alia sit hec species motus a motu physico', Albertus Magnus, *De Anima, Opera Omnia*, vii, ed. Cl. Stroick (Münster i. W., 1968), p. 211, lines 32–3.

[29] *ScG* I, 13 (Leonine, p. 31) and see *ScG* I, 53, which the Leonine Commission placed in the Appendix at p. 21*, 6–15, but which the current editors seem to regard as genuine. What Thomas ascribes to Plato he probably derives from Aristotle's reports (there is also *Metaphysics K*, 1071^{b}37), from Dionysius (see ch. II n. 74 above for references), and the *Liber de Causis* which uses 'rediens' to describe knowledge (see prop. 15 and Thomas's comment *In de Causis*, pp. 88ff.); cf. ch. III n. 35 above.

ipso sunt ipsa vita divina'[30] follows from the identity of God's life and
his thinking, together with the identity of his thinking and what he
thinks. This remarkable union is accomplished in the *respondeo* of the
article; it remains to the replies to the objections to make the necessary
separation between the modes of divine and finite being.

The first reply removes from God's life the form of motion belonging to physical creation. The second denies of lifeless material being
the life it has in God; a house is not itself alive because it is life in him.
The fourth makes certain that evils, and other forms of privative being,
are not given, by their life in God, a reality they do not possess. The
third is part of this negative process but it has, with the second, a positive character which in fact also enables the transition to the questions
on will.

As noted above, the differentiation of knowledge and will in
Aquinas depends partly on a distinction between the object as it is
known and comes to be within the knower and the object as willed. In
order that the object be further sought by will, beyond intellect, it
must in some way remain a further object in itself for love beyond its
possession in knowledge. In the reply to the third objection of this last
article of the final question on God's knowing, Thomas allows that
there is a sense in which material being has a truer existence outside
the divine intellect than it has within it. This did not appear in the
question 'de scientia Dei' where, as indicated above, things were said
to exist more perfectly in God than outside him and thus were able to
be known more perfectly in God's knowledge of himself than directly
through their exterior effects. The new position is as follows:

It must be said that if in the knowledge of natural things there were not matter,
but only form, in all ways natural things would be more truly in the divine
mind than in themselves.... But because by definition matter belongs to
natural things, it must be said that natural things have a truer being absolutely
in the divine mind than in themselves, because in the divine mind they are
uncreated, in themselves, however, they are created. But to be this particular
being, as a man or a horse, this they more truly possess in their own distinct
being than in the mind of God, because it belongs to the truth of man to be
material, but they do not have the materiality in the divine mind.[31]

---

[30] *ST* I, 18, 4; see n. 8 just above. Proclus draws the conclusion that being and intelligence are vitally in life from his general principle that all things are in all things,
Elements, prop. 103. Thomas knows the doctrine also from the *Liber de Causis*, prop. 12.
He finds however that the 'auctor huius libri' badly understands the teaching of Proclus
which Thomas finds agreeable with Aristotle; see *In de Causis*, prop. 12, p. 79, lines 2–19.

[31] 'Dicendum quod si de ratione rerum naturalium non esset materia, sed tantum

So next, the love, the appetite or will, which conjoined to intellect, creates the being of things as they are distinct from the divine thinking, must be considered. It too is a form of self-relation. In love God rests in himself through his own ecstasy.

Will is God's relation to himself as good. It is distinguished from the self-relation which is knowledge, wherein God possesses his being as true: 'sicut bonum addit rationem appetibilis supra ens, ita et verum comparationem ad intellectum' (I, 16, 3). Truth, and the act apprehending it, is prior to will and its object, because it is a more immediate relation to being 'verum respecit ipsum esse simpliciter et immediate' (I, 16, 4). Cognition also naturally precedes appetite in the attaining of an object, in so far as desire depends upon apprehension. This is a fundamentally Aristotelian way of relating the faculties. In Aristotle's theology the divine described as self-knowledge moves other beings because they desire what they know.[32] Thomas's ordering of will after intellect reflects his teaching at previous points in the *Summa* that truth is prior to good, that being is the most appropriate name of God, and that being is prior to good.[33] In the questions on the divine operations, this Aristotelian aspect of Thomas's thought comes through strongly, as indeed it often does for Neoplatonists when they are dealing with the second level of spiritual life.[34]

In Thomas, intellect dominates questions 14 to 26, as already indicated. We could indeed give more evidence for his intellectualizing of life, providence, and beatitude. It is of some significance that God's willing is a consequence of his knowing and Thomas's treatment of will is often just a reproduction in other terms of the treatment of knowing. For example, he writes 'Sicut alia a se intelligit intelligendo essentiam suam, ita alia a se vult volendo bonitatem suam' (I, 19, 2 *ad* 2). Moreover, God can properly be said to love because he is intellectual. 'Amor igitur et gaudium et delectatio, secundum quod significant actus appetitus sensitivi, passiones sunt; forma, omnibus modis veriori modo essent res naturales in mente divina per suas ideas quam in seipsis. . . . Sed quia de ratione rerum naturalium est materia, dicendum quod res naturales verius esse habent simpliciter in mente divina quam in seipsis, quia in mente divina habent esse increatum, in seipsis autem esse creatum. Sed esse hoc, utpote homo vel equus, verius habent in propria natura quam in mente divina, quia ad veritatem hominis pertinet esse materiale, quod non habent in mente divina', *ST* I, 18, 4 *ad* 3.

[32] *Metaphysics* Λ, 6.
[33] *ST* I, 13, 8 and I, 5, 2; see pp. 4–5 and 74–6 above.
[34] Cf. n. 23 above.

non autem secundum quod significant actus appetitus intellectivi. Et sic ponuntur in Deo.'[35]

It also belongs to Aristotle's influence on the treatise of the divine operations that the passions ('passiones animae') are distinguished from the habits which are moral virtues ('habitus moralium virtutum')[36] and that the consideration of providence follows the latter. To Aristotle's distinction Thomas owes his division of the question on God's love, 20, from that on his justice and mercy, 21. To the order of the *Ethics* in which the problem as to the nature of prudence is consequent on a consideration of the moral virtues, Thomas attributes his placing of his question on providence, and consequently its subordinates on predestination and the Book of Life. Aquinas is explicit in his prologue to question 20 that the basis of his theological division is one made in human psychology. When he takes up passions and human moral virtues in the *Summa*, Thomas is conscious of following Aristotle.[37] But more than Aristotle is behind the structure of the treatise on the divine operations.

If the priority of being, truth and knowing in Thomas has a positive relation to the fundamentals of Aristotle's way of thinking, the priority given to simplicity and goodness reflect the Neoplatonic criticism of Aristotle. Will and goodness must acquire a precedence, if God's simplicity hides him to our way of knowing, and if 'ei quasi ignoto coniungamur'.[38] When causing, God's goodness is prior, and the *Summa* proceeds from and returns to a God of whom we do not now have vision and who is never known comprehensively to us.[39] Conformity to a God, to whom we are unified through inclusion in his self-revealing activity of exit and return, determines the further development of the questions on the operations of God. There is

---

[35] *ST* I, 20, 1 *ad* 1. As well, the doctrine of the divine ideas finally reduces the divine art of making to knowing. 'Thomas often calls the divine art simply divine knowledge', Kovach, 'Divine Art', p. 668.

[36] *ST* I, 20, *prol.*

[37] 'Nam et post morales virtutes in scientia morali consideratur de prudentia, ad quam providentia pertinere videtur', *ST* I, 22, *prol.* 'In parte autem appetitiva inveniuntur in nobis et passiones animae, ut gaudium, amor, et huiusmodi; et habitus moralium virtutem, ut iustitia. . . . Unde primo consideramus de amore Dei; secundo, de iustitia Dei et misericordia eius', *ST* I, 20, *prol.* Thomas states at *ST* I, 49 that he is following Aristotle rather than the Stoics on the relation of the passions and virtue of the soul. His view of how prudence in the form of providence and its consequents should be ordered in an Aristotelian framework does indeed seem to reflect the procedure of the *Nicomachean Ethics*, where practical wisdom is discussed in book vi, the moral virtues having already been treated.

[38] *ST* I, 12, 13 *ad* 1.   [39] *ST* I, 13, 11 *ad* 2 and *ST* I, 5, 2 *ad* 1.

a strong sense of these activities as forms of self-relation and there is a movement outward from the simplicity of God in their course. As from the perfect self-return of immaterial being, it was deduced that such being knew itself and was conscious of the conformity of its being to its intellect and of its truth as exemplary idea to the being of other things, so it is now shown that to self-knowledge there is necessarily added the perfection of willing itself. The return of the simple being of God upon itself is what underlies the unity of knowing and willing for Aquinas.[40]

Understanding God to be self-related is absolutely necessary in order to conceive what it means for God to will. In will, God 'vult et se et alia. Sed se ut finem, alia vero ut ad finem' (I, 19, 2). This is both a different relation of God to himself than knowledge is, and, by adding it, we are more fully able to understand how God's power to cause is grounded in his nature. By willing and loving them God is more ade-quately related to things outside him as they are in themselves. If God's knowledge of material creation is abstracted from the perfec-tion added in his willing it, there is an inadequacy between the way these things are in themselves and how they are present to God in his knowledge. Such an abstraction is implied when, in question 14, will was spoken of as added to intellect when God moves to creation. It is also required for the distinction between God's 'scientia visionis' and his '[scientia] simplicis intelligentiae' (I, 14, 9). When will is joined to intellect, the relation 'ad res, secundum quod sunt in seipsis' is also given (I, 19, 3 *ad* 6).

So the movement outward in these questions is simultaneously a development in our knowledge of God, in the presence of creatures to God, and in our knowledge of the reason for their creation. There is the movement from will, God's relation to himself as the good end in which he rests, to love, God's ecstasy. Love moves outward to justice, mercy, providence, and predestination. In these God is for other things their law or measure—justice is for will and intellect what truth is for knowing—a measuring rooted in his liberal goodness or mercy,[41]

[40] The crucial texts are *Summa Theologiae* I, 14, 1: 'Unde cum Deus in summo im-materialitatis ... sequitur quod ipse sit in summo cognitionis'; I, 19, 1: 'Unde in quolibet habente intellectum est voluntas'; and I, 27, 5: 'actiones in natura intellectuali et divina non sunt nisi duae, scilicet intelligere et velle.... Relinquitur igitur quod nulla alia processio possit esse in Deo, nisi verbi et amoris.'

[41] 'Intellectus autem qui est causa rei, comparatur ad ipsam sicut regula et men-sura.... Iustitia igitur Dei, quae constituit ordinem in rebus conformem rationi sapien-tiae suae, quae est lex eius, convenienter veritas nominatur', *ST* I, 21, 2. 'Opus autem divinae iustitiae semper praesupponit opus misericordiae, et in eo fundatur', *ST* I, 21, 4.

and he is the reason in things, non-human and human, drawing them into their end, itself ultimately the divine goodness. Love, as 'vis unitiva etiam in Deo . . . quia illud bonum quod vult sibi, non est aliud quam ipse, qui est per suam essentiam bonus' (I, 20, 1 *ad* 3), has a reality for God's inner being not found in those more externalized designations of his activity. Thus, love is a proper name of God the Holy Spirit; it is a proper designation of an internal personal relation.[42] Finally, by this outward movement, the operation *ad extra* is reached. Power is 'principium effectus'.

Power implies the idea of a principle executing what will commands toward that which reason directs, which three coincide in God. Or it may be said that God's own knowledge or will, as it is the origin of effects, contains the notion of power. Hence the consideration of knowledge and will precedes in God the consideration of power, as cause precedes act and effect.[43]

The consequence of this development of the knowledge of God's nature, together with the understanding of how he can cause and have relation to the real independent existence of creatures, will be that, for Thomas, the proper conception of creation requires the knowledge of the Trinity.[44]

The transition from the divine knowledge, which 'importat relationem ad creaturas secundum quod sunt in Deo' (I, 14, 15) to relations 'ad res secundum quod sunt in seipsis (I, 19, 3 *ad* 6) makes the problem of expressing the divine self-relation consistently with the divine simplicity more and more difficult. Treating God as object of himself in will, Thomas is required once again to speak of him as moving upon himself. 'And this is what Plato meant when he said that the first mover moves himself.'[45] To express God's various relations to his creatures, his acts must be defined even more concretely. To such differences as 'scientia visionis' and '[scientia] simplicis intelligentiae'

---

[42] *ST* I, 37, 1.

[43] 'potentia importat rationem principii exequentis id quod voluntas imperat, et ad quod scientia dirigit; quae tria Deo secundum idem conveniunt. Vel dicendum quod ipsa scientia vel voluntas divina, secundum quod est principium effectivum, habet rationem potentiae. Unde consideratio scientiae et voluntatis praecedit in Deo considerationem potentiae, sicut causa praecedit operationem et effectum', *ST* I, 25, 1 *ad* 4.

[44] 'Dicendum quod cognitio divinarum Personarum fuit necessaria nobis . . . ad recte sentiendum de creatione rerum. Per hoc enim quod dicimus Deum omnia fecisse Verbo suo, excluditur error ponentium Deum produxisse res ex necessitate naturae. Per hoc autem quod ponimus in eo processionem amoris, ostenditur quod Deus non propter aliquam indigentiam creaturas produxit', *ST* I, 32, 1 *ad* 3. Cf. also *ST* I, 39, 8; I, 45, 6 and 7.

[45] 'Et secundum hoc Plato dixit quod primum movens movet seipsum', *ST* I, 19, 1 *ad* 3.

and 'scientia speculativa' and 'scientia practica',[46] there is added the difference between 'amor amicitiae' and 'amor concupiscentiae'. For 'Deus, proprie loquendo, non amat creaturas irrationales amore amicitiae, sed amore concupiscentiae' (I, 20, 2 *ad* 3). Just because his love is cause, in order to create the difference in things, God must love one thing more than another.[47] Because the statements about God's nature must show the grounds for the actual character of creation, it becomes increasingly difficult to make sense of the denial as real in God of the composition which defines the difference between creatures and God. What is the 'amor vis unitiva etiam in Deo, sed absque compositione' or the 'amor divinus ... vis concretiva absque compositione quae sit in Deo, inquantum aliis bona vult' (I, 20, 1 *ad* 3)? Must not God be self-divided by the self-knowing and loving which includes relation to external creation, if he is the unified one of the love, 'extra se in amatum translatus' (I, 20, 2 *ad* 1)?

It is not, however, simply with the outward movement culminating in the 'divina potentia' of question 25 that the treatise on the divine operations concludes. 'De divina beatitudine', question 26, effects a return to God's knowledge, which began the tract and which dominates it. Beatitude 'significat bonum perfectum intellectualis naturae'.[48] The perfection of such a nature will be an 'intellectualis operatio, secundum quam capit quodammodo omnia' (I, 26, 2). Thomas specifically excludes the possibility that 'beatitudo ei conveniat secundum rationem essentiae' or 'secundum voluntatem'; it is 'magis secundum rationem intellectus'.[49] Thus the statement of É. Pousset is not altogether precise. He is correct that beatitude concludes the entire first twenty-five questions of the *Summa*. Thomas says that it is the last member in a series: 'post considerationem eorum quae ad divinae essentiae unitatem pertinent'.[50] But this is not 'l'unité de l'être et de l'agir'. Beatitude does not specifically unite 'l'acte d'être et de la connaissance'; nor is the fact that they 'en Dieu, sont identiques' the salient point. As Pousset states himself, in God, will is 'aussi identique à l'être et à l'agir'.[51] Rather, it is precisely

---

[46] *ST* I, 14, 9 and I, 14, 16.

[47] *ST* I, 20, 3.

[48] *ST* I, 26, 1 and 2; *Comp. Theo.* i, 107, and *ScG*, *Liber Primus*, conclude with beatitude according to a similar reasoning.

[49] *ST* I, 26, 2 *obj.* 2 and *ad* 1.

[50] *ST* I, 26 *prol.*, see also the last words of the question.

[51] É. Pousset, 'Une relecture du Traité de Dieu dans la "Somme Théologique" de saint Thomas, I', *Archives de philosophie* 38 (1975), 561 n. 3.

as intellectual act, 'secundum rationem intellectus', that beatitude gathers together all the preceding perfections, and so happiness, by concluding the treatise on the divine operations, completes the second stage of the progressive revelation of the divine nature.

There can be no doubt that, like its corresponding member in the first series of divine attributes, i.e. question 11, 'de unitate Dei', the 'de divina beatitudine' involves a return to the point of departure which contains what intervenes. Happiness is a perfection which collects rather than removes. This is made clear by the first words of the first article; according to Boethius, happiness is 'status omnium bonorum aggregatione perfectus'. The first objection asks how such a thing is compatible with God's simplicity. This aggregation is not denied of God by Thomas but said to exist in him 'per modum simplicitatis' (I, 26, 1 *ad* 1). Specifically, happiness is presented as an intellectual activity containing will and power, rather than as a less complete relation to the object than they. Happiness knows the good it possesses—or, put otherwise, it is by knowledge that will enjoys its self-possession as its own end or good. Further, the intellectual nature, which is happy, is, as will, the source of good or evil, and has power over its acts. Intellect is the origin of will and power—this was already clear—and they are also thus the perfections of intellect. So, as a self-complete activity intellect contains them and is happy.[52] Beatitude is intellect knowing and enjoying its will and power, the happiness of God, and synthetically completes the divine operations. Beatitude also involves the subjective relation to God explicit in questions 12 and 13, i.e. the relation of rational creatures to God. Partly God is recognized to be happy 'secundum intellectum', because it is by intellect that we enjoy God in vision.[53] He is our blessedness. Objectively, he alone is happy since other intellects are happy by knowing him. Returning to the solutions in question 12, Thomas is able to place happiness in the subjective act of finite intellects through created grace.[54] The whole *de deo uno* is then

---

[52] 'Nihil enim aliud sub nomine beatitudinis intelligitur, nisi bonum perfectum intellectualis naturae, cuius est suam sufficientiam cognoscere in bono quae habet; et cui competit ut ei contingat aliquid vel bene vel male, et sit suarum operationum domina', *ST* I, 26, 1. 'Dicendum quod beatitudo, cum sit bonum, est obiectum voluntatis. Obiectum autem praeintelligitur actui potentiae. Unde secundum modum intelligendi prius est beatitudo divina quam actus voluntatis in ea requiescentis. Et hoc non potest esse nisi actus intellectus. Unde in actu intellectus attenditur beatitudo', *ST* I, 26, 2 *ad* 2. See also *ST* 1, 25, 1 *ad* 4.　　　　　　　　　　　　　　　　　[53] *ST* I, 26, 2 *sed contra*.

[54] 'ex parte ipsius obiecti, sic solus Deus est beatitudo, quia ex hoc solo est aliquis beatus, quod Deum intelligit. . . . Sed ex parte actus intelligentis beatitudo est quid creatum in creaturis beatis', *ST* I, 26, 3.

concluded by showing that God's happiness includes all happiness. So, as God's unity gathers into his simplicity all those positive perfections which its initially privative form seemed to deny, happiness gathers into his knowledge all the perfections of the acts of his creatures.[55]

In these questions on the divine operations Thomas has opened and developed the self-relation of the divine being to the point where it becomes increasing comprehensible how God is that self-division and plurality which is the Trinity of persons and why Christians regard the first principle so described as creator and true explanation of the existent world. Yet Thomas will pull back from regarding the transition to these descriptions of God as possible for reason. What lies behind this retreat is implicit in the tensions present within Thomas's treatment of the operations and is at root the same difficulty discovered in his consideration of the substantial names. This is the contrariety active in his return within Neoplatonic structures to more Hellenic philosophical positions. The general problem is the opposition of God's simplicity to the knowledge of him. The continuing specific difficulty for Thomas is how the content of what is known of God from the finite can be attributed to him if its mode is simplified.

In the questions on the operations the structures of thought belonging to the sciences of psychology and ethics are the means employed to order the theological material. The use of these patterns may be inessential as to content. Of the essence, however, are the self-reflective character of the divine acts, and the difference between the operations precisely in terms of the way subject and object of the activities are related. A mode, which the divine acts have in common with the finite spiritual form, is essential to their nature. It is also necessary to distinguish various forms of this mode if God is to be spoken of in theology as cause of what is other than him. Our argument has shown that God must divide and unite himself as subject and object of his acts and that these acts are many not only from the perspective of the created intellect viewing them, but also that the different forms of these self-relations are absolutely essential to distinguishing them from each other. The self-return which is knowledge is not the same as those which are truth and will. And so knowledge, truth, and will are not simply identical with the being of God. This comes out very clearly when, in the introductory question to the treatise on the Trinity,

---

[55] 'quidquid est desiderabile in quacumque beatitudine, vel vera vel falsa, totum eminentius in divina beatitudine praeexistit', *ST* I, 26, 4.

Thomas is at pains to show that the procession of love is not generation, which would have the consequence that it was indistinguishable
from the procession of the word or knowledge.

There is a difference between intellect and will, because the intellect is actualized by the thing understood coming to be in the intellect according to its likeness; will however is actualized, not because some likeness of the object of will
is in the will, but because the will has an inclination toward the thing willed.
The procession then which belongs to the nature of intellect, is according to
the nature of likeness, and so is able to have the character of generation. . . .
However, the procession belonging to the nature of will, is not considered
according to the character of likeness, but more according to character of
impulse and movement into something. And therefore . . . it proceeds in the
divine through the mode of love . . . for from love someone is said to be moved
and impelled toward something to be done.[56]

The different forms of relation to creation correspond to these different forms of self-relation. Unless the modes of finite composition are
in some way carried into the divine it will be nothing but blank incomprehensible unity. If this were the sum of Thomas's theology, it could
not proceed, as it does next, to the Trinity of persons.

---

[56] 'est differentia inter intellectum et voluntatem, quod intellectus fit in actu per hoc
quod res intellecta est in intellectu secundum suam similitudinem; voluntas autem fit in
actu, non per hoc quod aliqua similitudo voliti sit in voluntate, sed ex hoc quod voluntas
habet quandam inclinationem in rem volitam. Processio igitur quae attenditur secundum rationem intellectus, est secundum rationem similitudinis; et in tantum potest
habere rationem generationis. . . . Processio autem quae attenditur secundum rationem
voluntatis, non consideratur secundum rationem similitudinis sed magis secundum
rationem impellentis et moventis in aliquid. Et ideo quod procedit in divinis per
modum amoris . . . prout aliquis ex amore dicitur moveri vel impelli ad aliquid facien-
dum', *ST* I, 27, 4.

VI

Relatio est idem quod persona:
the Trinity of Persons
Questions 26 to 43

QUESTIONS 26 to 43 complete the consideration of God 'in se' in the *Summa Theologiae* by that procession or emanation which produces real relation and opposition within the divine essence. These real relations are subsistent divine persons. There are two main aspects of the structural analysis herein attempted. The first is a treatment of the internal structure of the treatise *de deo trino*. In this considerable assistance is derived from Bernard Lonergan's *Verbum*. The analysis must, however, be more extensive than his and, ultimately, conclusions other than his will be drawn about the logic operative in these questions. The second part is an examination of the connections between the treatise on the predications belonging to the divine unity and that on the Trinity of persons. Included in this must be some consideration of the significance of the different relations between metaphysical theology and scriptural theology which Thomas holds to exist in these two treatises. As the examination of the links and discontinuities within the whole 'de deo in se' will require venturing well outside the 'de deo trino' and will lead more easily to general conclusions, it is taken up after the internal structure has been sifted.

Bernard Lonergan writes the following (I have supplied the references to specific questions from Fr Lonergan's notes):

There is the order of our concepts *in fieri*, and then, processions [*q.* 27] precede relations [*q.* 28] and relations precede persons [*qq.* 29–43]. There is the order of our concepts *in facto esse* and then there are the persons as persons [*qq.* 30–2], the persons considered individually [*qq.* 33–8], the persons compared to the divine essence [*q.* 39], to the relations [*q.* 40], to the notional acts [*q.* 41]. Now these orders are inverse. The processions and the notional acts are the same realities. But the processions are in God prior, in the first order of our concepts, to the constitution of the persons. On the other hand, the notional acts are acts of the persons and consequent to the persons conceived as constituted. . . . He [Thomas] maintained a distinction between the property of the Father as relation and the same property as constitutive of the Father. As relation, the property is subsequent to generation; as constitutive, the same property is prior to generation . . . there are two systematic and inverse orders, necessarily what is prior in one order will be subsequent in the other.[1]

Leaving aside whatever else is said or implied here, there seems to be the grounds for asserting, in these questions, a circular motion of the same kind as we have discovered in the movement from simplicity to unity in questions 3–11, and from intellect to beatitude in questions 14–26. There is at least a return to the matters which began the treatise in those questions which conclude it.

Question 27 is 'de processione divinarum personarum'. It shows how the operations of intellect and will, which are internal to the divine essence, are productive of processions or origins. These words are used more or less as synonyms. The relations of origin, generation and spiration are treated in question 28, 'de relationibus divinis'. The relations are the persons as subsistences in the essence and their treatment commences properly at question 29, 'de personis divinis'. These are parallel to questions 40, 'de personis in comparatione ad relationes sive proprietates', and 41, 'de personis in comparatione ad actus notionales'. (Questions 42 and 43 are considered later in this chapter.) This appears immediately from the names of the notional acts: 'innascibilitas, paternitas, filiatio, communis spiratio et processio'. And Thomas is quite clear on the subject: 'notio dicitur id quod est propria ratio cognoscendi divinam personam. Divinae autem personae multiplicantur secundum originem.'[2] The relations of origin and the notional acts are two ways of regarding the same thing. 'Dicendum quod actus notionales secundum modum significandi tantum differunt a relationibus personarum, sed re sunt omnino idem.' This is the *ad secundum* of question 41, article 1. It goes on to consider the relations primarily in their character as origins or quasi-motions. The notions are abstract nouns grounded in the activities. For this reason their existence causes Thomas great difficulty. As substantives, they seem to provide a way to arrive at the subsisting persons by philosophical reason.[3] If the point be strained, questions 27

---

[1] B. Lonergan, *Verbum: Word and Idea in Aquinas*, ed. D. B. Burrell (Notre Dame, 1967), pp. 206–7.   [2] *ST* I, 32, 3.

[3] 'quarentibus quo sunt unus Deus, et quo sunt tres, sicut respondetur quod sunt essentia vel deitate unum, ita oportuit esse aliqua nomina abstracta, quibus responderi possit personas distingui. Et huiusmodi sunt proprietates vel notiones in abstracto significantes, ut paternitas et filiatio', *ST* I, 32, 2. See also I, 32, 1 and question I, 39, *passim*, but especially article 7.

and 41 are the specifically corresponding members; in effect, notional acts reach back to the origin of relations.

It is evident, on the face of it, that question 40, 'concerning the persons as compared to the relations or properties', draws the extensive treatment of the persons back to its earlier ground in the relations (*q.* 20). Article 4 of question 29 is 'utrum hoc nomen persona[e in divinis] significet relationem [vel substantiam]' and concludes 'hoc nomen persona significat relationem in recto, et essentiam in obliquo'. Article 1 of question 40 is similarly 'utrum relatio sit idem quod persona'. By the same arguments, it determines: 'Sed quia relatio, secundum quod est quaedam res in divinis, est ipsa essentia; essentia autem idem est quod persona, ut ex dictis patet; oportet quod relatio sit idem quod persona.' The shape of the treatise is then a movement from the activities within the essence to the persons and back again. Fr Lonergan finds a rationale for these opposed movements in the distinction between the order of our concepts *in fieri*, i.e. the order corresponding to the origin, production or becoming of things, factually or logically, and *in facto esse*, i.e. a knowing beginning with the thing produced and proceeding from it to the origins through which its being is made intelligible. The latter mode is the form under which the Trinity is made known to men, nor could we have discovered it by the alternative route. Because of the origins of sacred doctrine in divine revelation, the *Summa Theologiae* has an 'ordo disciplinae', the inverse of the human 'via inventionis'.[4] Thomas is explicit that human reason cannot invent the Trinity. But, 'Trinitate posita, congruunt huiusmodi rationes; non tamen ita quod per has rationes sufficienter probetur Trinitas Personarum.'[5] Thus, the circular motion in the treatise *de deo trino* derives from the joining and difference of the movements of man's knowledge from nature to God and from God to nature. This is the reason we have assigned to the circular motion of the *Summa* generally and of its parts. Still, a full analysis of the structure of the questions on the Trinity requires that other considerations be drawn into the argument.

What is chiefly to be added in order that the structure of the treatise on the Trinity might become more completely understood is the relation of unity and plurality in it. The direction forward from the operations, through the persons, to creation is in general a development of multiplicity. The self-related operations of knowing and willing,

---

[4] See W. J. Hankey, 'The Place of the Psychological Image', 104.
[5] *ST* I, 32, 1 *ad* 2.

which determine the divine processions, are a more unified form of being than that to which they give rise. This is why there is no power posited between the essence of God and his operations, from which the latter would derive. Indeed properly speaking, 'potentia activa est principium agendi in aliud' and 'maxime manifestatur in creatione'; power is the operation of God outside his essence.[6] In this perspective, Thomas says, 'Sed intelligere et velle non sunt tales actus qui designent processionem alicuius rei a Deo distinctae, vel essentialiter vel personaliter.'[7] Yet power is a notional act; 'Patri attribuitur et appropriatur.'[8] The Father is the source of all procession. In fact, because he is the ultimate origin of personal procession, the power of creation belongs properly to the Father. And because the power which creates has its first form in the 'potentia generandi', power in God is modified, as knowing and willing also are, in the personal relations.[9] That is, power has a different character in the Father than in the Son, and so on. In this way, the *de deo trino* occupies a position midway between the treatise on the operations and that on creation.

Putting the same point differently, Thomas maintains that, although the distinction of persons is real, it is the minimal distinction; 'distinctio personarum non debet esse nisi per id quod minimum distinguit, scilicet per relationem' (I, 40, 2 *ad* 3). Because the distinction is within a substance or nature, it can be compared to a relation of identity; 'per huiusmodi relationes non diversificatur substantia, sicut nec per rationem identitatis' (I, 28, 1 *ad* 2). It is a distinguishing not through a relation 'ad aliud' but 'ad se' (I, 29, 4 *ad* 1). This involves mutual opposition; 'oppositio relativa faciat pluralitatem realem in divinis' (I, 32, 3 *ad* 3). Still, mutual opposition demands intimate unity; 'oppositorum relatione unum est in altero' (I, 42, 5 *ad* 3). The reason

---

[6] *ST* I, 25, 1 and I, 45, 6 *ad* 2 respectively.

[7] *ST* I, 41, 4 *ad* 3.

[8] *ST* I, 45, 6 *ad* 2.

[9] The Father is 'principium totius divinitatis', *ST* I, 39, 8, and is called Father primarily because he generates a person (*ST* I, 33, 3 quoted below). Article 5 of question 41 is 'utrum potentia generandi significet relationem et non essentiam'. *ST* I, 42, 6 *ad* 3 and I, 45, 6 show how power is personally modified in being given and received. On this modification cf. Dom C. F. Gomes, OSB, 'La réciprocité psychologique des personnes divines selon la théologie de saint Thomas d'Aquin', *Atti dell'VIII Congresso Tomistico*, ed. A. Piolanti, iv, Studi tomistici 13 (Vatican City, 1981), who says: 'la puissance n'est pas "eodem modo" en chaque Personne, on est en droit de dire la même chose des autres attributs et en particulier de la conscience' (pp. 162–3). He refers us to '. . . Pater est sapiens ut concipiens, Filius vero sapiens ut verbum conceptum' which is *De Pot. q.* 9, *a.* 9, *ad* 6 (p. 250). He notes that *ST* I, 14, 2 *ad* 1 is the same as *De Veritate q.* 2, *a.* 2, *ad* 2 (p. 155 of Gomes).

for moving beyond the operations comes out in this reflection. For actions of this kind, the more complete the issuing the more perfect the return to the source. 'Sed id quod procedit ad intra processu intelligibili, non oportet esse diversum; imo, quanto perfectius procedit, tanto magis est unum cum eo a quo procedit' (I, 27, 1 *ad* 2). In contrast to operations *ad extra*, the source and result are equal. The penultimate question of the treatise has to do with the 'equality and likeness of the divine persons in respect to each other'.[10]

It is just this lack of equality between source and effect which marks off the first processions within the essence from the procession outside it, creation. 'It must be said that what first proceeds from unity is equality, and then comes multiplicity. And therefore from the Father, to whom, according to Augustine, unity is proper, the Son processes, to whom equality is appropriate, and then the creature comes forth to which inequality belongs.'[11] In fact, on this account, the elements of the created world must also be unequal to each other. Since none of them can individually mirror the divine perfection adequately, they represent it as best they can by embodying different goods variously, and so together they do better than any one could.[12] The unity of equality and of substance is lost in the procession *ad extra*. 'Dicendum quod cum creatura procedat a Deo in diversitate naturae, Deus est extra ordinem totius creaturae, nec ex eius natura est eius habitudo ad creaturas' (I, 28, 1 *ad* 3). He is really and essentially distinguished from creatures. 'Secundum rem quidem Deus distinguitur per essentiam a rebus quarum est per creationem principium' (I, 41, 4 *ad* 3). Yet, the two genera of procession are linked. The procession within the essence is the basis of that emanating outside the divine being.

The next chapter will elaborate this connection. At this point it is necessary to make clear only that the procession of creatures becomes intelligible through the procession of persons, and that

[10] 'De aequalitate et similitudine divinarum personarum ad invicem', *ST* I, 42.

[11] 'Dicendum quod primum quod procedit ab unitate, est aequalitas, et deinde procedit multiplicitas. Et ideo a Patre, cui, secundum Augustinum, appropriatur unitas, processit Filius, cui appropriatur aequalitas, et deinde creatura, cui competit inaequalitas. Sed tamen etiam a creaturis participatur quaedam aequalitas, scilicet proportionis', *ST* I, 47, 2 *ad* 2. It is Augustine's *De Doctrina Christiana* I, 5 (PL 34, 21) to which Thomas is referring.

[12] 'Produxit enim res in esse propter suam bonitatem communicandam creaturis, et per eas repraesentandam. Et quia per unam creaturam sufficienter repraesentari non potest, produxit multas creaturas et diversas, ut quod deest uni ad repraesentandam divinam bonitatem', *ST* I, 47, 1.

what differentiates the two is the dissimilarity of the relation between unity and plurality in them. Thomas is explicit:

divinae Personae secundum rationem suae processiones habent causalitatem respectu creationis rerum . . . cum de Dei scientia et voluntate ageretur, Deus est causa rerum per suum intellectum et voluntatem. . . . Unde et Deus Pater operatus est creaturam per suum Verbum, quod est Filius, et per suum Amorem, qui est Spiritus Sanctus. Et secundum hoc processiones Personarum sunt rationes productionis creaturarum, inquantum includunt essentialia attributa, quae sunt scientia et voluntas.[13]

Here Thomas reaches right back to the development of knowledge and will in the essence, and mediates that through the distinct persons of the treatise on the Trinity, to provide 'rationes' for creation. The movement toward creatures is evident at every level of this treatise just as it recurred again and again in the consideration of the operations: 'persona procedens in divinis procedit ut principium productionis creaturarum' (I, 33, 3 *ad* 1). Each of the persons is understood through such a relation. Something has been said already of the Father's appropriation of power. The word is similarly conceived; 'in Verbo importatur respectus ad creaturam Deus enim cognoscendo se, cognoscit omnem creaturam' (I, 34, 3). Thus, the Word is 'Sapientia genita et creata'.[14] Something will be said about the Spirit's relation to creation below.

The other side of this is that the creation is obviously not a specific act of one person of the Trinity, though its ground in power is particularly appropriated to the Father as the source of all procession, as stated above. The unity of the whole Trinity stands over against the multiplicity of creatures: 'creare convenit Deo secundum suum esse; quod est eius essentia, quae est communis tribus Personis. Unde creare non est proprium alicui Personae, sed commune toti Trinitati' (I, 45, 6). Creation signifies a divine action, 'quae est eius essentia cum relatione ad creaturam' (I, 43, 3 *ad* 1). Being is properly the object of the creator in creation and, as God is the proper producer of being—to create properly belongs to God alone—it is his being which is known from creation. Here once again we encounter the influence of Proclus, mediated through Dionysius and the *Liber de Causis*.[15] It is then the essential unity, not the plurality and distinction of persons, which unaided reasoning from creatures attains. 'Virtus autem creativa Dei

[13] *ST* I, 45, 6; see F. J. Ruello, 'Saint Thomas et Pierre Lombard'.
[14] *ST* I, 41, 3 *ad* 4 and see ch. V n. 18, p. 100 above.
[15] See Endnote 4, p. 165 below.

est communis toti Trinitati, unde pertinet ad unitatem essentiae, non ad distinctionem personarum. Per rationem igitur naturalem cognosci possunt de Deo ea quae pertinent ad unitatem essentiae, non autem ea quae pertinent ad distinctionem personarum' (I, 32, 1). The *de deo trino* is situated between the operations in the unity and the operation from the unity. The intelligibility of creation requires both that the procession of persons within the unity be developed, and that there be a return from these to the unity of essence. This is in fact what is to be found.

The circle of the questions on the Trinity begins with a movement from unity to plurality, i.e. from the unity of the activities to the distinction of persons. 'Et quia Personae divinae secundum relationes origines distinguuntur, secundum ordinem doctrinae prius considerandum est de origine sive de processione; secundo, de relationibus originis; tertio, de Personis' (I, 27, *prol.*). After this the persons can be treated individually. Question 29 is 'de personis divinis'; 30 is 'de pluralitate personarum in divinis'. Question 31 declares that 'trinitas' does not signify 'unam essentiam trium personarum' but rather 'significat magis numerum personarum unius essentiae' (I, 31, 1 *ad* 1). Because the Trinity teaches that there is plurality in God, the Trinity is not knowable by the reasoning from creatures which manifests instead the unity of essence. Examining the evidence, Thomas is convinced that the pagan philosophers did not arrive at consubstantial subsistences in the divine.[16] Thus it is clear why question 32, 'de divinarum personarum cognitione', which considers how we can know the Trinity though it is not discoverable by natural reason, follows 31, in which the Trinity is primarily given the significance of plurality. The following questions, 33–38, are thus 'de singulis Personis'.

The circle described by the treatise on the Trinity begins to turn back toward the divine unity even within the questions on the individual persons. The last person treated, the Holy Spirit, is the union of what differentiates Father and Son. The Spirit has a dual role in the theology of Thomas. His is the procession of will or love. Love is a force impelling to unity, but it also carries the subject out of himself and is an endeavour to attain union beyond the possession already given in knowledge. Will is necessarily added to knowledge for production or practice and involves a relation to things in themselves.

Just so, God the Spirit is God, both as perfectly united and resting in himself in love, and as translated ecstatically out of himself by love.

[16] *ST* I, 32, 1 *ad* 1.

The second role of the Spirit is displayed in question 43 on the mission of the persons, the transitional question between the *de deo trino* and the *de deo creante*. For the Spirit is the medium of the gracious indwelling of the Trinity and so he is the person to whom 'gift' is appropriated: 'omnia dona, inquantum dona sunt, attribuantur Spiritui Sancto, quia habet rationem primi doni, secundum quod est Amor' (I, 43, 5 *ad* 1). This follows from questions 37 and 38 which treat 'love' and 'gift', proper names of the Spirit. Their order and rationale are readily determined: 'Ratio autem gratuitae donationis est amor; ideo enim damus gratis alicui aliquid, quia volumus ei bonum. Primum ergo quod damus ei, est amor quo volumus ei bonum. Unde manifestum est quod amor habet rationem primi doni, per quod omnia dona gratuita donantur.[17] And so, because the Holy Spirit is love, he is the gift by which God bestows his other graces. The movement is outward to creatures from love. This is one side of the development in the *de deo trino* toward creation. The other side is also present in the three questions on the Holy Spirit which begin with 36, 'de persona Spiritus Sancti'. They involve the return to unity, since love for Neoplatonists, pagan and Christian, is the means of return.[18] In this perspective, one notices their situation between the questions on the Father and the Son considered as individual persons, on the one hand, and the questions comparing the essence and the persons (41), and treating the equality and likeness of the persons (42), on the other.

The Holy Spirit is called 'spirit', the general name for God, because he is what is common to Father and Son; 'ex ipsa communitate eius quod dicitur Spiritus Sanctus' (I, 36, 1). Even what is proper to the notion of spirit, 'impulsionem et motionem significare videtur', conveys the idea of making one. 'Est autem proprium amoris quod moveat et impellat voluntatis amantis in amatum.'[19] Because the persons are

---

[17] *ST* I, 38, 2; question 37 is 'de nomine Spiritus Sancti qui est amor', question 38 is 'de nomine Spiritus Sancti quod est donum'.

[18] On Proclus, see S. Gersh, *KINHΣΙΣ*, pp. 123–7. 'If love is an activity, it would be reasonable to conclude that love like activity manifests itself in two forms: (i) as the complete cycle of remaining, procession, and reversion, and (ii) as the third element in such a triadic formation' (p. 124). Thomas collects this doctrine from Dionysius: love is a complete activity in God by which he moves himself: *In de Div. Nom.* IV, vii–xii, esp. 369, 390, 439, 444, 455, 460. So in the *Summa Theologiae* love carries God out of himself (I, 20, 2 *ad* 1) and is the unifying bond (I, 37, 1 *ad* 3 and I, 39, 8). On Dionysius see Louth, *The Origins*, p. 176; Louth does not speak of the Neoplatonic source of Dionysius' doctrine. A. Wohlman, 'L'élaboration des éléments aristotéliciens dans la doctrine thomiste de l'amour', *Revue thomiste*, 82 (1982), 247–69, discusses the balance of Platonic and Aristotelian elements in Thomas's teaching; he traces the Platonic element to Dionysius (p. 250).   [19] *ST* I, 36, 1; cf. also *ST* I, 27, 4.

distinguished solely by relation, personality is nothing apart from the essence except the opposition expressed in the relations. 'Relationes autem personas distinguere non possunt, nisi secundum quod sunt oppositae' (I, 36, 2). Father and Son will thus be one except as they are opposed. 'Pater et Filius in omnibus unum sunt, in quibus non distinguit inter eos relationis oppositio' (I, 36, 4). They are evidently not opposed in that which makes them common principle of the Spirit. 'Sicut igitur Pater et Filius sunt unus Deus propter unitatem formae significatae per hoc nomen Deus; ita sunt unum principium Spiritus Sancti, propter unitatem proprietatis significatae in hoc nomine principium' (I, 36, 4). Nor is this incompatible with their also being two. 'Neque est inconveniens unam proprietatem esse in duobus suppositis, quorum est una natura' (I, 36, 4 *ad* 1). To put the matter somewhat paradoxically, the Holy Spirit is the return, under the form of personality, to the unity of essence of the Father and Son out of their personal opposition. They are two hypostases with one act and so he unites the two. 'If the subjects of the spiration are considered, then the Holy Spirit proceeds from the Father and Son in their plurality; for he proceeds from them as the unifying love of both.'[20] Thus, the Spirit is posited because of the unity out of division of the Father and Son. He is not the essence prior to their distinction but the return to that essential unity through relation, i.e. as person. Without him their personal union does not exist.[21] So the language about him as union and connection becomes theologically intelligible.[22]

The structure of the Godhead just exposed is in fact the application to it of the Neoplatonic logic of *exitus* and *reditus*, present from the beginnings of western trinitarian theology:

La contribution propre et géniale de saint Augustin, c'est d'avoir associé l'utilisation de l'"epistrophê',—de la conversion vers le principe, prônée par le néo-platonisme,—d'une 'epistrophê' aimante à l'analyse du donné biblique

---

[20] 'Si vero considerentur supposita spirationis, sic Spiritus Sanctus procedit a Patre et Filio ut sunt plures; procedit enim ab eis ut amor unitivus duorum', *ST* I, 36, 4 *ad* 1.

[21] 'excluso Spiritu Sancto, qui est duorum nexus, non posset intelligi unitas connexionis inter Patrem et Filium. Et ideo dicuntur omnia esse connexa propter Spiritum Sanctum; quia posito Spiritu Sancto, invenitur ratio connexionis in divinis Personis, unde Pater et Filius possunt dici connexi', *ST* I, 39, 8.

[22] The Spirit is 'nexus Patris et Filii inquantum est Amor' (*ST* I, 27, 1 *ad* 3) and 'nexus duorum' (*ST* I, 39, 8). Aquinas quotes Augustine's designation of the Spirit as 'aequalitatis unitatisque concordia' (*ST* I, 39, 8 *obj.* 2). Cf. J. Châtillon, '*Unitas, Aequalitas, Concordia vel Connexio*, Recherches sur les origines de la théorie thomiste des appropriations (*Sum. theol.*, I, q. 39, art. 7–8)', *Commemorative Studies*, ed. A. A. Maurer, i, pp. 337–79.

sur les relations aimantes entre le Père et le Fils pour découvrir dans l'Esprit la communion d'amour entre le Père et le Fils qui retourne à son Père dans l'amour.[23]

The intellectualizing of the Trinity in this way brings the Stoic and Neoplatonic systematizing of the sciences into Christian theology. Thomas finds in the *De Trinitate* of Boethius a treatise on the divisions and methods of the sciences.[24] The Neoplatonists carry forward the Stoic division of science into physics, logic and ethics and 'l'intuition fondamentale du stoïcisme, selon laquelle le Logos est l'objet commun des trois parties de la philosophie'.[25] Augustine picks up this tradition, but for him the interior relations of the persons of the Trinity found the relations of the parts of science.

Selon Augustin, la physique a pour objet Dieu comme cause de l'être, la logique Dieu comme norme de la pensée, l'éthique Dieu comme règle de vie. Cet ordre augustinien: physique, logique, éthique, correspond à l'ordre des Personnes divines dans la Trinité: le Père est le Principe de l'être; le Fils, l'Intelligence; l'Esprit-Saint, l'Amour. L'unité systématique des parties de la philosophie reflète ici l'intériorité réciproque des Personnes divines.[26]

Pierre Hadot also notes that in Augustine another triad—*natura, doctrina, usus*—in a like manner functions both in the sciences and in the relations of the divine persons.[27] Thomas employs it as well. 'Usus ergo quo Pater et Filius se invicem fruuntur, convenit cum proprio Spiritus Sancti, inquantum est Amor' (I, 39, 8). By a Neoplatonic logic, the Holy Spirit is, consequently, a certain gathering-in of the distinguished persons. Indeed, Thomas agrees with Augustine, not only in speaking of the Spirit as that whereby Father and Son enjoy each other, but also as 'dilectio, delectatio, felicitas vel beatitudo' (I, 39, 8). He thus recalls that aggregation in happiness which concluded the operations.

After the questions on the Holy Spirit, it is altogether reasonable that we should return to the unity of essence. Question 39, comparing the essence and persons, commences this work. Its first article maintains, in fact, that 'divina simplicitas hoc requirit, quod in Deo sit idem essentia et suppositum, quod in substantiis intellectualibus nihil est aliud quam persona'. The question goes on to show from this that

[23] B. de Margerie, *La Trinité chrétienne dans l'histoire*, Théologie historique 31 (Paris, 1975), p. 164.

[24] Cf. my 'The *De Trinitate* of St. Boethius'.

[25] P. Hadot, 'Les divisions des parties de la philosophie', p. 212.

[26] Ibid.   [27] Ibid., n. 80.

essential names are predicated of the persons and explains how this is done. This requires Thomas to raise again the problems of question 32, on how the divine persons are known. For, if essential predicates are appropriate to the persons, there must be some knowledge of the persons from the rational consideration of creatures. 'Sicut igitur similitudine vestigii vel imaginis in creaturis inventa utimur ad manifestationem divinarum Personarum, ita et essentialibus attributis. Et haec manifestatio Personarum per essentialia attributa appropriatio nominatur' (I, 39, 7).

As previously explained, questions 40 and 41, on the comparison of the persons first with the relations and then with the notional acts, draw the argument of the treatise back toward its starting-point in the operations. Question 42, on the equality and likeness of the persons, also considers their unity. As indicated above, equality is a relation of the terms of procession which belongs to that of the persons in contrast to that of creation. According to a scheme worked out in the last article of question 39, equality as a predicate of God connotes unity, 'unitatem importare'. 'Aequalitas autem importat unitatem in respectu ad alterum; nam aequale est quod habet unam quantitatem cum alio.' Indeed, equality proves to be a term exactly suited to explain the essential unity of the persons without dissolving their differences. In divine persons, it connotes both essence and relations. 'Aequalitas autem utrumque importat, scilicet distinctionem personarum, quia nihil sibi ipsi dicitur aequale; et unitatem essentiae, quia ex hoc personae sunt sibi invicem aequales, quod sunt unius magnitudinis et essentiae' (I, 42, 1 *ad* 4). So in equality, the argument returns to the unity of essence without leaving behind the distinction of persons. The structure of the *de deo trino* conforms in this way to those of the divisions already analysed. The unity to which simplicity returned was fuller than it. Beatitude consisted in the intellectual activity with which the operations began but it included the self-enjoyment belonging to will and the practical ease of infinite power which had not yet appeared in the 'de scientia Dei'. The final return of creatures to God will also involve such a development.[28] For though the all in all contains no more than what is in the source, the unity of the divine *principium* and what has come out of it makes the implicit explicit, both in fact and for knowledge and will. In Thomas what intervenes between beginning and end is

---

[28] See the conclusion of the *Summa contra Gentiles*. Thomas did not reach the last things in the *Summa Theologiae*.

included in the beginning as end. So equality comprehends both the self-distinction of the persons and the unity of essence.

The last question of the *de deo trino* concerns the mission of divine persons. Its very title suggests its appropriateness for providing a transition to the *de deo creante*. Something more will be said about it below as we take up comprehensively the problems of the connections between the sections of the *de deo*. Just now two points must be made to show how question 43 arises out of the immediately preceding questions and leads to those beyond.

First, we must be clear that the interpenetration of essence and person has been the main subject since the consideration of what belonged peculiarly to the Holy Spirit. It appeared in 39 as the persons were shown to be knowable through essential names, in 40 as the personal relations and essential, or notional, acts were related to each other (article 4), and in 41, as persons and notional acts were compared. What happens throughout is that the essential acts, and, by implication, the essence, are shown to be modified in the personal relations. Knowing, willing, power are modified as they are given or received in the relation of one person to another. This is a predominant consideration when thinking about equality and likeness in God. It gives content to Thomas's thinking that, as in God there is 'principium secundum originem, absque prioritate', it is necessary 'ibi esse ordinem secundum originem, absque prioritate' (I, 42, 3). This is 'ordo naturae'. So the final article of 42 works out the equality of Father and Son 'secundum potentiam' in so far as the absolute divine potency is given and received. The last words of the question are: 'Habet ergo Filius eamdem potentiam quam Pater, sed cum alia relatione. Quia Pater habet eam ut dans; et hoc significatur, cum dicitur quod potest generare. Filius autem habet eam ut accipiens; et hoc significatur, cum dicitur quod potest generari' (I, 42, 6 *ad* 3). Since power is the creative operation, the procession to creatures might follow immediately but the missions intervene.

The intervention of the missions is the analogue for grace of the procession of creatures. The gracious mission of the Trinity to the rational creature so as to dwell in it has two aspects, the persons severally and as a whole. This carries forward the point made just above in respect to the preceding questions, and reformulated constitutes the second point. The ultimate basis of the divine mission is the eternal procession. The order of origin or nature thus determines it. As we have seen, the Holy Ghost is the person especially sent; he proceeds from both the Father and Son, and, as love, he is the first gift and the basis of all other graces. But, since the Father is absolute principle and receives nothing, neither is he sent. 'Unde cum Pater non sit ab alio, nullo modo convenit sibi mitti, sed solum Filio et Spiritui Sancto, quibus convenit esse ab alio' (I, 43, 4). The other side is that the mission is the whole Trinity both sent and received. Moreover, this consideration concludes the question and the *de deo trino*. It had earlier been established that the indwelling of the whole Trinity was the purpose of the mission, 'per gratiam gratum facientem tota Trinitas inhabitat mentem' (I, 43, 5). When this purpose is in view, the Trinity as a whole is also perceived to be the sender; this is the final point of Thomas. 'Si vero Persona mittens intelligatur esse principium effectus secundum quem attenditur missio, sic tota Trinitas mittit Personam missam' (I, 43, 8). The significant point is that it is this 'tota Trinitas', persons and essence taken together, not the essence considered apart from the persons, which creates. Thomas wrote earlier: 'Virtus ... creativa Dei est communis toti Trinitati' (I, 32, 1); now he says 'creaturas visibiles tota Trinitas operata sit' (I, 43, 7 *ad* 3). So the return to a concrete unity, a unity in and through self-relation, is once again the transitional moment.

There is here, moreover, as in the return accomplished by concluding the divine operations with beatitude, a subjective element also. The God who is his intellect and will has a special affinity with his intelligent creatures. Although he is in everything by essence, power, and presence, he is sent only to rational creatures. God is in men as the known is in the knower and the loved in the lover.[29] According to this special mode, he establishes his own abode in man as his temple.

Thus there is a giving and receiving of the divine essence from God to man in the missions of the Word and Spirit. The similitude of intellectual natures provides for a relation of the creature to the Creator, the relation of created intellection to its principle. Man's intellectual motion is derived from God's. Thus, the divine persons proceed to bestow illumination and love upon men by the presence of the Word and Spirit respectively. Man is, then, returned to God when he receives and enjoys the divine persons present in him.[30]

The problem of the continuity between the *de deo trino* and what precedes it and follows it has two sides. One is the connection between it and what is more unified; the other is the connection with what is less. The two are themselves joined; for the embracing problem is how

---

[29] *ST* I, 43, 3.
[30] M. Carreker, '*Motus in Deo*', p. 77; at this point Mr Carreker cites *ST* I, 43, 3 *ad* 1.

relation to other is contained in and emerges from self-relation. It is easier to commence with the drive toward the procession of creatures.

The essential matters are before us. It is necessary only to draw them together and to fill out some elements. The treatment of God's operations moved from knowledge to will and power. By this movement the production of creatures became intelligible. God's power creates after will affirms the object known. The internal activities of knowing and willing determine the processions in the Trinity. The power of creation derives ultimately from the *potentia generandi* and, as power to create, it is given and received by the persons, so, in fact, this essential operation is an act of the whole Trinity. Since, in the Trinity, knowing and willing originate real distinction, a definite sense can be given to Thomas's statement that the procession of persons makes rational the procession of creatures. As well it becomes clearer why he both says that knowledge of the Trinity is necessary 'ad recte sentiendum de creatione rerum' (I, 32, 1 *ad* 3) and maintains 'similitudine vestigii vel imaginis in creaturis inventa utimur ad manifestationem divinarum Personarum' (I, 39, 7). Beyond this, we must recollect how a relation to creation is contained in the individual consideration of the persons.

Article 3 of question 33 asks 'Utrum hoc nomen Pater dicitur in divinis per prius secundum quod personaliter sumitur'. It concludes: 'Sic igitur patet quod per prius paternitas dicitur in divinis secundum quod importatur respectus Personae ad Personam, quam secundum quod importatur respectus Dei ad creaturam.' But the prior by no means excludes what is second. The immediately succeeding *ad primum* states that a person proceeding comes forth as a 'principium productionis creaturarum'. Moreover, as also indicated earlier, it is precisely the fact that the Father is the ultimate generating principle or underived source of persons that makes the *potentia creandi* appropriate to him. He is source of creatures because he is the source of persons.

There is a similar treatment of the Word. Article 3 of question 34 asks 'Utrum in nomine Verbi importetur respectus ad creaturam'. The answer is affirmative. Indeed, Thomas uses expressions close to those of Eriugena when the latter speaks of God as making himself in his Word: 'Sed quia Deus uno actu et se et omnia intelligit, unicum Verbum eius est expressivum non solum Patris, sed etiam creaturarum.'[31] As in the operations, knowledge has a different character owing to its

---

[31] *ST* I, 34, 3 and ch. V n. 18, pp. 100–1 above.

different objects. God's knowledge of himself is 'cognoscitiva'; of creatures, it is 'cognoscitiva et factiva'. So the procession of knowledge, the Word, is 'expressivum' of the Father; it is 'expressivum et operativum' of creatures.[32] This leads to Thomas commenting favourably on scriptural speech about Wisdom, begotten and created, 'quia sapientia creata est participatio quaedam Sapientiae increatae' or, alternatively, because both creation and generation are something the Son receives from the Father.[33]

It has already been stated how the name 'gift', ascribed to the Holy Spirit, involves a necessary relation to creatures. He is gift as origin of grace and the meaning of possession which is appropriate to having God as such a gift belongs only to the rational creature. 'Unde sola creatura rationalis potest habere divinam Personam' (I, 38, 1). This, however, does not prevent the name being appropriated to the Spirit as eternal person. Ultimately, the personal relation of Word and Spirit to creatures has the same basis in the origin of their processions. Love, like knowing, is an essential as well as a notional act—they designate both the unity of essence and a person. So the same kinds of things are said of the Spirit as those we have just noticed about the Word.

Unde sicut Pater dicit se et omnem creaturam Verbo quod genuit, inquantum Verbum genitum sufficienter repraesentat Patrem et omnem creaturam; ita diligit se et omnem creaturam Spiritu Sancto, inquantum Spiritus Sanctus procedit ut amor bonitatis primae, secundum quam Pater amat se et omnem creaturam. Et sic etiam patet quod respectus importatur ad creaturam et in Verbo et in Amore procedente, quasi secundario, inquantum scilicet bonitas et veritas divina est principium intelligendi et amandi omnem creaturam. (I, 37, 2 *ad* 3.)

Here Saint Thomas moves between the *de deo uno*, the *de deo trino*, and the *de deo creante* as if there were no fundamental difference in the way men come to know God in them. This is because relation to self and relation to other are united in God's being. The ground of this unification must now be further explored in terms of the connection of the *de deo trino* with the preceding questions by virtue of the modification being and acts receive through relation.

In the earlier chapters a self-relation, or reflexive circle, was uncovered in the divine being and acts. The acts were found to be differentiated by means of varying forms of this relation and this variety was discovered to involve different ways in which relation to others is bound up with self-relation. The facts, first that the proper character of

[32] Ibid.   [33] *ST* I, 41, 3 *ad* 4.

the persons includes a relation to creatures, and secondly, that the relation of persons to creatures varies from person to person, show that the same features are present in this section of the *de deo* as were found in earlier ones. What remains to be demonstrated is that the self-relation not only continues into the treatise on the Trinity but that it has here a different character on account of the greater distinction of the terms of relation in the Trinity itself as opposed to the being or the activities. This would be the same kind of difference as that between the goodness of the divine essence and the same thing manifest as will in the operations.

The crucial point is simply that the persons are nothing except subsistent relations in the divine essence. Indeed they are the divine being as given and received. Thomas says it is proper to speak of an 'esse acceptum, inquantum procedens ab alio habet esse divinum'.[34] What actually forms the persons is this being given and received in knowing and willing. But, as was said at the beginning of this chapter, there is a greater difference between the subject and object of these self-relations when they form the persons than when they are the acts of the essential unity. It is just this which, Thomas claims, makes the persons undiscoverable from the essence. Intellection and loving both involve identity a well as difference.

Sicut enim ex hoc quod aliquis rem aliquam intelligit, provenit quaedam intellectualis conceptio rei intellectae in intelligente, quae dicitur verbum; ita ex hoc quod aliquis rem aliquam amat, provenit quaedam impressio, ut ita loquar, rei amatae in affectu amantis, secundum quam amatum dicitur esse in amante, sicut et intellectum in intelligente. Ita quod cum aliquis seipsum intelligit et amat, est in seipso non solum per identitatem rei, sed etiam ut intellectum in intelligente et amatum in amante. (I, 37, 1.)

The distinction of the thing understood or loved, expressed in language about thinking as speaking a word, cannot be known to be actual in the divine simplicity. This causes the break between the methods of the treatises on the unity of essence and on the persons. More must be said of this below. What is before us so far is that in the persons the self-relation, already discovered in the divine essence, communicates itself in knowing and willing as something distinct, given and received.

The giving and receiving modifies the activities according to the difference the divine being has in the personal relations. 'Dicendum quod eo modo convenit Filio esse intelligentem, quo convenit ei esse

---

[34] *ST* I, 27, 2 *ad* 3; cf. Gomes, 'La réciprocité psychologique', pp. 166–7.

Deum, cum intelligere essentialiter dicitur in divinis. . . . Est autem Filius Deus genitus, non autem generans Deus. Unde est quidem intelligens, non ut producens verbum, sed ut Verbum procedens. . . .'[35] The Son understands not by producing a word, but as a word which comes from another. The distinction between the two is not 'secundum rem' but 'ratione sola'. Therefore, they remain one act of wisdom. Following Augustine, Thomas says: 'ut sic Pater et Filius simul tantum possint dici sapientia, non autem Pater sine Filio. Sed Filius dicitur sapientia Patris, quia est sapientia de Patre sapientia; uterque enim per se est sapientia, et simul ambo una sapientia' (I, 39, 7 *ad* 2). The same modification is true of activity of loving. The Spirit loves 'ut Amor procedens, non ut a quo procedit amor' (I, 37, 1 *ad* 4). And so there is also here one act, for the 'Father enjoys not only the Son, but also himself and us by the Holy Spirit.'[36] As stated before, power is also modified by being communicated in the ordered giving and receiving of the essence. The denials of motion proper (incomplete act as in bodies), which one expects to find in a treatise speaking of procession in God, are indeed present.[37] Yet, conforming to the just-described taking of active and passive into God, Thomas turns at one point from the negation of motion to an affirmation of receptivity. 'Et licet motus non sit in divinis, est tamen ibi accipere' (I, 42, 1 *ad* 3. 'Accipere' belongs to motion in the wider sense, the internal activity of intellectual being in which what is thought and loved is formed and is thus given by one side of the act and received by the other. Moreover, as giving and receiving acquire a meaning 'in divinis', and as the analogues of the agent and patient of motion become more distinct, as here in the questions on the Trinity, so in fact one comes nearer to the proper motion of the physical world than in the *de deo uno*. In sum, the *de deo trino* communicates with the *de deo uno* in virtue of the gradual development toward greater distinction in the terms of the various forms of self-relation in the divine. In such a view of the structure of theology, the next stage, a procession from the divine to creatures, does indeed become intelligible.

[35] *ST* I, 34, 2 *ad* 4; also I, 37, 1 *ad* 4: 'Dicendum quod sicut Filio, licet intelligat, non tamen sibi competit producere verbum, quia intelligere convenit ei ut Verbo procedenti; ita, licet Spiritus Sanctus amet, essentialiter accipiendo, non tamen convenit ei quod spiret amorem . . . quia sic diligit essentialiter ut Amor procedens, non ut a quo procedit amor.'

[36] '. . . Pater non solum Filium, sed etiam se et nos diligit Spiritu Sancto', *ST* I, 37, 2 *ad* 3.

[37] *ST* I, 41, 1 *ad* 2: 'in divinis non sit motus'; *ST* I, 42, 1 *ad* 3: 'motus non sit in divinis', and *ST* I, 27, 1. Cf. my 'Theology as System and as Science', p. 89 n. 29.

In actual fact, as we know, there is not a simple unimpeded progress in the *Summa Theologiae* of St Thomas. The treatise on the Trinity should not form one whole with what precedes and follows, because, in principle, faith is presupposed more directly in one part of the argument than in the treatise on God's unity. It is not obvious that Thomas's real practice here altogether conforms with his theory. Method in the theology of the *Summa* involves throughout a movement from the self-manifesting God; scriptural and ecclesiastical authority are used from the beginning. For the existence of the one God, 'there is what is said by the person of God in Exodus 3, "I am that I am"'.[38] Despite this instance, it is apparently generally the case that when Thomas is considering questions which are 'théologiques importantes' as distinct from those 'de nature philosophique', he chooses the arguments 'sed contra' from Scripture and the Fathers.[39] This is however not without exception even in the treatise on the Trinity[40] and it actually begins 'in fieri', from the activities which produce the processions. Even when it turns and proceeds 'in facto esse', from the persons posited, there is no noticeable shift in the kind of reasoning employed. Moreover, seen in terms of a circle which moves out from unity and returns to it, one notices that the end includes the intermediate plurality so that the two sides do not just remain in opposition. Still, reason and revelation in the *Summa* are very subtly intertwined. Faith is always in some sense presupposed. It must be difficult to detect the shift of which Thomas speaks. There is not sufficient reason, then, to doubt what he says about his method in the *de deo trino* and we must now attempt to explain that.

What is of significance is that the *ordo disciplinae* in theology, the order of intelligible teaching, starts with the unity of God. Reason is more adequately employed here than on the Trinity, understood as a doctrine about plurality in God. His unity presupposed, the problem, from the perspective of Thomas, is that reason cannot consistently discover real plurality in God. This is not the universal view of the scholastics of the High Middle Ages. For Richard of St Victor and Matthew of Aquasparta the problem is rather the reconciliation of the unity and the three persons, each of which 'considered by itself can both be proved by reason' and both of which are believed. Matthew writes,

---

[38] *ST* I, 2, 3 *sed contra*.

[39] L. Elders, 'Structure et fonction de l'argument *sed contra* dans la *Somme théologique* de saint Thomas', *Divus Thomas*, 80 (1977), 260.

[40] The exception is the *sed contra* of *ST* I, 28, 4.

Tertium est habitudo et connexio ad invicem credendorum. Quamvis enim ratione possit probari unitas divinae essentiae seorsum considerata, et trinitas personarum seorsum considerata, tamen quomodo simul stat unitas cum trinitate omnino est incomprehensibile.... Unde Richardus optime, *De Trinitate* IV libro, cap. 1, praemittens quomodo rationibus necessariis probatur unitas divinae essentiae, et quomodo similiter trinitas personarum dicit: 'Et quidem quaelibet harum considerationum et assertionum, cum per semetipsam solam et seorsum attenditur, nihil credibilius, nihil verius videtur. Si quando autem unam cum alia conferimus, et quomodo concorditer et simul stare possint attendimus, nisi fidei firmitas obsistat, protinus in ambiguum venit quidquid multiplex ratio persuasit.'[41]

By contrast, in the *Summa Theologiae*, reason can more easily approach the unity than the Trinity of God. Thomas's way of looking at the problem would seem to be determined by the priority he gives to the divine simplicity which we have found in so many contexts.

In this light one of the few developments in Thomas's thought discerned by historians acquires significance. This change from his position in the *Commentary on the Sentences*, through the *Disputed Questions*, first *De Veritate* and then *De Potentia*, to the *Summa contra Gentiles* and *Summa Theologiae*, is his coming to believe that all intellection involves the production of a mental word.[42] *Intelligere* is *dicere*. As long as Thomas held that the coming forth of a word—a formed concept— was not essential to intellection, there could be no demonstration on this basis of the Trinity. Once, however, this crucial step had been taken—by the time of the *De Potentia*—and once he combined it with placing the treatment of the Trinity immediately after the operations of knowing and willing, as in the *Summa Theologiae*, rather than before them, as in the *Sentences Commentary*, or separated from them, as in the *Summa contra Gentiles*, Thomas seems inevitably to be led to a demonstration of the three persons. Indeed some have held him to have made the attempt.[43] But, in fact, in the *Summa Theologiae* Thomas continues

[41] Matthew of Aquasparta, *Quaestiones de fide, Quaestiones Disputatae de fide et de cognitione*, Bibliotheca Franciscana Scolastica Medii Aevi I (2nd ed.; Quaracchi, 1957), I, v, p. 133.

[42] See, for example, J. de la Vaissière, SJ, 'Le sens du mot "verbe mental" dans les écrits de saint Thomas', *Archives de philosophie*, 3 (1925), 168–75; P. Vanier, *Théologie trinitaire chez saint Thomas d'Aquin*; B. Lonergan, *Verbum*. R. L. Richards, *The Problem of an Apologetical Perspective*, contains useful summaries of the historical work on this question and critical analysis of the conclusions drawn from it.

[43] See Richards, *The Problem of an Apologetical Perspective*. The most important is Cyprien Vagaggini, 'La hantise de "rationes necessariae" de saint Anselme dans la théologie de saint Thomas', *Actes du Congrès international du IXe centenaire de l'arrivée d'Anselme au Bec*, Spicilegium Beccense (Le Bec–Hellouin/Paris, 1959), pp. 103–40. See the discussion in my 'The Psychological Image', p. 104.

to make the same denials that natural reason can reach the Trinity which he makes in earlier works. The reason now given is that, though *intelligere* is by nature *dicere*, yet owing to the divine simplicity, we cannot know that any inner distinction applies to God's reason. We cannot know that what belongs to the understanding, as we experience it, belongs also to God's understanding. This is once again the problem of the difference of modes and the separation of form and content. Does the production of a distinct word in knowing apply only to our mode of knowledge or does it belong also to God's? Because of the simplicity of God this cannot be certainly answered. B. Lonergan puts it thus: 'Hence, though our *intelligence* is always a *dicere*, this canot be demonstrated of God's. Though we can demonstrate that God understands, for understanding is a pure perfection, still we can no more than conjecture the mode of divine understanding and so cannot prove that there is a divine Word.'[44] Thomas puts it as follows, relating the various elements:

licet ratio naturalis possit pervenire ad ostendendum quod Deus sit intellectus, modum tamen intelligendi non potest invenire sufficienter. Sicut enim de Deo scire possumus quod est, sed non quid est, ita de Deo scire possumus quod intelligit, sed non quo modo intelligit. Habere autem conceptionem verbi in intelligendo, pertinet ad modum intelligendi: unde ratio haec sufficienter probare non potest; sed ex eo quod est in nobis aliqualiter per simile coniecturare.[45]

In the *Summa Theologiae* Thomas speaks of intellection as universally characterized by the production of a mental word. 'Quicumque autem intelligit, ex hoc ipso quod intelligit, procedit aliquid intra ipsum, quod est conceptio rei intellectae ex vi intellectiva proveniens, et ex eius notitia procedens. Quam quidem conceptionem vox significat, et dicitur verbum cordis, significatum verbo vocis' (I, 27, 1). But, when considering how we know the Trinity, because the 'similitudo' of our intellect to God's is not sufficient for demonstration, we must proceed, as did Augustine, and 'per fidem venitur ad cognitionem' (I, 32, 1 *ad* 2). We cannot prove the Trinity from the first principles of reason, rather 'inducitur ratio, non quae sufficienter probet radicem, sed quae radici iam positae ostendat congruere consequentes effectus' (I, 32, 1 *ad* 2). Once again the incongruities in the system of Thomas result from a separation of form and content necessitated by the extreme tension within his thought between the opposed Neoplatonic

---

[44] Lonergan, *Verbum*, p. 196.
[45] *De Pot.*, q. 8, a. 1 *ad* 12 (p. 216).

logics of the finite and the infinite. What otherwise appears to belong universally to intellect is unknowable because of the divine simplicity, so the rational method of the *de deo uno* must be reversed in the *de deo trino*. But was not the momentum in fact too strong for the brakes?

VII

Relatio ad Creatorem: the Procession of Creatures from God, Questions 44 and 45

THE main problems involved in the transition from the treatise on God in himself to that on the procession of creatures from him have all been raised in considering the *de deo trino*. The difficulties in moving from simplicity to real distinction are parallel in Thomas to the discontinuity between faith and reason. It remains to notice how the unity of structure appears once creation has been reached in the downward descent.

Despite the fact that one is within and the other outside the divine essence, the language used of the emergence of the divine persons and of creatures is similar. Both are called processions. There is the treatment 'de processione divinarum personarum' and that 'de processione creaturarum'.[1] Both are also emanations. 'Word' is a proper name for the Son. 'Significat enim quandam emanationem intellectus; persona autem quae procedit in divinis secundum emanationem intellectus, dicitur Filius' (I, 34, 2). But he also enquires 'de modo emanationis rerum a primo principio, qui dicitur creatio' (I, 45, *prol.*). Both processions are understood in terms of relation. Because real relation in God is his essence, 'oportet quod relatio sit idem quod persona' (*ST* I, 40, 1). Creation is a relation to God. Creation is a relation not in God but in the creature: 'creatio in creatura non sit nisi relatio quaedam ad Creatorem'.[2] Creation, like the persons, proceeds from the divine operations, they from the internal acts of knowledge and love, it from the external act, power.[3] The power to create, like creation as object of the divine knowledge and love, is modified through the personal relations. It is ordered in accord with divine being; 'So even also the power of creating, although it is common to the three persons, belongs

---

[1] *ST* I, 27, *prol.* and I, 44, *prol.*
[2] *ST* I, 45, 3; for some indications of the Neoplatonic origins of this doctrine cf. ch. V n. 23.
[3] *ST* I, 45, 6 *ad* 3.

to them according to a certain order; for the Son has it from the
Father, and the Holy Spirit from both.'[4] The Father has 'creatio' as a
proper attribution because he does not have the 'virtus creandi' from
another. The Son has it from the Father. All things are said to be made
'through' him as a mediate cause 'sive principium de principio'. The
Spirit has it from both and 'creator' belongs to him because 'domi-
nando gubernet et vivificet quae sunt creata a Patre per Filium' (I, 45, 6
ad 2). Similarly both processions involve the coming into existence of
real distinction and so the origination of a plurality of substances.
From the facts that the relations in God are real and establish subsistences and that the relations are 'plures', 'Unde sequitur quod sint
plures res subsistentes in divina natura' (1, 30, 1). Similarly creation is
the coming into being of being; 'cum creatio sit emanatio totius esse
ab ente universale' (I, 45, 4 *ad* 1), 'Proprie vero creata sunt subsistentia' (I, 45, 4). Moreover, by an argument reported in the last chapter,
Thomas concludes that God intends the multiplicity and the variety of
the substances. The difference of the two kinds of procession also
comes out here. For from the principle that the aim of creation is to
represent the divine goodness in what is outside God, it follows not
only that the source and the result of the procession of creatures are
unequal but that created things must be unequal to each other.[5] In
sum, the processions of persons and creatures are different, but the
language used of them is the same. As we ascended to the knowledge
of God from our knowledge of creatures, so we now descend using the
same concepts. The way up is the way down.

The common ground between Thomas and the Neoplatonists at
this point is evident enough. There is his language; 'procession' and
'emanation' are used as equivalent to 'creation'. More deeply significant perhaps are the doctrines that the derived is really related to the
first principle, but not the contrary, and that the first is the direct
cause of the substantial being of all else. The ultimate source of these
teachings is Proclus.[6]

Thomas's synthesis of Porphyry and Proclus, in maintaining that
God is known as *esse* because he is the cause of being, involves the
final step in one of those gradual interminglings of opposed positions
which is so deeply subversive of their original meaning and purpose.

---

[4] 'ita etiam et virtus creandi, licet sit communis tribus Personis, ordine tamen quo-
dam eis convenit; nam Filius habet eam a Patre, et Spiritus Sanctus ab utroque', *ST* I,
45, 6 *ad* 2.
[5] *ST* I, 47, 1 and 2, cf. p. 119 above.
[6] Cf. Endnote 4, p. 165 below and ch. V, n. 23, p. 103 above.

Another doctrine of St Thomas, closely related to this and exposing how he has assimilated and united their divergent traditions, needs to be added to the list. This is the idea that creation is by participation. Particular beings, because they are not absolutely primary, have existence divided from essence and hence participate in the first act of being, God. Creation is this participation: 'creation is the emanation of all being from the universal existence' (I, 45, *prol.*). Thomas unites Plato and Aristotle, joining causation and participation in the very first article of the questions considering the procession of creatures. He begins by returning to the simplicity of God. 'It has been shown above, when treating the divine simplicity, that God is being itself subsisting through itself. And again it was shown that subsisting being is not able to be except as one. . . . It follows, therefore, that all other things are not God's being but participate the act of being.'[7] Because all else participates the first being, it must be caused by it. 'Hence Plato said that it is necessary to posit unity before all multiplicity. And Aristotle said, in the second book of the *Metaphysics*, that "what is most existent and most true is the cause of all being and of all truth".'[8] Being itself functions like a Platonic separate form. 'Sed sicut hic homo participat humanum naturam, ita quodcumque ens creatum participat, ut ita dixerim, naturam essendi; quia solus Deus est suum esse, ut supra dictum est' (I, 45, 5 *ad* 1).

Fr Geiger's *La participation dans la philosophie de s. Thomas d'Aquin* brought out forcefully Thomas's Neoplatonism on this point. Since twentieth-century Thomists were so deeply committed to finding a philosophy in Thomas founded on what they regarded as his unique ontology, they found it necessary to discover some way of interpreting his Neoplatonism congruent with it. Professor C. Fabro's *Participation et causalité selon s. Thomas d'Aquin*, and indeed much else by him, endeavoured the interpretation and conciliation. On the one hand, Thomas's dependence on the Christian Platonism of Dionysius was

---

[7] 'Ostensum est autem supra, cum de divina simplicitate ageretur, quod Deus est ipsum esse per se subsistens. Et iterum ostensum est quod esse subsistens non potest esse nisi unum. . . . Relinquitur ergo quod omnia alia a Deo non sint suum esse, sed participant esse', *ST* I, 44, 1.

[8] 'Unde et Plato dixit quod necesse est ante omnem multitudinem ponere unitatem. Et Aristoteles dicit, in II *Metaphy.*, quod "id quod est maxime ens et maxime verum, est causa omnis entis et omnis veri"', *ST* I, 44, 1. Among the sources for 'Plato dixit' cited ad loc. by the Ottawa editors are instructively 'Secundum AUGUSTINUM, *De Civit. Dei*, Lib. viii, cap. 4 (PL 41, 231)—*In Sent.*, Lib. I, dist. ii, qu. 1, a. 1, haec eadem veritas recitatur ex DIONYSIO, *De Div. Nom.*, cap. 13, 2 (PG 3, 980)—cf. PLOTINUM, *Ennead* v, Lib. iii, cap. 12 . . . PROCLUM, *Instit. Theol.*, prop. V. . . .'

drawn into the light. But, on the other, Thomas was discovered to have transformed this essentialism by means of a philosophical twist Fr Fabro was best able to explicate by reference to Heidegger.[9] Similarly, as we have tried to show in chapter I above, the great Neo-platonic circle involved in the return of creation to its divine source was reinterpreted by Fr Chenu in existentialist terms. His aim was by maintaining the existence of two returns in the *Summa* — one natural in the *Secunda Pars*, the other gracious in the *Tertia Pars* — to insist on a fundamental difference between Thomas and his Neoplatonic sources. In virtue of holding to an independent Christian return founded on contingent historical facts, Aquinas was supposed to have prevented the reduction of his theology to any pagan philosophical form. These existentialist reformations of Thomas now fail to con-vince and it remains to see him within the history of Christian Neo-platonism where these structures are fundamental.

The final exit and return in the *Summa* commences, as did the series within the *de deo in se*, with a proof based on the four causes of Aristotle but reordered to form this Neoplatonic circle. Like question 2 article 3, 'Utrum Deus sit', question 44 as a whole, 'de processione creaturarum a Deo et de omnium entium prima causa', orders the causes by beginning with the efficient or moving cause and passing through the material and formal to conclude with the final cause. Thomas designates the content of the four articles as follows:

Primo: utrum Deus sit causa efficiens omnium entium.
Secundo: utrum materia prima sit creata a Deo. . . .
Tertio: utrum Deus sit causa exemplaris rerum. . . .
Quarto: utrum ipse sit causa finalis rerum. (I, 44, *prol.*)

In fact, the *ad secundum* and *ad tertium* of article 2, itself explicitly about whether God causes matter, helps to make clear that the 'tertia via' of the proof for God's existence, 'sumpta ex possibile et necessario', is from the material to its cause.[10] For they answer problems raised in objections 1 and 2 respectively concerning the 'primum principium passivum' and what is 'tantam in potentia'. Pure matter is what has the possibility for existence. The order of the five ways and of the articles of question 44, although the members correspond to the causes of Aristotle, is different from that given in any of the Philosopher's lists. Aristotle catalogues the causes at *Physics* ii, 3 ($194^{b}23$–$195^{a}3$).

---

[9] Most recently: C. Fabro, 'L'interpretazione dell'atto in S. Tommaso e Heidegger', *Atti del Congresso Internazionale Tommaso d'Aquino*, i (Naples, 1975), pp. 119–28.

[10] *ST* I, 2, 3; cf. ch. II n. 22 and ch. III nn. 31–2 and Endnote 2, p. 163.

Thomas retains Aristotle's order when he comments on them as follows: 'ex quo fit aliquid cum insit' (section 178), 'species et exemplum' (section 179), 'a quo est principium motus' (section 180), 'finis' (section 181).[11] Material cause is designated 'ex quo fit aliquid' here and at *Metaphysics Δ* 2 (1013ª24). There are two lists at *Physics* II, 7 (198ª1–14). The second is the same as the catalogue at *Physics* ii, 3. Thomas, again correctly, as in all his reports of these lists, gives the order in an introductory phrase to his comment: 'reducendo quaestionem propter quid in quamlibet dictarum quatuor causarum scilicet *formam, moventem, finem et materiam*'.[12] It seems that the first three in this list, or the last three members in the one at *Physics* ii, 3 are kept together because they 'often coincide'.[13]

The catalogues in the *Metaphysics* occur at *A*, 3 (983ª24–32), *α*, 2 (994ª19–994ᵇ27) and *Δ*, 2 (1013ª24–1013ᵇ3). Thomas in his commentary writes of the first as follows:

Causae autem *quadrupliciter* dicuntur: quarum una est ipsa causa formalis.... *Alia* vero causa est materialis. *Tertia* vero causa est efficiens, quae est unde principium motus. *Quarta* causa est finalis, quae opponitur causae efficienti, secundum oppositionem principii et finis. Nam motus incipit a causa efficiente et terminatur ad causam finalem.[14]

This comment would provide a rationale for his own ordering in the *Summa* but not Aristotle's. 'The fourth cause is the final, which is opposed to the efficient, according to the opposition of source and end. For motion begins from efficient cause and halts at the final cause.'

There are two lists in chapter 2 of book *α*. They belong to Aristotle's demonstration that there is no infinite regress of the causes, i.e. to his equivalent of Thomas's five ways. Here they are:

Primo quidem in genere causae materialis....
Secundo exemplificat in genere causae efficientis....
Tertio exemplificat in genere causarum finalium....
Ultimo facit mentionem de causa formali.[15]

Postquam Philosophus praemisit quod causae entium non sunt infinitae, hic *probat propositum*.... Primo ostendit propositum *in causis efficientibus* vel moventibus. Secundo in causis materialibus.... Tertio in causis finalibus.... Quarto in causis formalibus.[16]

---

[11] St Thomas Aquinas, *In octo libros Physicorum Aristotelis Expositio*, ed. P. M. Maggiolo (Turin/Rome, 1954), II, v, 178–81.

[12] *In Phys.* II, xi, 241.

[13] *Physica* ii, 7, 198ª25.

[14] *In Meta.* I, iv, 70.

[15] *In Meta.* II, ii, 300.

[16] *In Meta.* II, iii, 301.

This second list has an order closest to that of Thomas's in the *Summa*; indeed, it would be the same logically if the formal cause were taken as the end sought. The last is at *Metaphysics Δ*, 2. Thomas comments:

Dicit ergo primo, quod *uno modo* dicitur causa id ex quo fit aliquid.... *Alio autem modo* dicitur causa, species et exemplum, id est exemplar; et haec est causa formalis.... *Tertio modo* dicitur causa unde primum est principium permutationis et quietis; et haec est causa movens vel efficiens.... Quarto modo dicitur causa finis.[17]

Of the six listings of the causes by Aristotle given above, two from the *Physics* and four from the *Metaphysics*, only the first and the last, *Physics* ii and *Metaphysics Δ*, 2, have the same order. These two and *Metaphysics A*, 3 simply pair off the two opposed causes, matter and form, moving and final. *Physics* ii, 7 and the first of the two listings at *Metaphysics α*, 2 place mover and end between form and matter, or matter and form. Only the second list at *Metaphysics α*, 2 begins with the moving cause but, as noted, it does not conclude with the final but the formal cause. There is no evident reason for the order in the last three lists.

Thomas uses the causes to structure his writing only twice in the first forty-five questions of the *Summa Theologiae*; in both cases he uses the same order. He places matter and form between the moving and final causes. Proper motion, as distinguished from activity generally, belongs to the material.[18] When seen in relation to the divine causality, it involves a going out from simple immaterial being to matter which is raised to formal perfection as the good, or end, it lacks. In causing, God, as the principle of all procession, i.e. the Father, knows the form by which he acts in the Son and loves the Son and himself as end in the Spirit.[19] Thus understood, the order Thomas uses in distinction from his sources in Aristotle has a reason. The source of motion is the obvious beginning just as its opposed cause, the final, is appropriate end. As noted, he says, glossing Aristotle, who also mentions their opposition, 'motion begins from efficient cause and ends at final cause'.[20] 'Prima autem et manifestior via est, quae sumitur ex parte motus.' The moving cause is an obvious point from which to start the ways to God within a theology which also begins from him. These ways ended: 'Ergo est aliquid intelligens, a quo omnes res naturales ordinantur ad finem, et hoc dicimus Deum' (I, 2, 3). But 'intelligere et velle' are

---

[17] *In Meta.* v, ii, 763–5 and 771.   [18] See ch. III n. 40 and ch. V.
[19] See ch. II n. 75 and ch. VI.   [20] *In Meta.* I, iv, 70.

motions as 'actus perfecti' and as such display the 'rediens ad essentiam suam'. This return is perfect in the divine being. Its *exitus* and
reditus become fully manifest in the processions of persons founded in
God's activities of knowledge and love; these in turn make intelligible
the procession and return of creatures. The five ways begin the theological development by which revelation becomes intelligible to us,
just as knowledge of the divine persons is necessary for the right idea
of creation. To achieve this unity Aquinas unites Plato and Aristotle,
the knowledge of infinite principle and its finite representation.

Plato understood by motion any given operation so that to understand and to
judge are a kind of motion. Aristotle likewise approaches this manner of speaking in the *De Anima*. Plato accordingly said that the first mover moves himself
because he knows himself and wills or loves himself. In a way this is not
opposed to the reasons of Aristotle. There is no difference between reaching a
first being that moves itself, as understood by Plato, and reaching a first being
that is absolutely unmoved as understood by Aristotle.[21]

The structure of theology, as set out in the *Summa Theologiae*, imitates
this motionless divine motion which has itself as source and end and
whose power has perfect mastery over the means. Theology is imitating God and is thus the 'perfectior' way of knowing. It begins with
God in himself and treats all else 'sub ratione Dei' when it draws what
has come out from him back to him because he is 'principium rerum et
finis rerum' and gives reality its structure. The unity of reality, as of
theological system, derives from the unity of the causes in God.
'Dicendum quod cum Deus sit causa efficiens, exemplaris et finalis
omnium rerum, et materia prima sit ab ipso, sequitur quod principium
omnium rerum sit unum secundum rem.'[22]

---

[21] *ScG* I, 13; cf. ch. V n. 29 above.

[22] *ST* I, 44, 4 *ad* 4. An excuse must be added for terminating the treatment of creation
two-thirds of the way through a section. The 'de productione creaturarum' is divided:
'primo quidem, quae sit prima causa entium; secundo, de modo procedendi creaturarum a prima causa; tertio vero, de principio durationis rerum' (*ST* I, 44, *prol.*). The
third consideration corresponds to question 46. The reason a stop can be made at 45 is
that a beginning in time is not necessary to the notion of creation. Creation is 'emanationem totius entis a causa universali, quae est Deus' (*ST* I, 45, 1). That the emanation
has a beginning in time is not known to reason but only to faith. 'Dicendum quod mundum non semper fuisse, sola fide tenetur, et demonstrative probari non potest, sicut et
supra de mysterio Trinitatis dictum est' (*ST* I, 46, 2). Once posited, it can be made intelligible but it cannot strictly be demonstrated, since time does not enter into the 'quod
quid est', the universal knowledge, of a thing through which demonstration takes place.
Hence some who think the world eternal speak of it as created: 'Dicendum quod illi qui
ponerent mundum aeternum, dicerent mundum factum a Deo ex nihilo. . . . Et sic etiam
recusant aliqui creationis nomen, ut patet ex Avicenna in sua *Metaph.*' (*ST* I, 46, 2 *ad* 2).

VIII

Upon the Shoulders of Giants: some Philosophical and Theological Implications[1]

THE thought of St Thomas is not adequately understood from the perspective of an anti-modern ontological realism like that of one side of the Thomistic revival. Thomas is genuinely a medieval thinker poised between antiquity and modernity. His is not the unthought being discovered in a return to pre-Classical philosophic myth; his doctrine of being cannot be assimilated to that of Heidegger. Because subjectivity and being are so intimately unified in Thomas's thought, the transcendental Thomists, by going some way with modern critical philosophy, expose aspects of it unknown to the realists, but they miss the concreteness and objectivity of divine science in Thomas which remains hidden to existential eyes. Both contemporary schools are blind to the Neoplatonic origins and structure of his doctrine. There is, then, something to be learned from those who would look at Thomas from the perspective which appreciates the negative theology of the Neoplatonists. But if their henological theology is motivated by an acceptance of Heidegger's critique of Western ontology, they are not likely to discern the balance of elements in Thomas's *Summa Theologiae*. For the identification there of being and thought in the simplicity of God, and the consequent affirmative predication of him, must in the end repel all who turn to Neoplatonism in flight from onto-theo-logy. Still, that there is something in Thomas to attract these divergent tendencies in contemporary thought displays the comprehensiveness of Thomas's synthesis. Yet it must be admitted that our examination of the actual structure of the initial questions of the theological *Summa* also shows St Thomas not to have been altogether

---

[1] An early version of this chapter, entitled 'A Vindication of St. Thomas Aquinas as an Hellenic Theologian', was presented as a paper to the Seventh Annual Sewanee Mediaeval Colloquium, April 1980, University of the South, Tennessee, and as lectures for the Harvard Divinity School and the Philosophy Department of the Memorial University of Newfoundland.

successful at unifying the opposing tensions of his system and not to have found a form which could constructively resolve their warfare. His solution to the problem of the one and the many is not final. It is not clear, however, that there is any better answer by which it might be judged, and no one will deny that his was a magnificent attempt.

If we are not satisfied with the context in which Thomas's *Summa* has usually been presented over the last century, and if we claim some theological and philosophical relevance for him, we are obliged to provide at least a sketch of what can be said for and against his system from our alternative standpoint. Our principal revision of the standard contemporary account of Thomas's work is to have placed his Aristotelianism within the context of the ongoing development of Neoplatonism, pagan and Christian. This has entailed distinguishing between the Neoplatonic schools which influenced him and the diverse Christian philosophic and spiritual traditions related to them. Some implications of this recasting of the framework of his thought are now to be examined.

The most general consequence is a revision of the notion of Hellenism and Platonism with which contemporary Christian theologians often work. It is wrong to identify Hellenic philosophy with Plato, and Neoplatonism is not simply a following of him or even of the Hellenic alternatives to him. As A. H. Armstrong has written: 'certainly nobody who knew the *Enneads* would insult Plotinus himself by calling his interpretation of Plato "scholarly"'.[2] Sir Richard Southern has shown that the Platonism of the High Middle Ages actually involved a turning away from interest in the works of Plato himself.[3] When Aquinas cites Plato neither the words nor the doctrine are often to be found in a Platonic dialogue.[4] The Neoplatonisms investigated in looking for the sources of Aquinas have opposing spiritual and philosophic directions. The essence of Neoplatonism—if it exists—is not to be captured by citing texts of Plato; certainly it will escape if the tradition of their

---

[2] 'The Background of the Doctrine "That the Intelligibles are not Outside the Intellect"', p. 394; reprinted in *Plotinian and Christian Studies*.

[3] *Platonism, Scholastic Method, and the School of Chartres*, The Stenton Lectures (1978) 12 (Reading, 1979).

[4] 'There was [*sic*] available to the Latin West in the thirteenth century only three works of Plato—the *Meno*, the *Phaedo* and the *Timaeus*. It is certain that Saint Thomas did not use either the *Meno* or the *Phaedo* and there is no convincing evidence that he was directly acquainted with either Cicero's or Chalcidius' translations of the *Timaeus*. His knowledge of Plato and Platonism came therefore, certainly for the most part, from other sources'; R. J. Henle, *Saint Thomas and Platonism: A Study of the* Plato *and* Platonici *Texts in the Writings of Saint Thomas* (The Hague, 1956), pp. xxi–xxii.

varied interpretation is not added. Neoplatonism is not a single one-sided dogmatism to which philosophies recognizing plurality, change, and experience must be opposed. Nor can one set against it religious life and its recognition of faith and feeling, scriptural and traditional authority, celebration, ascetic practice, and sacramental union. It is a dynamic tradition constituting in its varied forms the greater part of the history of philosophy.

Neither can a Christianity accepting the authority of the Scriptures and tradition absolutely oppose itself to Hellenistic Platonism. It is not accidental that a considerable part of the Scriptures was written in Greek. The Judaism of the time of Jesus defined itself in and against its Hellenistic setting and was profoundly affected by it. The adoption of the modes of thought of the Hellenistic schools and of Neoplatonism, as their greatest synthetic product, was not simply an apologetic device of Christians. Doctrine and the formal statement of it became essential to Christianity. Nor have the Christian theologians, unlike the followers of Muhammad, proved able to terminate their association with philosophy, the thinking the Greeks invented. Indeed the theologies of the Church are fated to an intimate marriage with the history of philosophy, and to remain faithful to revelation and reason, only by a most discriminating plunder of the Egyptians. Contemporary Thomism misunderstood Thomas partly because it did not appreciate the difference between the existentialism it assumed and the Neoplatonized Aristotle Thomas found philosophically authoritative.

A result of our study is that we have come to appreciate how deeply Hellenistic and Christian forms are enmeshed. Oppositions set up between Christian doctrine and paganism turn out to correspond to oppositions within the tradition the Greeks initiated, e.g. reason and tradition, reason and the union before and beyond *ratio*. As Tertullian's warfare between Athens and Jerusalem was at least in part a struggle between the Stoa and the Platonists, so the antagonism between Augustinian spirituality and Aristotelian science was also assimilated in part to a difference between two Christian Neoplatonic traditions, and such a division between Neoplatonic schools was the real origin of the strife invented between the so-called existential ontology of Exodus and Greek essentialism.[5] A consciousness of this should make us aware of the degree to which the historical dynamic of Christian theology conforms to that of philosophy. Indeed the life and

[5] See introduction above and my 'Aquinas' First Principle'.

differences of the pagan schools were carried on in one form or another by the Christian theologians after Christians closed the academies. History provides the evidence for that unity of the two theologies, scriptural and philosophical, in which Aquinas believed and which is essential to his theological practice. They are both aspects of one thinking which is both human and divine or, alternatively, they are two forms of revelation.[6] It continually turns out that any other course than this broad ecumenical way does not limit revelation to Scripture but makes revelation theologically incomprehensible. Of course, as a result of its intimate connection with the Hellenic tradition, Christianity must share its fate. Because Thomists accepted much of the Heideggerian account of the nemesis of the imputed forgetting of Being for which Plato was held responsible, and which had become the destiny of Western philosophy and theology together with their practical consequences, they struggled to enable Thomas to escape Heidegger's net.[7] If our account be accepted, a more complete answer to Heidegger is required.

The theology of St Thomas is to be judged as a part of this tradition of philosophic theology. The escape-routes are closed. Thomas did not anticipate the logic of modern science, nor is his system founded on a specific biblical revelation of being to which only he was adequately sensitive and which made his doctrine true no matter what science or philosophy might say. Nor yet does he squeeze through an opening he had made for contemporary existential man turning from intellectual form and encompassing system to the world, nature, and historical contingency. The knowledge of all things in a God best understood through Aristotle's modification of Platonic self-subsistent forms is not so direct for Thomas as for the Augustinians, but it is none the less his whole aim. This knowledge is the conclusion of philosophy and the beginning of theology, and his *Summa* is throughout their meeting. If Thomas cannot escape the Hellenistic tradition, or even the Middle Ages, those who would defend him must support also the tradition to which he belongs. They cannot turn him against his colleagues in the hope of giving him the sole benefit. None the less his captivity may be turned in his favour. He need no longer bear the whole burden of Christian philosophy alone.

---

[6] See Endnote 1, p. 162 below and ch. II, especially nn. 24 and 25, pp. 42–3 above, and my 'Theology as System and as Science'.

[7] See introduction above, and my 'Aquinas' First Principle' and 'Pope Leo's Purposes'.

Instead, together with his predecessors and successors, he is to be evaluated as a great contributor to a theological tradition endeavouring, and evidently to some degree succeeding, in solving the problem of the one and the many in all its diverse forms. Infinite and finite, abstract and concrete, spirit and matter, intuition and ratiocination, reason and sense are reconciled. He and his Christian co-workers are faced with divisions between creator and created, nature and grace, for example, which, though they have their pagan analogues, are more severe than those confronting theologians who did not accept the Judaeo-Christian revelation.[8] Moreover, it is clear that his high place among his fellows in the thirteenth century derives from the depth of his understanding of the contrarieties and tensions present for theology and his construction of a unity from them. As we have seen, these tensions are represented in the Neoplatonic and Aristotelian directions of his thought, or, put another way, in the Platonic and Aristotelian directions of his Neo-platonism, or, perhaps best, in the Hellenistic and Hellenic directions of his Christianity. But this comprehensiveness has its costs. Our analysis has discovered incoherences in his system.

While denying of God the mode of the finite, Thomas holds that proper predications are made of him.[9] He affirms that God's acts are all one in his simplicity and yet distinguishes them as diverse forms of self-relation.[10] God's trinitarian distinction is rationally derived in an intelligible sequence in the *Summa Theologiae* and yet denied to be so.[11] These and many more difficulties arise from Aquinas' attempt to draw together the one and the many in the manner they appeared to him. The manifold problems of his predecessors remain imperfectly resolved in his system.

His denial of the mode of the finite to the infinite, so destructive for

---

[8] See chs. I, VI, and VII on creation and grace in pagan philosophy. I do not accept, nor would St Thomas recognize, the sharp oppositions established by many Thomists and other modern scholars between the pagan Greek and the Christian understandings of God and his power to make the world. Better approaches may be seen in Jean Trouil-lard, 'Procession néoplatonicienne et création judéo-chrétienne', in S. Gersh, *From Iamblichus*, and in G. Lafont, 'Le *Parménide*', pp. 78ff. I do not take Aristotle to represent God as closed up in his own self-knowledge unable to know the world, and so not the source of its being or its effective good, but only the origin of modifications in it. The texts in *Metaphysics* seem sufficient, but useful discussions are found in J. Maritain, 'Marginal Notes on Aristotle', *Bergsonian Philosophy and Thomism*, pp. 349–77 and J. P. Atherton, 'The Validity of Thomas' Interpretation of *ΝΟΗΣΙΣ ΝΟΗΣΕΩΣ*', *Atti del Congresso Internazionale Tommaso d'Aquino*, i (Naples, 1975), pp. 156–62. Both defend Aquinas' interpretation of Aristotle on these points.

[9] See ch. IV above.   [10] See ch. V above and R. T. Wallis, 'Divine Omniscience'.
[11] See ch. VI above.

maintaining real knowledge of God, stems from his judging with the Platonists against Aristotle that, in identifying God with the activity of νοῦς so as to make him the intelligible source of nature, the principle is in danger of being reduced to the division of the finite. His contrary elevation of the self-related activity of being into the simplicity of God has its source in Thomas's equal appreciation of Aristotle's criticism of Plato, that, if the first principle is only an empty abstract unity, the cause of division falls outside it, and the Good is not the complete end and perfect cause of reality. Thus God would become only one of the principles.[12] Similarly Thomas finishes the transformation of the Neoplatonic hypostases into predicates of God's being which Dionysius began but did not complete. This work of Dionysius Thomas understands anachronistically, yet with profound philosophical sense, to belong to what he calls the Areopagite's following of Aristotle.[13] But this is just the problem of how the real plurality of predicates can be affirmed and yet the division of simplicity denied. Is it not better to throw over this whole confused tangle? Or are we so inescapably enmeshed in it that, like Aquinas, we have no choice but to make the best of it?

One might begin making some decision about this by looking at the dissolution of Thomas's edifice. As compared with his medieval predecessors, Aquinas makes a sharper distinction between faith and reason than they. Gone for example are the 'rationes necessariae' of Anselm's reasonings about the Trinity and incarnation. The three subsistences in the one essence are not discoverable to the theology which is a part of philosophy.[14] The same kind of difference is made in respect to method.

For Adelard of Bath, both the way up and the way down, which, as also for Thomas, must be united to produce true thinking, belonged to reason. They were the differing directions of the thought of Aristotle and Plato respectively. In his *De Eodem et Diverso*, written in the first decade of the twelfth century, he writes:

Unus eorum [*in margin minio ascriptum* Plato] mentis altitudine elatus pennisque, quas sibi indui obnixe nisus, ab ipsis initiis res cognoscere aggressus

---

[12] See *Metaphysica* Λ, 987^{b}19ff.; for Thomas see n. 29 below.

[13] See ch. II n. 56 and ch. IV n. 47. Throughout his exposition of the *Liber de Causis* Thomas associates Dionysius and Aristotle in this reduction; see for example *In de Causis*, prop. 3, p. 23, lines 21–4; prop. 18, p. 103, lines 16–23. Modern scholarship assigns the step to Dionysius; see S. Gersh, *From Iamblichus*, p. 11, and A. H. Armstrong, 'Negative Theology, Myth and Incarnation', n. 19.

[14] See my 'The Psychological Image of the Trinity' and ch. VI above.

est, et quid essent, antequam in corpora prodirent, expressit, archetypas rerum formas, dum sibi loquitur, definiens. Alter autem artificialiter callens [*in margine ascriptum* Aristoteles], ut lectores complices facultate instrueret, a sensibilibus et compositis orsus est. Dumque sibi eodem in itinere obuiant, contrarii dicendi non sunt. Amat enim et compositio diuisionem et diuisio compositionem, dum utraque alteri fidem facit. Unde si quid in digitis et articulis abaci numeralibus ex multiplicatione creuerit, id utrum recte processerit, divisione eiusdem summae probatur.[15]

For Thomas, on the contrary, the difference between Plato and Aristotle is not in their points of departure. Because of his nature, man must necessarily begin with the things of sense.[16] The opposition between the two greatest Hellenic philosophers is instead in the mode of existence they ascribe to the forms of natural things. Making them separate in reality, Plato errs; though the Fates compensate him, for Thomas thinks him a safer man to follow than Aristotle on certain questions respecting the existence of the angelic separate substances.[17] In any case, for Thomas, natural man cannot begin from the knowledge of these or of God. The natural and the scriptural theologies form the unity of divine science, but it is the proper privilege of sacred doctrine to begin from the self-revelation of separated substance recorded in the canonical books. Man's soul, altogether descended into the temporal and sensible world, and adapted to the knowledge of it and of himself through it, is not naturally able to commence with the knowledge possessed by God and the blessed. But Thomas's way of uniting the content and distinguishing the starting-points and directions of the theologies is fragile and scarcely survives him.

[15] Adelard of Bath, *Traktat De Eodem et Diverso*, ed. H. Willner, Beit. zur Gesch. der Phil. des Mittelalters, Texte und Untersuchungen 4/1 (Münster, 1903), p. 11, lines 6–16. This passage is discussed in R. W. Southern, *Platonism, Scholastic Method, and the School of Chartres*, pp. 10–11.

[16] See ch. II above.

[17] In the first five chapters of *De Sub. Sep.*, Thomas compares and contrasts the positions of Plato and Aristotle. On the side of Aristotle he says: 'Et ideo Aristotiles manifestiori et certiori via processit ad investigandum substantias a materia separatas, scilicet per viam motus' (cap. ii, p. D44, lines 10–13). But if proceeding from the moving sensible is more accessible and certain, the dependence of the result upon this procedure is a considerable limitation of it, and so Plato in some respects does better than Aristotle by using a different method. 'Haec autem Aristotilis positio certior quidem videtur, eo quod non multum recedit ab his quae sunt manifesta secundum sensum, tamen minus sufficiens videtur quam Platonis positio' (cap. ii, p. D45, lines 97–100). Aristotle's worst error is tying the number of the angels to the number of heavenly motions. Thomas reproves him at *ST* I, 50, 3, where he approves what 'dicit Dionysius, XIV cap. *De Cael. Hier.*: "Multi sunt beati exercitus supernarum mentium, infirmam et constrictam excedentes nostrorum materialium numerorum commensurationem."'

John Duns Scotus does not hold that the way up from sensible existents is capable of arriving at a true knowledge of God.[18] But it is not
just the theological views of his successors which must have prevented
them from following Aquinas; their increased historical knowledge
must also have affected their opinions. St Thomas could not have read
the *Elements of Theology* by Proclus until 1268, when William of
Moerbeke finished the translation which Aquinas used when commenting on the *Liber de Causis*. If current scholarly opinion is correct,
the treatises *de deo* of his various works, including that of the *Summa
Theologiae*, were already completed by then.[19] What he found in the
Elements was a work clearly written by a pagan and beginning theologically with the One. This is the opposite order to that found in the
Philosopher's *Metaphysics* and is not clearly preserved in the *Liber de
Causis*, which for most of his life Aquinas ascribed to Aristotle. Of
course Thomas could explain away this discrepancy between fact and
theory by means of the distinction between the *via inventionis* and the
ordo disciplinae, and Proclus and Thomas are in fundamental accord
about the place of the human soul, but still questions must have
occurred to him.

The next generation had no escape. The *Elements* was known to
them. They found proofs of God's superessential reality which
depended on the physical inappropriate to him, and they felt the need
to distinguish what Christians knew from what natural man could
attain. While they constructed their philosophical theology through a
sharply Proclan logic, they thought it necessary to distinguish this
from what was primarily authoritative for the Christian theologian.
The union of Aristotle and Proclus in Dionysius provided sufficient
authority for Thomas's innovations, but, once the Proclan origins of
Dionysius and the *Liber de Causis* had become explicit, Dionysius no
longer sufficed to Christianize the enterprise. Nowhere is this strange
polarity more marked than in Duns Scotus. His thinking is more
Proclan than Thomas's but the opinions of Proclus have no authority
for the Scotistic doctor.[20] Others separated the theology which is a part

---

[18] See Endnote 2, p. 163.

[19] See ch. II n. 38; J. A. Weisheipl, *Friar Thomas d'Aquino*, p. 361, dates the *Prima Pars*
between 1266 and 1268; L. E. Boyle (ch. I n. 6 above) puts it in 1267. On the much-
disputed date of the *Compendium Theologiae*, cf. the Leonine edition of 1979, whose
editors say 'Le "*De fide*" serait à peu près contemporain du "*De potentia*" (1265–1267)',
p. 8.

[20] John Duns Scotus, *Lectura in Librum Secundum Sententiarum, a distinctione prima ad sextam, Opera Omnia* (Commissio Scotistica) xviii (Vatican City, 1982), *Lect.* ii, *d.* 3, *pars* 2,

of philosophy from that based on the Scriptures, not by their different starting-points, but because the first treats the nature of things in relation to the First Principle 'secundum ordinem providentie naturalis', the second, 'secundum ordinem voluntarie providentie'.[21] According to Ulrich of Strasburg, the second is 'more fully manifest in supernatural works such as miracles, the distribution of grace and virtues'.[22] Thus the unity of natural and gracious theology comes to be broken. Adelard of Bath's reconciliation of the upward and downward movements of knowledge could not satisfy Aquinas because faith was more than the preliminary form of reason. For the successors of Thomas, philosophy once again contained both motions, but the contrary directions no longer sufficed to distinguish Christian from pagan theology. So we pass instead to a fundamental separation between the character of their contents.

Reflection on the historical error made by Thomas can, however, enable an insight into what necessitates the theological unification of the two directions of thought. We may perhaps bridge again the chasm opening between the two theologies after Thomas, though not exactly on his terms. The alternative to this cleavage is that the One, which is both the ground of the unity of the phenomenal, and also the source of our knowing it as unified, i.e. of our having experience, be recognized equally with the phenomenal flux as a philosophical starting-point. Thomas acknowledges the necessity of both beginnings but divides them between philosophical and scriptural theology. Modern philosophy connects them. This appears in the discovery of the necessity of the categories and their unity for experience and its rationality. This is the argument of Kant's first *Critique*. For Descartes, the certainty of knowledge takes a more medieval form in that it depends upon the consciousness of the unity of the human soul with God, a unity really, if not apparently, prior to its experience of itself in the world.[23]

---

q. 3 (pp. 351–2): 'Ad illud *De causis*, dicendum ille liber accipitur ab Avicenna . . . et a Proclo similiter accipitur [est curandum]. Et ideo non est curandum de illo [scil. libro]; unde nullus doctor debet inniti illis propositionibus.'

[21] Attributed to Theodoric of Freiberg, *De subiecto theologiae*, appendix II, of Berthold of Moosburg, *Expositio super Elementationem Theologicam Procli*, ed. L. Sturlese, presentazione E. Massa, Temi e testi 18 (Rome, 1974), p. xci.

[22] Ulrich of Strasburg, *La 'Summa de Bono', Livre* I, Introduction et édition critique par J. Daguillon, Bibliothèque thomiste 12 (Paris, 1930), i, 2, 2, p. 32: the text reads 'plenius manifestet in operibus supernaturalibus, sicut sunt miracula, distributiones gratie et virtutum' and goes on 'et in institutione preceptorum et in efficacia sacramentorum'.

[23] See Descartes, *Méditations*, in *Œuvres et lettres*, textes présentés par A. Bridoux, 2 vols., Bibliothèque de la Pléiade, 40 (Paris, 1952). In the second meditation the 'je

Modern philosophy depends upon the adoption by rationalists and empiricists of one of the two starting-points, the sense-experience of nature or the rational knowledge of God and the soul. Contemporary philosophy, in so far as it commences with language, admits that some sort of grammatical structure and unity is the condition of any human experience. Seen in this way Thomas's theological Neoplatonism has a philosophical justification and a rational inescapability in his historical circumstances. Can it also be given a theological vindication?

The inadequacy of Classical Hellenic philosophy from the perspective of the Hellenistic Neoplatonists is just that it fails to subordinate everything to an absolute ruling unity. But this is also what Christianity finds inadequate in the religion of the Hellenic world: this is its idolatry. Among the Neoplatonists, the criticism is primarily of Aristotle and the impossibility for knowing, with its self-division, to be the first principle. Their criticism also took the form of reducing the independence of Aristotle's various sciences, drawing them into one system. While Plato was turned against Aristotle in this critical process by the Neoplatonists, he also was subjected to an unconscious criticism in the same direction when their view of him became explicit in Iamblichus' systematizing of the dialogues.[24]

Augustine and other Christian Platonists are at one with this direction of pagan Platonism. Where they think themselves to divide is on the enfleshment of the Word.[25] It is the same later Neoplatonists, who feel a strong need for the sensuous and cultic to effect the ascent towards the One, who are most polemically anti-Christian. But this movement toward the world is both a philosophic need for later Platonism and a permanent religious necessity for Christians. The human soul entirely descended into the temporal world and conscious of its weakness and sin—the human soul of Iamblichus, Proclus, and their followers—needs grace mediated through the sensible world to

pense' and its self-certainty seemed primary but, in *Méditation troisième*, Descartes recognizes his finitude by reflecting that he began with doubt, a doubt judged by a certainty it sought. Since 'ce qui est plus parfait ... ne peut être une suite et une dépendance du moins parfait' (p. 290), it follows that he must in fact know God first and himself after. 'Et je ne me dois pas imaginer que je ne conçois pas l'infini par une véritable idée, mais seulement par la négation de ce qui est fini ... j'ai en quelque façon premièrement en moi la notion de l'infini, que du fini, c'est-à-dire de Dieu, que de moi-même' (p. 294). Hobbes and Hume say exactly the opposite about the relation of the conception of the finite to the infinite.

[24] See H.-D. Saffrey, 'La *Théologie platonicienne* de Proclus, fruit de l'exégèse du *Parménide*'; G. Lafont, 'Le *Parménide* de Platon', and C. Andresen, 'The Integration of Platonism', on the systematizing of Plato through his own *Parménides*.

[25] See Augustine, *Confessiones*, vii, 11 ff.

ascend again. As E. R. Dodds has shown, the situations of pagan and Christian theologians are strictly parallel.[26]

It is through the later Neoplatonic philosophical forms that the Christians can find the means of thinking their religion. It is this which makes the return towards the more concrete philosophy of Aristotle a philosophical movement of late Neoplatonism which Boethius, Eriugena, Anselm, and Aquinas will identify with and carry forward when the pagan schools are closed. What is Neoplatonic in Thomas is seen to be necessary just as its correction is also required. We require both the Neoplatonic and Aristotelian beginnings if we continue to be both philosophers and Christians. Because Thomas's problems are still our own difficulties, though no doubt in different forms, we ought to explore them in more detail. As the *Elements of Theology* of Proclus has throughout appeared as the system most useful for explaining the origins of theological structure in Aquinas, its problems may illumine his.

Dr James Lowry has exposed the two contrary logics of the *Elements*: the logic of the infinite which gives the system its structure as unity, and the logic of the finite which gives it a structure as exit and return. Dr Lowry goes on to say that the interrelation of the movement of the total work as 'form with its content as informed beings to light a tension . . . between its principles and what is principled'.[27] It has been a chief aim of our analysis of the first forty-five questions of the *Summa Theologiae* to show how the Proclan logic of the finite has penetrated the infinite in Thomas's work. Thus, although there is an ordering of the divine names in the *de deo* of the *Summa* so that the more unified are higher, the principle and the principled are not so greatly in danger of falling apart as in Proclus. Consequently, the problems Dr Lowry finds in the *Elements* do not occur to the same degree, or at least not in the same way, in the *Summa*.

The unification by Thomas of the principle of division, being, with the One, or, put alternatively, the simplification of being, is both the

---

[26] E. R. Dodds, *Pagan and Christian in an Age of Anxiety*, and the concluding chapters and appendix II, pp. 283–311, of his *The Greeks and the Irrational*. The argument is taken up by A. H. Armstrong in a number of articles cited above, cf. especially introduction, n. 23. See also A. Smith, *Porphyry's Place*; A. Louth, *The Origins of the Christian Mystical Tradition*; R. L. Wilken, 'Pagan Criticism of Christianity: Greek Religion and Christian Faith', *Early Christian Literature and the Classical Intellectual Tradition*, ed. W. R. Schoedel and R. L. Wilken, Théologie historique 54 (Paris, 1979), pp. 116–34; and P. Rorem, 'Iamblichus and the Anagogical Method in Pseudo-Dionysian Liturgical Theology', *Studia Patristica*, xvii (1), ed. E. A. Livingstone (Oxford, 1982), pp. 453–60.

[27] See Lowry, *The Logical Principles*, ch. v, p. 75.

first priority in Thomas's *Summa* and the primary form of the identification of God with what returns upon itself. It is the division between these in Proclus which allows the hypostasizing of what are, in Thomas, attributes: 'putting attributes and subjects of attributes on the same level'. Consequently the problems of the relation of the henads and being do not recur for Thomas. In Proclus being as an hypostasis belongs below the henads; but, because they are multiple, it is also a principle of them. The ground of the solution of this problem was worked out for Thomas by Dionysius in turning the hypostases into attributes. Thomas develops the implications of the Dionysian solution by bringing the division of being as self-relation or return into the divine unity. At all levels, both those within God—his essence, operations, and personal processions—and that outside it, creation, God is self-related spirit. As we saw, this common form enables Thomas to tie the *Summa* together.

A difficulty like that which emerged in the relation of being and the henads for Proclus occurs in the ordering to each other of being, life, and thought. Dr Lowry sets it out as follows:

the hierarchical orders of the γένη of Being are the henads, intelligences, souls, and bodies. All of them are existent. But life and thought are what determine the further differences. It would seem naturally that since all four orders have existence the attributive hierarchy would be unity, thinking, life, and being. But Proclus does not allow this attributive hierarchy. He rather maintains that while unity is first, being is second, life third, and thought fourth.[28]

The two orders have different reasons. As more general and abstract, being is higher and life is next. But when in Proclus the relation of reality to motion is considered, the sequence is the One, henads, intelligences, souls, and bodies. Evidently there is a problem in reconciling these. There is a similar difficulty for Thomas. It is shown when he orders the names of God differently depending on whether we are thinking of them absolutely, in which case being is highest, or causally, according to which good is the first divine name. The dilemma manifests itself more intensely in Proclus, because of his hypostasizing of these abstractions, but the shadows of the Proclan difficulty are still present in Thomas's distinction between the kinds of attributes, and his ordering of them from the essential, through the operational to the personal. Thomas's corrective is twofold. Besides the reduction of the hypostases to attributes, he chooses the Aristo-

[28] *The Logical Principles*, ch. v, p. 77.

telian order in which the most completely actual is highest. Aquinas makes God the possessor of beatific life because he is thinking. Here, at any rate, the more concrete is prior. It cannot then be said of Thomas, as of Proclus: 'Being as hypostatical ground is reduced below that which it comprehends. In like manner life and thought are also reduced below that which they comprehend or to abstractions.'[29] James Lowry holds with St Thomas that the error of Proclus is to have made the 'principle of quantity' highest.[30] Whether or not this is so, there is certainly an inadequacy between form and content in this part of the *Elements*.

Dr Lowry thinks that the inadequacy of the principle to the principled in Neoplatonism has the result that 'since philosophy cannot explain what is beyond it, an intuitive extra-logical leap must render the unexplainable explained'.[31] And so 'its adherents place religion above philosophy'. But, if instead thought were truly elevated to the principle and if it were able to know it, the fundamental problem would be solved:

The result would be to show that the triad of ὄν, ζωή and νοῦς is the structure of the One as μονή, πρόοδος, and ἐπιστροφή. This result would be to reverse their hierarchical order from the priority of ὄν to the priority of νοῦς, but this no longer in a linear way but circularly. That is, νοῦς would be seen as existing and as the totality of life in its productive ability of thinking itself— as producing a world which is its own activity. Such a principle would be able to allow for the triadic principles of the Procline philosophy since its own activity as νοῦς would in fact be that of subject and object as self-consciously the same. And in allowing for the principles of the Procline philosophy, it would be completing in pure philosophical form the entire history of Greek philosophy in general and of Neoplatonism in particular.[32]

Judged by this Aristotelian–Hegelian standard, the verdict for St Thomas is ambiguous.[33] Certainly the logic of the infinite and that of the finite are united in the Godhead, linear and circular are joined,

---

[29] Ibid., p. 79.

[30] Ibid., p. 77. For Thomas on the idea of unity among the Platonists there is *In Meta.* I, x, 159, p. 47: 'Unde cum unum opinaretur esse substantiam entis, quia non distinguebat inter unum quod est principium numeri, et unum quod convertitur cum ente....' See also ibid. I, x, 160, p. 47. At ibid. XII, vii, 2525, p. 591, Thomas writes: 'Et ne videatur incidere in opinionem *Platonis*, qui posuit primum principium rerum ipsum unum intelligibile, ostendit consequenter differentiam inter unum et simplex: et dicit, quod unum et simplex non idem significant, sed unum significat mensuram ... simplex autem significat dispositionem....' There is also *ST* I, 30, 3 and I, 11 *passim*.

[31] Lowry, *The Logical Principles*, p. 86.

[32] Ibid., p. 86.

[33] See Endnote 5, pp. 166–7.

and his philosophy can be given an idealist interpretation because of the unity of the divine thinking and being. On the other side, faith stands above reason *in via* and the philosophical rationality within the theological structure cannot be completely realized. The inequality between simplicity and plurality has this result. As well, the inequality produces the ambiguities about the knowability of God, about the propriety of any predication, and about the real signification of different and multiple predicates. Furthermore, this imbalance between simplicity and plurality leads to the division between the character of our approach to the unity of God and to his trinitarian personality. Because division or composition is the mark of the finite and distinguishes it from the simple God, Thomas is unable to integrate it fully into theology proper. Yet without division and without incorporating the logic and structure of the world into divinity, the different levels of his spiritual universe would collapse into each other, the whole medieval system of religious mediation would break down, and ultimately how there is any revelation of God would become incomprehensible.

In attacking the angelology of Aquinas, Karl Rahner is looking for a Catholic theology not so tied as Thomas's is to a Neoplatonic system of emanation.[34] Because Thomas cannot think how the finite as division is capable of being fully taken into God, he is forced, like all Neoplatonists, to confess him to be hidden by what reveals him. God is manifest in what, because of its composition, is by nature opposed to the absolutely first; all reality subsequent to the One must fail to disclose the inmost divine reality. From Proclus to Thomas there is

[34] See K. Rahner, 'Angel' in *Sacramentum Mundi: An Encyclopedia of Theology*, ed. K. Rahner *et al.*, 6 vols., i (London, 1968), pp. 27–35. After endeavouring a reduction of angelology to Christology and anthropology, Fr Rahner writes of the medievals, 'Similarly the problem of the nature of the angels as "higher" than that of man was affirmed in a way that took for granted too readily and indiscriminately neo-Platonic conceptions of scales and degrees. For it must not be overlooked that the intellectual nature of man cannot so easily be characterized as inferior to that of the angels. That nature possesses absolute transcendence . . .' (p. 31).

'The essentially "incidental" character of Christian angelology has been well brought out by K. Rahner' says K. Foster, 'Angelogy in the Church and in St. Thomas', Appendix I, in St. Thomas Aquinas, *Summa Theologiae*, ix (Blackfriars, 1968), p. 302. But Thomas says: 'necesse est ponere, ad hoc quod universum sit perfectum, quod sit aliqua incorporea creatura' (*ST* I, 50, 1). The deduction here is from the divine nature as known: 'Deus . . . producit per intellectum et voluntatem' (ibid.). The angelic nature is not for the sake of what is below it but exists for its own part in God's glory (*ST* I, 50, 3). In this perspective the universe must be much more an angelic than a human place both numerically and qualitatively (ibid. and I, 50, 4 *ad* 3). Separate substances are not, as in Rahner's theological anthropology, mere abstractions.

certainly a movement in the form in which this dilemma is presented, and the direction is toward the more positive knowledge of God, but the inner dilemma is not resolved.

Part of the change within this specific historical sequence appears when Dionysius somewhat ambiguously transforms the hypostases into attributes. But the Neoplatonism of Dionysius and Eriugena dictates that the predicates belong properly to the creatures from which they are borrowed, and only metaphorically to God as cause. There is again a development from Dionysius to Thomas in attributing the names properly and affirmatively to the very being of God. Yet how this can be so remains incomprehensible because the division inherent in predication is external to the Neoplatonic simplicity of the divine. Consequently, that through which God is revealed remains outside him in the last analysis and human intellect is appropriated to the angels; men only participate in it.[35]

Irreconcilably uniting Aristotelian science with Neoplatonic systematic theology, Aristotle's complete noetic activity with the One of Proclus, Aquinas may appear as contradictory as he seems comprehensive. For an existentialist like Fr Rahner, Thomas is at once too idealist in endeavouring a knowledge of God in himself and not in the world, and equally too attached to those mediatorial structures which prevent man being simultaneously both immediately transcendent toward God and in the world. A rationalistic Hegelian like Dr Lowry criticizes the Neoplatonism which prevents the full transformation of faith into reason. A contemporary Calvinist blames him for rending the seamless garment of faith and reason woven by the earlier medieval theologians and releasing independent secularity into the world.[36] No doubt these opposed critical stances are not equally well founded, but they indicate the degree of unresolved contrariety in the system of Aquinas. Thomas's Neoplatonism can be defended; philosophical, theological, and historical reasons compel it. But the comprehensiveness of the Neoplatonic systems is equally essential to them and impossible for them. The demand·that the One be manifest as universal principle, which its nature as absolutely first requires, cannot be satisfied if the principle is undivided simplicity. The

---

[35] See Endnote 3, p. 165 below.

[36] F. A. Schaffer, *Escape from Reason* (London, 1968), pp. 9–13; for him, in the distinction by Thomas of nature and grace, 'we have the real birth of the humanistic Renaissance' (p. 10) and the opening of the 'sphere of the autonomous' (p. 11). See W. Pannenberg, *Basic Questions in Theology*, trans. in part by G. H. Kehm, Library of Philosophy and Theology, 3 vols., i (London, 1970), p. 13.

dynamism and comprehensiveness of the tradition is magnificently displayed in Thomas's development and correction of it, but eventual shipwreck also seems inevitable.

Yet nothing brings out the virtues of the old Platonic tradition like its contemporary alternatives. Process theology has been made the standard from which Thomas's emphasis on God's simplicity has been judged and found wanting. But both the historical and theological aspects of this endeavour seem inadequate to the task. B. Z. Cooper's *The Idea of God: a Whiteheadian Critique of St. Thomas Aquinas' Concept of God* fails to examine the structural complexity of Thomas's thought and to take into account the diversity and movement in the Hellenic and Hellenistic traditions.[37] They are represented as dogmatic assertions that static simplicity is the divine—if this were so there would be no hypostases save the One, or, in Thomas's alternative, no return of God upon himself. The account is feebly supported on a one-sided interpretation of a few texts of Plato; Aristotle and the Hellenistic developments are ignored.[38] Theologically and philosophically the position of Dr Cooper seems to amount to the demand that certain aspects of the moral, ontological, and cognitional structures of finitude be absolutized just as they are.

[37] B. Z. Cooper, *The Idea of God: A Whiteheadian Critique of St. Thomas Aquinas' Concept of God* (The Hague, 1974). For a more developed treatment of the critique of Aquinas by process theologians cf. my 'Aquinas and the Passion of God', *Being and Truth, Essays in Honour of John Macquarrie*, ed. A. Kee and E. Long (London, 1986), pp. 318–33.

[38] It is remarkable how even very sophisticated treatments of the Hellenic and Hellenistic worlds (a description not to be extended to include Dr Cooper's work) both ignore the special character of Aristotle's philosophy, including his criticism of Plato, precisely at the same point in which these moderns find Hellenism lacking, and also interpret Plato one-sidedly. See, for example, C. N. Cochrane, *Christianity and Classical Culture: A Study of Thought and Action from Augustus to Augustine* (London, 1944). For Professor Cochrane, Aristotle is identified with Plato on the relation of form and matter, and so the changing and the substantial or stable are separate worlds (pp. 81, 225 ff.). Professor G. C. Stead's paper 'The Concept of Mind and the Concept of God', as presented to the Eighth International Conference on Patristic Studies in Oxford, 1979, is subject to similar limitations. The development of historiography by the Greeks and the essential role history plays for Aristotle in finding his scientific objects and the principles of them (see especially the *De Anima*, the *Physics*, the *Metaphysics* and, differently, the *Politics*) becomes incomprehensible when his philosophy is viewed in this way. His notions of substance and activity are taken to exclude change and historical connection in R. G. Collingwood, *The Idea of History* (Oxford, 1946), pp. 20–1, and 42–5—see Leo Strauss, 'On Collingwood's Philosophy of History', *The Review of Metaphysics*, 5 (1952), 559–86. This understanding of Greek thought as anti-historical belongs together with a Christian 'new orthodoxy' exemplified in theologians like K. Lowith and Reinhold Neibuhr, who set up a polemical opposition between Greek pagan and Christian ideas of time. On this 'new orthodoxy' see W. W. Wagar, 'Modern Views of the Origins of the Idea of Progress', *The Journal of the History of Ideas*, 28 (1967), 55–70.

As we have seen, Thomas is more willing than his philosophical fathers to go a considerable distance in understanding the divine through the structures of finite reality, but he remains conscious of the difference. His refusal to go further is not simply to be laid at the door of his Platonism; it is from Neoplatonism that a motion is found which he takes into the inmost being of God. Thomas's construction has its incoherence, but it is not clear that the Whiteheadian alternative as presented by Dr Cooper is more than a radical anthropomorphism destructive of divinity, a *Götterdämmerung*.

There is, however, a more positive side to these process and dialectical theologies, namely their capacity to give meaning to the eschatological character of the Christian religion. But this is an area in which the Neoplatonic theologies with their emphasis on the return into God are naturally strong—unless, of course, it be insisted that the heavenly kingdom take a Marxist form. And so, even here, Thomas may be thought to understand at least as well as our contemporaries the philosophical necessities for the power of God over the future. It is the particular genius of the Proclan Neoplatonism, as compared with its Plotinian alternative, to articulate what in the πρόοδος and its principle is necessary for the perfection of the return.[39] This is the very purpose of Thomas's insistence on the absolute perfection of the divine and God's freedom *ad extra* which critics of classical theology find so objectionable. Indeed, the inadequacy and contingency of the created as compared with the infinite potentiality of God belong equally to this conception. For God's freedom and omnipotence are exalted so as to be able to draw all things into their end, to encompass time and matter. It is sophistical in reason and unjust in practice to demand the result if the means are not provided, and St Thomas maintains that even God is bound by the necessity to will the means if he wills the end.

It is because the contemporary alternatives seem so one-sided and are not more evidently solutions to the problems which Thomas faced, and partly solved, that we return to him and to the tradition of theology and philosophy in which his *Summa Theologiae* appears: theology as the science of the first principle and this as the total knowledge of reality in its unity. Thomas's conception of this was even wider than that of his predecessors and the polarities were perhaps more strongly opposed and differentiated than ever before. None the less, against all this he endeavours to draw everything together into

[39] See ch. I n. 55 and my 'Aquinas' First Principle', 148–50.

one system under one divine thinking in which, by God's generosity, we are participants. Philosophically and theologically the present time may almost be defined by its turning away from this high enterprise. Its rejection is more directly of the Hegelian philosophy which attempted to unite even more widely opposed and developed elements. In Hegel's world, political freedom, natural science, historical consciousness and science, secular philosophy, and the idea of Christianity as supernatural revelation had all grown stronger and more independent of each other than in Thomas's time.[40] These divisions were embodied in the institutions of modernity. Partly the revival of Thomism occurred in reaction against this modernity, and even specifically against Hegel.[41] Pope Leo hoped for a resolution of the destructive conflicts of his world that did not go so far as Hegel went in recognizing the forms of modern freedom and the autonomy of the different aspects of human endeavour this freedom demanded. And so he attempted a cure for 'the evils now overwhelming us and the evils we greatly fear' which would not be as total a speculative rationality as Hegel required. The aim of the Thomist revival was to promote a modern Christianity more directly under the authority of the Church than Hegel would allow.[42] The result was a Thomism which united faith and reason less completely than either Hegel or St Thomas had done.

Within the Church, this Thomism has collapsed both theoretically and practically. But may not Thomas have another contemporary calling than as a warrior against modern freedom? Might it not be better that those who appreciate his enormous accomplishment make common cause against those who give up or oppose the work of synthetic reason, the labour of constructing a *summa*? The common aim would be a theological activity which was not a movement from one dogmatically asserted partial position after another, which did not reduce intellect to a tool for practice, and which would provide the

---

[40] My interpretation of Hegel conforms most nearly to that presented by E. Fackenheim, *The Religious Dimension of Hegel's Thought* (Bloomington, Indiana, 1967).

[41] See Endnote 5, pp. 166–7, below and introduction. My 'Making Theology Practical' is an extended treatment of the character of anti-Hegelian Thomism.

[42] See J. A. Doull, 'The Logic of Theology since Hegel', *Dionysius*, 7 (1983), 129–36. 'It was idle, said Hegel to look for true religion where there were not true secular institutions' (129). The opposition of the religious revival of the nineteenth century to the institutions of the modern state stems from what is common to the reactionary church and the nineteenth-century post-Hegelian revolutionaries: 'Revolution and the reaction from it to tradition and divine authority were forms of the same: the one the separation of the human from the divine, the other their immediate unity' (131).

basis of a rigorously intellectual ecumenism in the broadest sense.[43] It would have to show again that there can be no philosophy or theology without a science of first principles and none which does not seek the unity of the opposed and divided. No doubt the task is more than human, but in attempting it we would become again the heirs of Aristotle and Plato, their Neoplatonic critics and adaptors, and the Christian theology which once felt itself elevated by standing on the shoulders of these giants.

[43] The necessary ecumenism is suggested in C. Andresen's way of integrating Platonism and early Christian theology which gets beyond the opposition of philosophers and theologians: 'The Integration', esp. pp. 412–13; in Jean Trouillard's way of embracing Neoplatonic philosophy within the Christian religion: 'Procession néoplatonicienne', esp. pp. 25–6; in G. Lafont's endeavour to stay with both metaphysical and anti-ontological philosophical approaches, which 'se vérifier l'une l'autre': 'Le *Parménide* de Platon', p. 80; in W. Beierwaltes's reaching out to both Hegel and Heidegger, thus bringing the Neoplatonic tradition to our time: 'Image and Counter-image', pp. 238–40; and in J. A. Doull's way of uniting the tradition and modern freedom.

ENDNOTES

Endnote 1. L. Ducharme, 'L'idée de la métaphysique dans les écrits du premier enseignement parisien de saint Thomas d'Aquin', *Colloque commemoratif saint Thomas d'Aquin, Église et théologie*, 5, 2 (1974), 155–69, finds Thomas both affirming and denying that metaphysics has God as its subject (p. 161). He concludes that 'saint Thomas décrit surtout la métaphysique comme science divine, théologie des philosophes' (p. 168), but is ambiguous about whether God is its subject because God is both the subject, and principle of the subject (when this is expressed as 'being *qua* being').

There is in Thomas no difficulty about a principle becoming an object of science. This is indeed usual, e.g. 'sicut musica credit principia tradita sibi ab arithmetico, ita doctrina sacra credit principia revelata sibi a Deo', *ST* I, 1, 2. Of course the real problem is whether the same science can have the same things both as principles and as subject. But even the controversial texts affirm this.

Crucial texts are Thomas's commentaries on Boethius' *De Trinitate* and on Aristotle's *Metaphysics* and the *Summa contra Gentiles*, iii, 25 and iv, 1. *In de Trin.* v, 4 is usually cited by those who would divide the two theologies. In fact it teaches that they meet. The divine is able to be treated in two ways: 'res divinae, quia sunt principia omnium entium et sunt nihilominus in se naturae completae, dupliciter tractari possunt . . .'. They are not just abstract principles, but things in themselves. Yet, the two ways of looking at separate substances start at opposite points. 'Per lumen naturalis rationis pervenire non possumus in ea nisi secundum quod in ea per effectus ducimur.' We arrive at God but do not start with him, and thus being, as our beginning, is the formal subject of the science. The other theology has not this limitation. 'Est autem alius modus cognoscendi huiusmodi res, non secundum quod per effectus manifestantur, sed secundum quod ipsae se ipsas manifestant.' It therefore begins with *Deus* as its *subiectum*. In a particular science there would be a difficulty about the principles becoming themselves subjects (or objects), i.e. something treated by the science. Metaphysics, theological science in its philosophical aspect, is not however a particular science. This is not only due to the generality of its subject, *commune ens*, but because it treats its own principles. Indeed, because it is also the science of principles, it is theology!

A fundamental integrity is present in Thomas's thought because philosophy is not involved in a vicious circle of always treating its objects by principles known elsewhere and assumed by it. First philosophy turns its eyes upon the *per se nota* which it arrives at through effects—effects being just what are known through another. 'philosophus primus . . . probat . . . per alia principia per se nota. Et sic non est aliquis circulus in diffinitione' (*In de Trin.* v, 1 *ad* 9, p. 172, lines 16–20). These 'naturae completae', which are 'in se res quaedam' (ibid., v, 4) are able to be given a kind of demonstration: 'cum per eos [effectos] pervenerimus ad cognitionem causarum primarum ... ex quibus probabantur demonstratione quia'. Just as demonstration 'propter quid' derives from them (ibid., v, 1 *ad* 9, p. 172, line 22–p. 173, line 1).

At root the unity of Thomas's thought stems from the unity of Aristotle's *Metaphysics*—as R. D. Crouse argues in '*Philosophia Ancilla Theologiae*', and 'St. Thomas, St. Albert, Aristotle: *Philosophia Ancilla Theologiae*'. It depends on the unity in that work of the science of being as being and the science of separate substances, i.e. on metaphysics being onto-theo-logy. One knows, of course, that modern scholarship denies this unity, e.g. W. Jaeger, *Aristoteles: Grundlegung einer Geschichte seiner Entwicklung* (Berlin, 1923). But this is not Aquinas's view: 'Secundum igitur tria praedicta, ea quibus perfectio huius scientiae attenditur, sortitur tria nomina. Dicitur enim scientia divina sive *theologia*, inquantum praedictas [separatas] substantias considerat; *Metaphysica*, inquantum considerat ens.... Dicitur autem *prima philosophia*, inquantum primas rerum causas considerat' (*In Meta.*, *proem.*, p. 2). These separate substances do actually become objects of knowledge in this science: 'secundum sententiam Aristotelis humanus intellectus potest pertingere ad intelligendum substantias simplices' (ibid., ix, xi, 1916, p. 458); 'cum haec scientia sit de premis causis et principiis, oportet quod sit de Deo' (ibid., i, iii, 64, p. 19). 'Patet ... quae sit natura huius scientiae, quia est speculativa, libera, non humana, sed divina: et quae est eius intentio, qua oportet habere quaestionem et totam methodum et totam hanc artem. Intendit enim circa primas et universales rerum causas, de quibus etiam inquirit et determinat. Et propter harum cognitionem ad praedictum terminum pervenit, ut scilicet non admiretur cognitis causis' (ibid., i, iii, 68, p. 20).

Endnote 2. L. Elders, 'Le problème de l'existence', 181. Importantly, Thomas does not proceed from a bare logical distinction but from the fact that 'invenimus ... in rebus quaedam quae sunt possibilia esse et non esse cum quaedam inveniantur generari et corrumpi', *ST* I, 2, 3. Because of his view of the situation of man's soul, proof of God's existence or of the subject of theology is not possible without the mediation of sense. Avicenna and Scotus try to overcome the dependence of God on the sensible which this seems to imply. They argue from the opposition of possible and necessary given independently of any particular sensible thing—though they would not concede that they were thereby talking only of logic or 'second intentions' any more than Anselm would. Avicenna's title at cap. 1, 6 is: 'Capitulum in initio loquendi de necesse est et de possibile esse, et quod necesse esse non habet causam et quod possibile est et causatum et quod necesse esse nulli est coaequale in esse nec pendet ab alio in esse', *De Philosophia Prima* 1, 6, p. 43, lines 3–6. For Scotus see John Duns

Scotus, *De Primo Principio: A Revised Text and Translation* by E. Roche, Franciscan Inst. Publications, Philosophy Series 5 (New York/Louvain, 1949). É. Gilson explains that the motive of these proofs from the concepts of the possible and the necessary is to reflect in the proof the freedom from the sensible which belongs to the divine object. This will remind one of Anselm's endeavour to find an argument reflecting the simplicity of God and the unity of content and form, of 'an sit' and 'quid sit' in him. '... if we start from physical bodies, we will finally succeed in proving the existence of their primary cause, but ... it will remain a physical cause ... the God whose existence physics can demonstrate does not transcend the physical order', *History*, p. 456. Despite the intentions of Scotus and Avicenna, the commentators generally interpret the notion of being on which the argument depends as 'derived by intelligence from the data of sense experience', A. M. Goichon, 'The Philosopher of Being', *Avicenna Commemorative Volume*, ed. V. Courtois (Calcutta, 1956), p. 109. D. Saliba, *Étude sur la Métaphysique d'Avicenne* (Paris, 1926), p. 103, writes: 'Nous voyons que, dans cette preuve, il faut tout d'abord admettre l'existence des êtres possibles comme un postulat lequel nous est donné par les sens.' See also D. Chahine, *Ontologie et théologie chez Avicenne* (Paris, n.d.); É. Gilson, 'Avicenne et le point de départ de Duns Scot', *Arch. hist. doct. lit. du moyen âge* 2 (1927), 89–149, and id., *History*, pp. 206–16 and 455–63. But this destroys the proofs and is a consequence of the philosophical presuppositions brought to the works by the commentators. These presuppositions are expressed by Gilson in a passage from *Réalisme thomiste*, p. 215: 'l'appréhension de l'être par l'intellect consiste à voir directement le concept d'être dans n'importe quelle donnée sensible'.

St Thomas is not dependent on Avicenna in the third way. Apparently following Averroes, he rejects Avicenna's definition of necessity: 'he defined necessity not in terms of essence and existence but in terms of unalterability, following Aristotle's definition of the necessary as that which cannot be otherwise (*Metaphysics Δ*, 1015ᵃ34)', A. Kenny, *The Five Ways*, p. 48. The Master of Balliol is reporting the results of G. Jalbert, *Nécessité et contingence chez saint Thomas d'Aquin et chez ses prédécesseurs*, Editions de l'Université d'Ottawa (Ottawa, 1961). Dr Jalbert finds that the movement in St Thomas's thought 'est fortement marqué par le rejet de la conception d'Avicenne à mesure que se précise celle d'Aristote fondée sur le rôle de la forme comme principe de nécessité et celui de la matière comme source de la contingence' (pp. 238–9). In this T. C. O'Brien and L. Elders agree (although Fr Elders does not associate the *tertia via* with the material cause except accidentally, 'Les cinq voies', p. 141; for Kenny see ch. II n. 22, p. 42 above). All told, Thomas has a view of theology which permits him neither to sacrifice its freedom—its descent from above—nor its connection with the sensible. He uses both Avicenna and Averroes at the point of their opposition.

Endnote 3. Cf. *ST* I, 12, 2 as quoted at n. 12, p. 85 above. The balance of Aristotelian and Neoplatonic elements in Aquinas is no more difficult to judge and understand than where one is attempting to understand in what sense and by what power humans know intellectual and simple realities. At I, 12, 12 obj. 1 he cites Boethius: 'ratio non capit simplicem formam' (*De consolatione philosophiae* v, 4 (PL 63, 847)) which he explains as follows: 'ratio ad formam simplicem pertingere non potest, ut sciat de ea quid est; potest tamen de ea cognoscere, ut sciat an est', I, 12, 12 *ad* 1. This must be contrasted with Aristotle's teaching on knowledge of the simple: *Metaphysics* Θ, 1051^{b}30–3, *De Anima* iii, 6. Thomas understands this true immediate grasp of essences to apply only to the knowledge of the sensible things to which our form of cognition is suited. Thus his comment on *De Anima* iii, 6, 430^{b}20. Aristotle is discussing our knowledge of points and units, but Thomas adds: 'et inde est etiam quod omnia que transcendunt hec sensibilia nota nobis, non cognoscuntur a nobis nisi per negationem, sicuti de substanciis separatis . . .', *Sentencia libri de anima* III, v, p. 227, lines 187–91. The root of the difference lies in their different conceptions of the relation of *ratio* and *intellectus* or divided and intuitive reason in man. For Aristotle, man may be characterized by practical intellect (cf. *Nic. Eth.* vi, 2, 1135^{b}4–5), but practical intellect exists only in virtue of theoretical intellect and, while this belongs primarily to the gods, man shares in it (*Metaphysics A*, 2, 982^{b}27–983^{a}24 and *Nic. Eth.* x, 7, 1178^{a}2). For Thomas, in contrast, man has this unified intellectual power only through a participation mediated by the angels: '[Intellectus] non est enim secundum hominem quantum ad naturam compositam, est autem propriissime secundum hominem quantum ad id quod est principalissimum in homine; quod quidem perfectissime invenitur in substantiis superioribus, in homine autem imperfecte et quasi participative', *In Ethica* x, 11 (Leonine xlvii, ii, p. 588, lines 155–60). There is also: 'Unde quamvis cognitio humanae animae proprie sit per viam rationis, est tamen in ea aliqua participatio illius simplicis cognitionis quae in superioribus substantiis invenitur, ex quo etiam intellectivam vim habere dicuntur; et hoc secundum illum modum quem Dionysius in VII cap. *De divinis nominibus* assignat. . . . Et hanc quidem differentiam angelorum et animarum Dionysius in VII cap. *De divinis nominibus* ostendit. . . . Id autem quod sic participatur non habetur ut possessio, id est sicut aliquid perfecte subiacens potentiae habentis illud, sicut dicitur in I *Metaphysicæ* quod cognitio Dei est divina et non humana possessio', *De Veritate*, ii, *q.* xv, *a.* 1, pp. 479–80, lines 312–19, 324–6, 346–51. Cf. *De Sub. Sep.* iv, p. D47, lines 15–24. See J. Peghaire, '*Intellectus' et 'Ratio' selon s. Thomas d'Aquin*, p. 288.

Endnote 4. *ST* I, 45, 4 *et* 5. As opposed to the Plotinian teaching that the One is cause of the highest spiritual beings and that they in turn cause what is below, the Proclan doctrine is that the One is the cause of the substantial being of things at every level below him. Transformed, this means that they reveal his being since theirs is his proper effect. For Proclus, see *Elements*, props. 57, 101, 138–40, 157 and Dodds's comments at pp. 230–2. Thomas finds the doctrine that substantial being is the proper and revealing effect of God in Dionysius and the *Liber de Causis*, which scholars find to be remarkably close together on this point. 'Si alia causa nominetur a suo effectu, oportet quod principalius nominetur Deus per ipsum esse a primo effectu per quem omnia fecit; huiusmodi autem est ens; ergo principalius nominatur Deus per ipsum esse', *In de div. nom.*, v, i, 636. Cf. his comments on propositions 3, 4, 9, 12, *In librum de causis*, where he uncovers the teaching of Proclus and the *auctor libri* that the characteristic effect of God is the being of things. 'Ipsum enim esse est communissimus effectus primus et intimior omnibus aliis effectibus; et ideo soli Deo competit secundum virtutem propriam talis effectus: unde etiam, ut dicitur in lib. *de Causis* [propos. IX] intelligentia non dat esse, nisi prout est in ea virtus divina', *de Pot.*, *q.* 3, *a.* 7, pp. 58–9. See also *q.* 7, *a.* 2, *ST* I, 105, 5 and *ST* I–II, 66, 5 *ad* 4. There seems to be a difference between Proclus and both the author of the *Liber* and Dionysius of importance here. A. Pattin writes in the introduction to his edition of the Liber de Causis: 'Le *Liber de Causis*, édition établie à l'aide de 90 manuscrits avec introduction et notes', *Tijdschrift voor Filosofie*, 28 (1966), 90–203: 'Dans le texte . . . se trouve la distinction entre *dare ens per modum creationis* et *dare uitam non per modum creationis immo per modum formae* (prop. 17, l. 56–57 et l. 57–59). Cette distinction, qui manque totalement dans les *Élements de théologie* de Proclus est à vrai dire déjà la célèbre distinction scolastique entre *esse causam per modum creationis* et *esse causam per modum informationis ou specificationis*' (pp. 97–8). In n. 35 he refers us to the *De Potentia* of Aquinas, *q.* 3, *a.* 1 for the celebrated scholastic distinction: 'Et inde est quod in lib. *de Causis* [prop. 18], dicitur, quod esse eius est per creationem, vivere vero et caetera huiusmodi, per informationem' (Pession, p. 39). S. Gersh, *From Iamblichus*, stresses the crucial role of the doctrine of creation in Dionysius (e.g. p. 205). Studies of importance on the doctrine of the *Liber de Causis* include Saffrey's introduction to his edition and his 'L'etat actuel des recherches'. Also, there is Leo Sweeney, 'Doctrine of Creation in *Liber de Causis*', *An Étienne Gilson Tribute, presented by his North American Students with a Response by É. Gilson*, ed. C. J. O'Neil (Milwaukee, 1959), pp. 274–89: 'the *Esse creans* of the *Liber de Causis* makes everything simply to be by an act of genuine creation' (p. 289). Studies of the relation between Thomas's teaching and that of Dionysius and the *auctor libri* include: C. Fabro, *Participation et causalité*, pp. 171–244; K. Kremer, *Die neuplatonische Seinsphilosophie*, pp. 299–313 and 300–96; F. van Steenberghen, *Introduction*, pp. 100–1; F. Ruello, 'La mystique de l'Exode', p. 243.

Endnote 5. The use of a Hegelian standard for judging St Thomas is not so arbitrary as might first appear. S. Gersh finds it appropriate for evaluating Dionysius in just that respect in which he is one with Thomas. In *From*

Iamblichus, p. 3, he writes of Dionysius that he 'both preserves the externally cognitative emanation theory of the pagan Neoplatonists and anticipates the Eriugenian immanently self-differentiating Godhead, he stands mid-way, in effect, between Spinoza and Hegel'. J. Moltmann, *The Trinity and the Kingdom of God: The Doctrine of God*, trans. M. Kohl (London, 1981), pp. 16 ff., locates Thomas in a historical, philosophical theological continuum moving toward Hegelian absolute subjectivity. Idealist interpretations are to be found in P. Rousselot, *L'Intellectualisme de saint Thomas* (2nd edn.; Paris, 1924) and J. N. Findlay, *Plato: The Written and Unwritten Doctrines*, International Library of Philosophical and Scientific Method (London, 1974), pp. 393–5; see also D. Bradley, 'Rahner's *Spirit in the World*: Aquinas or Hegel?', *The Thomist*, 41 (1977), 167–99. G. van Riet, 'Le problème de Dieu chez Hegel', *De Deo in philosophia S. Thomae et in hodierna philosophia: Acta VI Congressus Thomistici Internationalis*, Bibl. Pont. Acad. Rom. S. Thom. Aquin. 6, 3 vols. (Rome, 1965); i, pp. 205–13, is sympathetic, but in general Hegel was hated as the presiding devil of modern spirituality, from whose cauldron poured forth the worst excesses of subjective philosophy and self-certain secular freedom. B. Lakebrink, *Perfectio omnium perfectionum: Studien zur Seinskonzeption bei Thomas von Aquin und Hegel*, Studi tomistici 24 (Vatican City, 1984) sets the Thomistic 'Analektik' and the Hegelian 'Dialektik', together with their contents, altogether against each other. A good survey of Thomist attitudes is found in G. A. McCool, 'Twentieth-Century Scholasticism' and J. Macquarrie, *Twentieth-Century Religious Thought: The Frontiers of Philosophy and Theology, 1900–1970*, rev. edn. (London, 1971), pp. 254–6, 279, 288, 392, shows how the various realisms of our time have this anti-Hegelianism in common. Heidegger was in fact chosen against Hegel. Compare the articles in the section on Hegelian and Marxist dialectic with those on existentialism in *Sapientia Aquinatis: Communicationes IV Congressus Thomistici Internationalis* (Rome, 1955) and see C. Fabro, *Participation et causalité*, pp. 635–6; id., 'Le retour au fondement de l'être'; id., 'L'interpretazione dell'atto'; J. D. Jones, 'The Ontological Difference for St Thomas and Pseudo-Dionysius'. W. Luijpen, OSA, 'Heidegger and the Affirmation of God', *De Deo in philosophia S. Thomae*, i, pp. 303–10. But W. Beierwaltes, 'Image and Counterimage', draws on both Heidegger and Hegel to give contemporary force to the Neoplatonic tradition.

BIBLIOGRAPHY

In general, the bibliography contains only works to which reference is made in the notes either directly or obliquely. The writings of Plato and Aristotle cited are not listed; they are always quoted from the Oxford Classical Texts series. Similarly, Patristic and medieval authors are included only if quotations are from editions other than those in the *Patrologia Latina* and *Patrologia Graeca*. For Aquinas, the texts recommended by the current Leonine editors have been used. This is not always the one in Leonine *Opera Omnia*.

Abelard, Peter. *Theologia 'Summi Boni'*, ed. H. Ostlander. Beit. zur Gesch. de Phil. und Theo. des Mittelalters 35, 2/3.

— *Theologia Christiana. Opera Theologica*, ed. E. M. Buytaert. Corpus Christ. Cont. Med. 12. 2 vols. Brepols, 1964, ii.

Ackeren, G. F. van. *Sacra Doctrina: The Subject of the First Question of the Summa Theologiae of St. Thomas Aquinas*. Rome, 1952.

Adelard of Bath. *Traktat De Eodem et Diverso*, ed. H. Willner. Beit. zur Gesch. der Phil. und Theo. des Mittelalters, Texte und Untersuchungen 4/1. Münster, 1903.

Albertus Magnus. *De Anima*, ed. Cl. Stroick. *Opera Omnia* (Cologne) 7. Münster i. W., 1968.

— *Super Dionysium de Divinis Nominibus*, ed. P. Simon. *Opera Omnia* 37(1). Cologne, 1972.

— *Summa Theologiae sive de Mirabili Scientia Dei: Libri I Pars I, Quaestiones 1–50*, ed. D. Seidler. *Opera Omnia* 35(1). Cologne, 1978.

Anawati, G. C. 'Saint Thomas d'Aquin et la *Métaphysique* d'Avicenne'. *Commemorative Studies*, ed. A. A. Maurer (q.v.), i, pp. 449–65.

Anderson, J. F. *St. Augustine and Being*. The Hague, 1965.

Andresen, C. 'The Integration of Platonism into Early Christian Theology'. *Studia Patristica*, xv, ed. E. A. Livingstone. Texte und Untersuchungen 128 Berlin, 1984, pp. 399–413.

Anselm. *Opera Omnia*, ed. F. S. Schmitt. 6 vols. Edinburgh, 1946–61.

Aquinas, St Thomas. *Compendium Theologiae. Opera Omnia* (Leonine) xlii. Rome, 1979.

— *Contra Gentiles*. Introduction historique par A. Gauthier, trad. franç. par R. Bernier *et al.* 4 vols. Paris, 1951–61.

— *De Ente et Essentia. Opera Omnia* (Leonine) xliii. Rome, 1976.

— *De Rationibus Fidei ad Cantorem Antiochenum, Opera Omnia* (Leonine) xl (Pars B–C). Rome, 1968.

— *De Spiritualibus Creaturis*, ed. M. Calcaterra et T. S. Centi. *Quaestiones Disputatae*, ii. Turin/Rome, 1965.

—— *De Substantiis Separatis. Opera Omnia* (Leonine) xl (Pars D–E). Rome, 1968.

—— *Expositio super Boetium de Hebdomadibus*, ed. M. Calcaterra. *Opuscula Theologica*, ed. R. M. Spiazzi. 2 vols. Turin/Rome, 1954, ii.

—— *Expositio super librum Boethii de Trinitate*, ed. B. Decker. Studien und Texte zur Geistesgeschichte des Mittelalters 4. Leiden, 1959.

—— *In Aristotelis libros Peri Hermeneias et Posteriorum Analyticorum Expositio*, cum textu ex recensione Leonina, ed. R. M. Spiazzi. Turin/Rome, 1955.

—— *In duodecim libros Metaphysicorum Aristotelis Expositio*, ed. M. R. Cathala et R. M. Spiazzi. Turin/Rome, 1964.

—— *In librum Beati Dionysii de Divinis Nominibus Expositio*, ed. C. Pera. Turin/Rome, 1950.

—— *In librum de Causis Expositio*, ed. C. Pera. Turin/Rome, 1955. [H.-D. Saffrey's edition is used for text but Pera's remains valuable because of its indices.]

—— *In octo libros Physicorum Aristotelis Expositio*, ed. P. M. Maggiolo. Turin/Rome, 1954.

—— *Quaestiones Disputatae de Potentia*, new edn., ed. P. M. Pession, *Quaestiones Disputatae*, 2 vols. ii. Turin/Rome, 1964.

—— *Quaestiones Disputatae de Veritate. Opera Omnia* (Leonine) xxii–xxiv. 3 vols. Rome, 1970–5.

—— *Scriptum super libros Sententiarum Magistri Petri Lombardi*, editio nova, R. P. Mandonnet et M. F. Moos. 4 vols. Paris, 1929–47.

—— *Sentencia libri de Anima. Opera Omnia* (Leonine) xlv. Rome, 1984.

—— *Sentencia libri Ethicorum. Opera Omnia* (Leonine) xlvii, 2 vols. Rome, 1969.

—— *Summa contra Gentiles. Opera Omnia* (Leonine) xiii–xv. Rome, 1918–30.

—— *Summa Theologiae*, edito altera emendata. edidit Commissio Piana. Ottawa, 1953.

—— *Summa Theologiae*. Lat. text and Engl. trans., intr., notes, appendices and glossaries by the Dominicans from English-speaking Provinces, 60 vols. Blackfriars: London, 1963–76.

—— *Summa Theologica*, trans. by Fathers of the English Dominican Province, 22 vols. London, 1911–28.

—— *Super Evangelium S. Ioannis lectura*, ed. V revisa, cura P. Raphaelis Cai. Rome, 1952.

—— *Super Librum de Causis Expositio*, ed. H.-D. Saffrey. Textus Philosophici Friburgenses 4/5. Fribourg/Louvain, 1954.

Armstrong, A. H. 'The Apprehension of Divinity in the Self and Cosmos in Plotinus'. *The Significance of Neoplatonism*, ed. R. Baine Harris. Norfolk, Va., 1976, pp. 187–98. Reprinted in *Plotinian and Christian Studies* (q.v.).

—— 'The Background of the Doctrine "That the Intelligibles are not Outside the Intellect"'. *Les Sources de Plotin*, Entretiens Hardt 5. Vandœuvres/Geneva, 1960, pp. 393–413. Reprinted in *Plotinian and Christian Studies* (q.v.).

Armstrong, A. H. 'Elements in the Thought of Plotinus at Variance with Classical Intellectualism'. *The Journal of Hellenic Studies* 93 (1973), 13–22. Reprinted in *Plotinian and Christian Studies* (q.v.).

—— 'The Escape of the One. An Investigation of Some Possibilities of Apophatic Theology Imperfectly Realized in the West'. *Studia Patristica*, xiii, Texte und Untersuchungen 116, Berlin, 1975, pp. 77–89. Reprinted in *Plotinian and Christian Studies* (q.v.).

—— 'Eternity, Life and Movement in Plotinus' Accounts of νοῦς'. *Le Néoplatonisme*. Colloques internationaux du CNRS, Royaumont, 1969. Paris, 1971, pp. 677–774. Reprinted in *Plotinian and Christian Studies* (q.v.).

—— *Introduction to Ancient Philosophy*. 1st edn. London, 1947; 2nd edn. London, 1949; 3rd edn. London, 1957; 4th edn. London, 1965.

—— 'Man in the Cosmos: A Study of Some Differences between Pagan Neoplatonism and Christianity'. *Romanitas et Christianitas*, ed. W. den Boer *et al.* Amsterdam/London, 1973, pp. 5–14. Reprinted in *Plotinian and Christian Studies* (q.v.).

—— 'Negative Theology'. *The Downside Review*, 95 (1977), 176–89. Reprinted in *Plotinian and Christian Studies* (q.v.).

—— 'Negative Theology, Myth and Incarnation'. *Néoplatinisme: mélanges offerts à Jean Trouillard* (q.v.), pp. 47–62.

—— 'Pagan and Christian Traditionalism in the First Three Centuries A.D.' *Studia Patristica*, xv, ed. E. A. Livingstone. Texte und Untersuchungen 128, Berlin, 1984, pp. 414–31.

—— 'Philosophy, Theology and Interpretation: the Interpretation of Interpreters'. *Eriugena: Studien zu seinen Quellen*, ed. W. Beierwaltes (q.v.), pp. 7–14.

—— 'Platonic *Eros* and Christian *Agape*'. *The Downside Review*, 79 (1961), 105–21. Reprinted in *Plotinian and Christian Studies* (q.v.).

—— 'Platonic Love: a Reply to Professor Verdenius'. *The Downside Review*, 82 (1964), 199–208. Reprinted in *Plotinian and Christian Studies* (q.v.).

—— *Plotinian and Christian Studies*. Variorum Reprints Collected Studies 103. London, 1979.

—— 'Plotinus' Doctrine of the Infinite and Christian Thought'. *The Downside Review*, 73 (1954/5), 47–58. Reprinted in *Plotinian and Christian Studies* (q.v.).

—— 'Reason and Faith in the First Millenium A.D.'. *Proceedings of the American Catholic Philosophical Association* 40, Washington, 1966, pp. 104–9. Reprinted in *Plotinian and Christian Studies* (q.v.).

—— 'St. Augustine and Christian Platonism'. The St. Augustine Lecture, 1966. Villanova, 1967. Reprinted in *Plotinian and Christian Studies* (q.v.).

—— 'Salvation: Plotinian and Christian'. *The Downside Review*, 75 (1957), 126–39. Reprinted in *Plotinian and Christian Studies* (q.v.).

—— 'The Self-Definition of Christianity in relation to later Platonism'. *Jewish and Christian Self-Definition*, ed. E. P. Sanders. London, 1980, pp. 74–99.

—— 'Some Advantages of Polytheism'. *Dionysius*, 5 (1981), 181–8.

—— 'Spiritual or Intelligible Matter in Plotinus and St. Augustine'. *Augustinus Magister*. Communications du Congrès international augustinien, Paris, 1954. 3 vols, Paris, 1955, i, pp. 277–83. Reprinted in *Plotinian and Christian Studies* (q.v.).

—— 'Tradition, Reason and Experience in the Thought of Plotinus', *Atti del Convegno internazionale sul tema Plotino e il Neoplatonismo in Oriente e in Occidente, Roma, 1970.* Rome, 1974, pp., 171–94. Reprinted in *Plotinian and Christian Studies* (q.v.).

—— 'Was Plotinus a Magician?' *Phroenesis*, 1 (1955), 73–9. Reprinted in *Plotinian and Christian Studies* (q.v.).

—— (ed.). *Cambridge History of Later Greek and Early Medieval Philosophy*. Cambridge, 1967.

Atherton, J. P. 'The Validity of Thomas' Interpretation of ΝΟΗΣΙΣ ΝΟΗΣΕΩΣ'. *Atti del Congresso Internazionale Tommaso d'Aquino nel suo settimo centenario*, 9 vols. i. Naples, 1975, pp. 156–62.

Aubenque, P. 'Les origines néoplatoniciennes de la doctrine de l'analogie de l'être'. *Néoplatonisme: mélanges offerts à Jean Trouillard*. Les Cahiers de Fontenay 19–22. Fontenay-aux-Roses, 1981, pp. 63–76.

—— 'Plotin et le dépassement de l'ontologie grecque classique'. *Le Néoplatonisme*. Colloques internationaux du CNRS, Royaumont, 1969. Paris, 1971, pp. 101–8.

Audet, Th. A. 'Approches historiques de la *Summa Theologiae*'. *Études d'histoire littéraire et doctrinale*. U. de Montréal, Publ. de l'Institut d'études médiévales 17. Montreal/Paris, 1962, pp. 7–29.

Averroes. *Commentaria in I Physicorum*. Aristotle, *Opera*, iv. Venice, 1574.

Avicenna Latinus. *Liber de Philosophia Prima sive Scientia Divina*, i–iv, ed. S. van Riet with 'introduction doctrinale', 'Le statut de la métaphysique' by G. Verbeke. Louvain/Leiden, 1977.

—— *Metaphysica sive Prima Philosophia*. Venice, 1495.

Banning, J. van. 'Saint Thomas et l' *Opus imperfectum in Matthaeum*'. *Atti dell'VIII Congresso Tomistico Internazionale*, ed. A. Piolanti (q.v.), viii (1982), pp. 73–85.

Barnard, Ch.-A. 'Les formes de la théologie chez Denys l'Aréopagite'. *Gregorianum*, 59 (1978), 39–69.

Bataillon, L.-J. 'Sur quelques éditions de textes platoniciens médievaux'. *Rev. sc. ph. th.* 6 (1977), 243–61.

Beach, J. D. 'Separate Entity as the Subject of Aristotle's *Metaphysics*'. *The Thomist*, 20 (1957), 75–95.

Beierwaltes, W. ed. *Eriugena: Studien zu seinen Quellen: Vorträge des III. internationalen Eriugena-Colloquiums, Freiburg im Breisgau, 27.–30. August 1979*. Abhandlungen der Heidelberger Academie der Wissenschaften 1980, 3. Heidelberg, 1980.

—— *Identität und Differenz*. Frankfurt am Main, 1980.

—— 'Image and Counterimage: Reflections on Neoplatonic Thought with

Respect to its Place Today'. *Neoplatonism and Early Christian Thought: Essays in Honour of A. H. Armstrong*, ed. H. J. Blumenthal and R. A. Markus. London, 1981 pp. 236–48.

Beierwaltes, W. '*Negati Affirmatio*, or the World as Metaphor: a Foundation for Medieval Aesthetics from the Writings of John Scotus Eriugena'. *Dionysius*, 1 (1977), 127–59.

—— *Proclus: Grundzüge seiner Metaphysik*. Frankfurt am Main, 1965.

Benoit, P. 'Saint Thomas et l'inspiration des écritures'. *Atti del Congresso Internationale Tommaso d'Aquino nel suo settimo centenario*, 9 vols. iii. Naples, 1976, pp. 19–30.

Bernardus Silvestris. *Cosmographia*. Trans. with introduction and notes by Winthrop Wetherbee. New York/London, 1973.

Berthold of Moosburg. *Expositio super Elementationem Theologicam Procli, 184–221, de animalibus*, ed. L. Sturlese, presentazione E. Massa. Temi e testi 18. Rome, 1974.

Blanchette, O. 'Philosophy and Theology in Aquinas: On Being a Disciple in our Day'. *Atti del Congresso Internationale Tommaso d'Aquino nel suo settimo centenario*, 9 vols. ii. Naples, 1976, pp. 427–31.

Blumenthal, H. J. and R. A., Markus, ed. *Neoplatonism and Early Christian Thought: Essays in Honour of A. H. Armstrong*. London, 1981.

Boethius. *De interpretatione*, ed. C. Meiser. 2nd edn. Leipzig, 1880.

—— *The Theological Tractates and the Consolation of Philosophy*, ed. H. F. Stewart and E. K. Rand. Loeb Classical Library. London and New York, 1926.

Bonaventure. *Commentaria in IV Libros Sententiarum Magistri Petri Lombardi. Opera Theologica Selecta*, editio minor, 5 vols. i. Quaracchi, 1934.

—— *Itinerarium mentis in Deum. Opera Theologica Selecta*, editio minor, 5 vols. v. Quaracchi, 1964.

—— *Quaestiones Disputatae de scientia Christi. Opera Omnia*. 10 vols. v. Ad Claras Aquas, Quaracchi, 1891.

—— *The Soul's Journey into God, The Tree of Life, The Life of St. Francis*. Intro. by E. Cousins. The Classics of Western Spirituality. London, 1978.

Booth, E. G. 'St Augustine's *de Trinitate* and Aristotelian and neo-Platonist Noetic'. *Studia Patristica* xvi, ed. E. A. Livingstone. Texte und Untersuchungen 129. Berlin, 1985, pp. 487–90.

Boyle, L. E. '"Alia Lectura Fratris Thome"'. *Mediaeval Studies* 45 (1983), 418–29.

Bradley, D. J. M. 'Aristotelian Science and the Science of Thomistic Theology'. Paper delivered at the Seventh Annual Sewanee Mediaeval Colloquium. The University of the South, Sewanee, Tennessee, April, 1980. *Heythrop Journal*, 22 (1981), 162–71.

—— 'Rahner's *Spirit in the World*: Aquinas or Hegel?' *The Thomist*, 41 (1977), 167–99.

—— 'Religious Faith and the Mediation of Being: the Hegelian Dilemma in Rahner's *Hearers of the World*'. *The Modern Schoolman*, 55 (1978), 127–46.

—— 'Transcendental Critique and Realist Metaphysics'. *The Thomist*, 39 (1975), 631–67.

Breton, S. 'Actualité du néoplatonisme'. *Études néoplatoniciennes*, ed. J. Trouillard. Neuchâtel, 1973, pp. 110–26.

—— *Être, monde, imaginaire*. Paris, 1976.

—— 'L'idée de transcendental et la genèse des transcendentaux chez saint Thomas d'Aquin'. *Saint Thomas d'Aquin aujourd'hui*, ed. L'Association de Professeurs de Philosophie des Facultés Catholiques de France. Recherches de philosophie 6. Paris, 1963, pp. 45–74.

—— 'Origine et principe de raison'. *Rev. sc. ph. th.* 58 (1974), 41–57.

—— 'Le théorème de l'Un dans les *Éléments de Théologie* de Proclus'. *Rev. sc. ph. th.* 58 (1974), 561–83.

zum Brunn, É. 'La dialectique du "magis esse" et du "minus esse" chez saint Augustin'. *Le Néoplatonisme*. Colloques internationaux du CNRS, Royaumont, 1969. Paris, 1971, pp. 373–80.

—— 'L'exégèse augustinienne de "Ego sum qui sum" et la "métaphysique de l'Exode"'. *Dieu et l'être: exégèse d'Exode 3, 14 et de Coran 20, 11–24*, ed. Centre d'études des religions du livre, CNRS. Études augustiniennes. Paris, 1978, pp. 141–64.

—— 'La "métaphysique de l'Exode" selon Thomas d'Aquin'. *Dieu et l'être: exégèses d'Exode 3, 14 et de Coran 20, 11–24*, ed. Centre d'études des religions du livre, CNRS. Études augustiniennes. Paris, 1978, pp. 245–69.

Brush, J. E. *Language and Verification in Thomas Aquinas: A Contribution to Fundamental Theology*. Zurich, 1984.

Busa, R. (ed.). *Index Thomisticus*. Sect. i, 10 vols.; sect. ii(1), 23 vols.; sect. ii(2), 8 vols.; sect. iii, 6 vols. Frommann-Holzboog: Stuttgart-Bad Cannstatt, 1975.

Cameron, A. 'La fin de l'Académie'. *Le Néoplatonisme*. Colloques internationaux du CNRS, Royaumont, 1969. Paris, 1971, pp. 281–90.

Carreker, M. L. '*Motus in Deo*: Motionless Motion and its Relation to the Doctrine of the Trinity of St. Thomas Aquinas'. Unpublished MA Thesis. Department of Classics, Dalhousie University, Halifax, 1983.

Centre d'Études des Religions du Livre. *Dieu et l'être: exégèses d'Exode 3, 14 et de Coran 20, 11–24*. Études augustiniennes, Paris, 1978.

Chadwick, H. 'The Authenticity of Boethius' Fourth Tractate'. *The Journal of Theological Studies* 31 (1980), 551–6.

—— *Boethius: the Consolations of Music, Logic, Theology and Philosophy*. Oxford, 1981.

—— 'The Christian Platonism of Boethius'. Valedictory lecture, Christ Church, Oxford, June, 1979.

Chahine, D. *Ontologie et théologie chez Avicenne*. Paris, n.d.

Chaix-Ruy, J. 'Hegel et saint Thomas: dialectique et logique'. *Sapientia Aquinatis: Communicationes IV Congressus Thomistici Internationalis, Romae, 1955*. Bibl. Pont. Acad. Rom. S. Thom. Aquin. 1 and 2. 2 vols. Rome, 1955, i, pp. 212–20.

Charles, A. 'La raison et le divin chez Proclus'. *Rev. sc. ph. th.* 53 (1969), 458–81.

Charles-Saget, A. *L'architecture du divin: mathématique et philosophie chez Plotin et Proclus.* Collection d'études anciennes. Paris, 1982.

Châtillon, J. '*Unitas, Aequalitas, Concordia vel Connexio*: Recherches sur les origines de la théorie thomiste des appropriations (*Sum. theol.* I, q. 39, art. 7–8)'. *Commemorative Studies*, ed. A. A. Maurer (q.v.), i, pp. 337–79.

Chenu, M.-D. 'Création et histoire'. *Commemorative Studies*, ed. A. A. Maurer (q.v.), ii, pp. 391–9.

—— *Nature, Man and Society in the Twelfth Century: Essays on New Theological Perspectives in the Latin West.* Selected, ed. and trans. from *La théologie au douzième siècle* by J. Taylor and L. K. Little. Chicago and London, 1968.

—— *S. Thomas d'Aquin et la théologie*, Maîtres spirituels 17. Paris, 1959.

—— 'S. Thomas innovateur dans la créativité d'un monde nouveau'. *Atti del Congresso Internazionale Tommaso d'Aquino nel suo settimo centenario*, 9 vols. i. Naples, 1975, pp. 39–50.

—— 'La théologie comme science au XIIIe siècle'. *Arch. hist. doct. lit. du moyen âge*, 2 (1927), 31–71.

—— *La théologie comme science au XIIIe siècle.* 3rd edn. revised, Bibliothèque thomiste 33. Paris, 1957.

—— *La théologie au douzième siècle.* Études de phil. médiévale 45. Paris, 1957.

—— *Toward Understanding St. Thomas*: translation of *Introduction à l'étude de saint Thomas d'Aquin.* Trans. with authorized corrections and bibliographical additions by A.-M. Landry and D. Hughes. Library of Living Catholic Thought. Montreal/Paris, 1950; Chicago, 1964.

Cochrane, C. N. *Christianity and Classical Culture: A Study of Thought and Action from Augustus to Augustine.* London, 1944.

Colin, P. 'Contexte philosophique de la restauration du thomisme en France à la fin du XIXe siècle'. *Atti dell'VIII Congresso Tomistico Internazionale*, ed. A. Piolanti (q.v.) ii, 1982, pp. 57–84.

Colish, M. L. 'Avicenna's Theory of Efficient Causation and its Influence on St. Thomas Aquinas'. *Atti del Congresso Internazionale Tomasso d'Aquino nel suo settimo centenario.* 9 vols. i. Naples, 1975, pp. 296–307.

Collingwood, F. (ed.). '*Summa de Bono* of Ulrich of Strasbourg, *Liber III, Tractatus 2, Cap. I, II, III, Tractatus 3, Cap. I, II*'. *Nine Mediaeval Thinkers.* ed. J. R. O'Donnell. PIMS, Studies and Texts 1. Toronto, 1955, pp. 293–308.

Collingwood, R. G. *The Idea of History.* Oxford, 1946.

Congar, M. J. 'Théologie'. *Dictionnaire de théologie catholique.* xv(1). Paris, 1946.

Cooper, B. Z. *The Idea of God: A Whiteheadian Critique of St. Thomas Aquinas' Concept of God.* The Hague, 1974.

Corbin, M. *Le chemin de la théologie chez Thomas d'Aquin.* Bibl. des archives de phil., nouv. sér. 16. Paris, 1974.

Coreth, E. *Metaphysics*, ed. and trans. J. Donceel. New York, 1968.

Corsini, E. *Il trattato de Divinis Nominibus dello Pseudo-Dionigi e i commenti neoplatonici al Parmenide.* Turin, 1962.

Courcelle, P. *Les lettres grecques en Occident de Macrobe à Cassiodore*. Paris, 1948.

Courtès, P.-C. 'L'être et le non-être selon saint Thomas d'Aquin'. *Revue thomiste*, 67 (1967), 387–436.

—— 'L'Un selon saint Thomas'. *Revue thomiste*, 68 (1968), 198–240.

Cousins, E. H. 'The Indirect Influence of the Koran on the Notion of Reason in the Christian Thought of the Thirteenth Century'. *Actas del V Congresso Internacional de Filosofía Medieval*. 2 vols. Madrid, 1979, i, pp. 651–6.

—— (ed.). *Bonaventure: The Soul's Journey into God, the Tree of Life, the Life of Saint Francis*. The Classics of Western Spirituality. London, 1978.

Crouse, R. D. 'The Doctrine of Creation in Boethius, the *De hebdomadibus* and the *Consolatio*'. *Studia Patristica* xvii (1), ed. E. A. Livingstone. Oxford, 1982, pp. 417–21.

—— 'Honorius Augustodunensis: the Arts as *via ad patriam*'. *Arts libéraux et philosophie au moyen âge: Actes du quatrième Congrès international de philosophie médiévale, Montréal, 1967*. Montreal/Paris, 1969, pp. 531–9.

—— 'Honorius Augustodunensis, Disciple of Anselm?' *Die Wirkungsgeschichte Anselms von Canterbury*, Analecta Anselmiana, ed. F. S. Schmitt, iv(2). Frankfurt, 1975.

—— '*In Multa Defluximus: Confessions* x, 29–43, and St. Augustine's Theory of Personality'. *Neoplatonism and Early Christian Thought*, ed. H. J. Blumenthal (q.v.), pp. 180–5.

—— '*Intentio Moysi*: Bede, Augustine, Eriugena and Plato in the Hexameron of Honorius Augustodunensis'. *Dionysius*, 2 (1978), 137–57.

—— '*Philosophia Ancilla Theologiae*: Some Texts from Aristotle's *Metaphysics* in the Interpretation of Albertus Magnus'. *Actas del V Congreso Internacional de Filosofía Medieval*, 2 vols. Madrid, 1979, i, pp. 657–61.

—— '*Recurrens in te unum*: the Pattern of St. Augustine's *Confessions*'. *Studia Patristica* xiv, ed. E. A. Livingstone. Texte und Untersuchungen 117. Berlin, 1976, pp. 389–92.

—— 'St. Augustine's *De Trinitate*: Philosophical Method'. *Studia Patristica* xvi, ed. E. A. Livingstone. Texte und Untersuchungen 129. Berlin, 1985, pp. 501–10.

—— 'St. Thomas, St. Albert, Aristotle: *Philosophia Ancilla Theologiae*'. *Atti del Congresso Internazionale Tommaso d'Aquino nel suo settimo centenario*, 9 vols, i. Naples, 1975, pp. 181–5.

—— '*Semina Rationum*: St. Augustine and Boethius'. *Dionysius*, 4 (1980), 75–86.

Damascius Successor. *Dubitationes et solutiones de primis principiis*, ed. C. A. Ruelle. 2 vols. Paris, 1889.

Delvigne, T. 'L'inspiration propre du traité de Dieu dans le *Commentaire des Sentences* de saint Thomas'. *Bulletin thomiste, Notes et communications* (1932), 119*–22*.

Descartes, R. *Méditationes. Œuvres et lettres*. Textes présentés par A. Bridoux. Bibliothèque de la Pléiade 40. 2 vols. Paris, 1952.

Dewan, Lawrence, OP. '*Objectum*. Notes on the Invention of a Word'. *Arch. hist. doct. lit. du moyen âge* 48 (1981), 37–96.

—— 'St. Thomas and the Divine Names'. *Science et esprit*, 32 (1980), 19–33.

Dezza, P. 'La preparazione dell'Enciclica "Aeterni Patris": il contributo della Compagnia di Gesù'. *Atti dell'VIII Congresso Tomistico Internazionale*, ed. A. Piolanti (q.v.), i, 1981, pp. 51–65.

Dodds, E. R. *The Greeks and the Irrational*. Sather Classical Lectures 25. Berkeley and Los Angeles, 1951.

—— *Pagan and Christian in an Age of Anxiety: Some Aspects of Religious Experience from Marcus Aurelius to Constantine*. Wiles Lectures, 1963. Cambridge, 1965.

Dondaine, H.-F. '"Alia lectura fratris Thomae"? (*Super I Sent*.)'. *Mediaeval Studies*, 42 (1980), 308–36.

—— *Le Corpus Dionysien de l'Université de Paris au XIIIe siècle*. Rome, 1953.

—— 'Saint Thomas et Scot Érigène'. *Rev. sc. ph. th.* 35 (1951), 31–3.

Doucet, V. *Commentaires sur les Sentences, supplément au répértoire de F. Stegmueller*. Ad Claras Aquas, Quaracchi, 1954.

Doull, J. A. 'Augustinian Trinitarianism and Existential Theology'. *Dionysius*, 3 (1979), 111–59.

—— 'The Logic of Theology since Hegel'. *Dionysius*, 7 (1983), 129–36.

Ducharme, L. 'L'idée de la métaphysique dans les écrits du premier enseignement parisien de saint Thomas d'Aquin'. *Colloque commemoratif saint Thomas d'Aquin, Église et théologie*, 5, 2 (1974), 155–69.

Duclow, D. F. 'Dialectic and Christology in Eriugena's *Periphyseon*'. *Dionysius*, 4 (1980), 99–118.

Duméry, H. 'L'Être et l'Un'. *Miscellanea Albert Dondeyne*. Bibliotheca Ephemeridum Theologicarum Lovaniensium 35. Louvain, 1974, pp. 331–50.

—— 'Le néant d'être'. *Les Études philosophiques*. July–Sept. 1973, 315–27.

Durantel, J. *S. Thomas et le pseudo-Denis*. Paris, 1919.

Elders, Leo. SVD. 'Les cinq voies et leur place dans la philosophie de saint Thomas'. *Quinque sunt viae*, ed. L. Elders. Studi tomistici 9. Vatican City, 1980, pp. 136–46.

—— 'Le Commentaire sur le quatrième livre de la *Métaphysique*'. *Atti del Congresso Internazionale Tommaso d'Aquino nel suo settimo centenario*, 9 vols., i. Naples, 1975, pp. 203–14.

—— 'L'ordre des attributs divins dans la *Somme théologique*'. *Divus Thomas*, 82 (1979), 225–32.

—— 'Le problème de l'existence de Dieu dans les écrits de s. Thomas d'Aquin (A propos du livre de F. van Steenberghen)'. *Divus Thomas*, 86 (1983), 171–87.

—— 'Structure et fonction de l'argument *sed contra* dans la *Somme théologique* de saint Thomas'. *Divus Thomas*, 80 (1977), 245–60.

Eriugena, John Scotus. *Homélie sur le prologue de Jean*. Intro., texte critique, trans. et notes de É. Jeauneau. Sources chrétiennes 151. Paris, 1969.

— *Periphyseon, de divisione naturae*, ed. I. P. Sheldon-Williams with the collaboration of L. Bieler. Script. lat. Hiberniae 7, 9, 11. 3 vols. Dublin, 1968–81.

— *Periphyseon: on the Division of Nature*. Trans. M. L. Uhlfelder with summaries by J. A. Potter. Library of Liberal Arts 157. Indianapolis, 1976.

Evans, G. R. *Anselm and a New Generation*. Oxford, 1980.

— *Anselm and Talking about God*. Oxford, 1978.

— *Old Arts and New Theology*. Oxford, 1980.

— 'Thierry of Chartres and the Unity of Boethius' Thought'. *Studia Patristica*, xvii(1), ed. E. A. Livingstone. Oxford, 1982, pp. 440–5.

Fabro, C. 'L'"esse" tomistico et il "Sein" hegeliano'. *Sapientia Aquinatis: Communicationes IV Congressus Thomistici Internationalis, Romae, 1955*. Bibl. Pont. Acad. Rom. S. Thom. Aquin. 1 and 2. 2 vols. Rome, 1955, i. pp. 263–70.

— 'Il nuovo problema dell'essere e la fondazione della metafisica'. *Commemorative Studies*, ed. A. A. Maurer (q.v.), ii, pp. 423–57.

— 'L'interpretazione dell'atto in S. Tommaso e Heidegger'. *Atti del Congresso Internazionale Tommaso d'Aquino nel suo settimo centenario*, 9 vols., i. Naples, 1975, pp. 119–28.

— *Participation et causalité selon s. Thomas d'Aquin*. Chaire card. Mercier 2. Louvain/Paris, 1961.

Fackenheim, E. *The Religious Dimension of Hegel's Thought*. Bloomington, Indiana, 1967.

Fairweather, E. R. *A Scholastic Miscellany: Anselm to Ockham*. Library of Christian Classics 10. London, 1956.

Farrer, A. *Finite and Infinite*. Westminster, 1943.

Faucon, P. *Aspects néoplatoniciens de la doctrine de saint Thomas d'Aquin*. Lille/Paris, 1975.

Festugière, A. M. J. (ed.). *La Révélation d'Hermès Trismégiste*. Études bibliques. 4 vols. Paris, 1944–54.

Finance, J. de. *Être et agir dans la philosophie de saint Thomas*. Bibliothèque des Archives de philosophie. Paris, 1945.

Findlay, J. *Plato: The Written and Unwritten Doctrines*. International Library of Philosophical and Scientific Method. London, 1974.

Foster, K. 'Angelology in the Church and in St. Thomas'. Appendix 1, *Summa Theologiae* ix. Blackfriars, 1968, pp. 301–5.

Garrigues, M.-O. 'L'œuvre d'Honorius Augustodunensis: inventaire critique'. Unpublished Ph.D. diss. Univ. de Montréal, 1979.

— (ed.). 'Honorius Augustodunensis, *De anima et de Deo, quaedam ex Augustino excerpta, sub dialogo enarata*'. *Recherches augustiniennes* 12 (1977), 212–78.

Garrigou-Lagrange, R. *De Deo Trino et Creatore*, ed. altera revisa. Turin, 1951.

— *De Deo Uno*. Paris, 1938.

— 'Dialectique hégélienne et métaphysique thomiste'. *Sapientia Aquinatis: Communicationes IV Congressus Thomistici Internationalis, Romae, 1955*. Bibl. Pont. Acad. Rom. S. Thom. Aquin. 1 and 2, 2 vols. Rome, 1955, i. pp. 271–81.

Geiger, L. B. 'Les idées divines dans l'œuvre de s. Thomas'. *Commemorative Studies*, ed. A. A. Maurer (q.v.), i, pp. 175–209.

—— *La participation dans la philosophie de s. Thomas d'Aquin*. Bibliothèque thomiste 23. Paris, 1942.

Genuyt, F. M. *Vérité de l'être et affirmation de Dieu: essai sur la philosophie de saint Thomas*. Bibliothèque thomiste 42. Paris, 1974.

Gersh, S. E. *From Iamblichus to Eriugena: an Investigation of the Prehistory and Evolution of the Pseudo-Dionysian Tradition*. Studien zur Problemgeschichte der antiken und mittelalterlichen Philosophie 8. Leiden, 1978.

—— 'Ideas and Energies in Pseudo-Dionysius the Areopagite'. *Studia Patristica*, xv, ed. E. A. Livingstone. Texte und Untersuchungen 128, Berlin, 1984, pp. 297–300.

—— *ΚΙΝΗΣΙΣ 'ΑΚΙΝΗΤΟΣ: A Study of Spiritual Motion in the Philosophy of Proclus*. Leiden, 1973.

Gervais, J. 'La place et le sens des questions 12 et 13 dans la *Prima Pars* de la *Somme Théologique*'. *Rev. de l'Univ. d'Ottawa* 19 (1949), sect. spéc. 80*–4*.

Ghellinck, J. de. *Le mouvement théologique du XIIᵉ siècle: études, recherches et documents*. 2nd edn. Museum Lessianum, sect. hist. 10. Bruges, 1948.

Giannini, G. 'Parmenide, Heidegger e S. Tommaso'. *Sapientia Aquinatis: Communications IV Congressus Thomistici Internationalis, Romae, 1955*. Bibl. Pont. Acad. Rom. S. Thom. Aquin. 1 and 2. 2 vols. Rome, 1955, i, pp. 482–8.

Gilson, É. 'Avicenne et le point de départ de Duns Scot'. *Arch. hist. doct. lit. du moyen âge*, 2 (1927), 89–149.

—— *Being and Some Philosophers*. 2nd edn. Toronto, 1952.

—— 'De la notion d'être divin dans la philosophie de saint Thomas d'Aquin'. *De Deo in philosophia S. Thomae et in hodierna philosophia. Acta VI Congressus Thomistici Internationalis*. Bibl. Pont. Acad. Rom. S. Thom. Aquin. 6. 3 vols. Rome, 1965, i, pp. 113–29.

—— *The Christian Philosophy of Thomas Aquinas*. London, 1961.

—— *The Elements of Christian Philosophy*. Garden City, 1960.

—— *L'être et l'essence*. 2nd edn. revue et augmentée. Paris, 1962.

—— *History of Christian Philosophy in the Middle Ages*. London, 1955.

—— *La philosophie au moyen âge*. 2nd edn. Paris, 1944.

—— 'Le réalisme méthodique'. *Philosophia Perennis, Abhandlungen zu ihrer Vergangenheit und Gegenwart*, ed. F.-J. von Rintelen. 2 vols. Regensberg, 1930, ii, 744–55.

—— *Réalisme thomiste et critique de la connaissance*. Paris, 1939.

—— '*Quasi Definitio Substantiae*'. *Commemorative Studies*, ed. A. A. Maurer (q.v.), i, pp. 111–29.

—— 'Trois leçons sur le thomisme et sa situation présente'. *Seminarium*, new series 5, no. 4 (1965), 682–737. Reprinted as *Les Tribulations de Sophie*. Paris, 1967.

—— 'Une sagesse rédemptrice'. *Jacques Maritain, son œuvre philosophique*. Bibliothèque de la Revue thomiste. Paris, 1949, pp. 3–5.

Glorieux, P. 'La somme "Quoniam Homines" d'Alain de Lille'. *Arch. hist. doct. lit. du moyen âge*, 20 (1953), 113–364.

Goichon, A. M. 'The Philosopher of Being'. *Avicenna Commemorative Volume*, ed. V. Courtois. Calcutta, 1956.

Gomes, C. F., OSB. 'La réciprocité psychologique des personnes divines selon la théologie de saint Thomas d'Aquin'. *Atti dell'VIII Congresso Tomistico*, ed. A. Piolanti (q.v.). iv, Studi tomistici 13, Vatican City, 1981, pp. 152–71.

Gorce, M.-M. *L'essor de la pensée au Moyen Âge: Albert le Grand—Thomas d'Aquin*. Paris, 1933.

—— 'Le problème des trois Sommes: Alexandre de Halès, Thomas d'Aquin, Albert le Grand'. *Revue thomiste*, 26 (1931), 293–301.

Grabmann, M. *La Somme théologique de saint Thomas d'Aquin*, trans. by F. van Steenberghen from *Einführung in die Summa des hl. T. von Aquin*. Freiburg i. B., 1919/Paris, 1925.

—— *Thomas von Aquin: Eine Einführung in seine Persönlichkeit und seine Gedankenwelt*. Munich, 1920.

Grisey, G. 'The "Four Meanings" of "Christian Philosophy"'. *The Journal of Religion*, 41–2 (1961–2), 103–18.

Hadot, P. 'Apophatisme et théologie négative'. *Exercices spirituels et philosophie antique*. Études augustiniennes. Paris, 1981, pp. 185–93.

—— 'Dieu comme acte d'être dans le néoplatonisme. A propos des théories d'É. Gilson sur la métaphysique de l'Exode'. *Dieu et l'être: exégèses d'Exode 3, 14 et de Coran 20, 11–24*, ed. Centre d'études des religions du livre, CNRS. Études augustiniennes. Paris, 1978, pp. 57–63.

—— 'La distinction de l'être et de l'étant dans le *De Hebdomadibus* de Boèce'. *Die Metaphysik im Mittelalter*, 2 vols, ed. P. Wilpert. Miscellanea Mediaevalia 13, Berlin, 1963, ii, pp. 147–53.

—— 'Les divisions des parties de la philosophie dans l'Antiquité'. *Museum Helveticum*, 36 (1979), 201–23.

—— 'L'être et l'étant dans le néoplatonisme'. *Études néoplatoniciennes*, ed. J. Trouillard *et al*. Neuchâtel, 1973, pp. 27–39.

—— 'Exercices spirituels antiques et "philosophie chrétienne"'. *Exercices spirituels et philosophie antique*. Études augustiniennes. Paris, 1981, pp. 59–74.

—— '"Forma Essendi": interprétation philologique et interprétation philosophique d'une formule de Boèce'. *Les études classiques*, 38 (1970), 143–56.

—— *Porphyre et Victorinus*. Études augustiniennes. 2 vols. Paris, 1968.

—— 'La présentation du platonisme par Augustin'. *Kerygma und Logos: Festschrift für Carl Andresen*, ed. A. M. Ritter. Beiträge zu den geistesgeschichtlichen Beziehungen zwischen Antike und Christentum. Göttingen, 1979, pp. 272–9.

Hales, Alexander of. *Glossa in Quatuor Libros Sententiarum Petri Lombardi*. Ad Claras Aquas, Quaracchi, 1951.

—— *Summa Theologica*. 4 vols. Ad Claras Aquas, Quaracchi, 1924–48.

Hankey, W. J. 'Aquinas' First Principle: Being or Unity?' *Dionysius*, 4 (1980), 133–72.

—— 'Aquinas and the Passion of God'. *Being and Truth, Essays in Honour of John Macquarrie*. Edited by A. Kee and E. Long. London, 1986, pp. 318–33.

—— 'The *De Trinitate* of St. Boethius and the Structure of the *Summa Theologiae* of St. Thomas Aquinas'. *Atti del Congresso Internazionale di Studi Boeziani, Pavia, 5–8 ottobre, 1980*, ed. L. Obertello. Rome, 1981, pp. 367–75.

—— 'Making Theology Practical: Thomas Aquinas and the Nineteenth Century Religious Revival'. *Dionysius*, 9 (1985), 85–127.

—— 'Pope's Leo's Purposes and St. Thomas' Platonism'. *Atti dell'VIII Congresso Tomistico Internazionale sull'Enciclica 'Aeterni Patris' e nel centenario della fondazione dell'Accademia S. Tommaso, Rome, 1980*, ed. A. Piolanti (q.v.), 1982, viii, pp. 39–52.

—— 'The Place of the Proof for God's Existence in the *Summa Theologiae* of Thomas Aquinas'. *The Thomist*, 46 (1982), 370–93.

—— 'The Place of the Psychological Image of the Trinity in the Arguments of Augustine's *de Trinitate*, Anselm's *Monologion*, and Aquinas' *Summa Theologiae*'. *Dionysius*, 3 (1979), 99–110.

—— 'The Structure of Aristotle's Logic and the Knowledge of God in the *Pars Prima* of the *Summa Theologiae* of Thomas Aquinas'. *Sprache und Erkenntnis im Mittelalter*, ed. A. Zimmermann. Miscellanea Mediaevalia 13/2, Berlin/New York, 1981, pp. 961–8.

—— 'Theology as System and as Science: Proclus and Thomas Aquinas'. *Dionysius*, 6 (1982), 83–93.

Harvanek, R. F. 'History and "Aeterni Patris"'. *Notes et documents, Institut International 'J. Maritain'*. v, 16 (July–September 1979), 1–12.

Henle, R. J. *Saint Thomas and Platonism: A Study of the Plato and Platonici Texts in the Writings of Saint Thomas*. The Hague, 1956.

Hennesey, J. 'Leo XIII's Thomistic Revival: A Political and Philosophic Event'. *Celebrating the Medieval Heritage: A Colloquy on the Thought of Aquinas and Bonaventure*, ed. D. Tracy. *The Journal of Religion*, 58 Supplement (1978), S185–S197.

Iamblichus. *Les Mystères d'Égypte*. Texte établi et traduit par É. des Places. Collection des Universités de France. Paris, 1966.

Inge, W. R. *The Philosophy of Plotinus*. 2nd edn., 2 vols. London, 1923.

Jacquin, A.-M. 'Les "*Rationes Necessariae*" de saint Anselme'. *Mélanges Mandonnet: Études d'histoire littéraire et doctrinale du moyen âge*. Bibliothèque thomiste 13 and 14. Paris, 1930, ii, pp. 67–78.

Jaeger, W. *Aristoteles: Grundlegung einer Geschichte seiner Entwicklung*. Berlin, 1923.

Jalbert, G. *Nécessité et contingence chez saint Thomas d'Aquin et ses prédécesseurs*. Éditions de l'Université d'Ottawa. Ottawa, 1961.

Jeauneau, É. 'La division des sexes chez Grégoire de Nysse et chez Jean Scot Érigène'. *Eriugena: Studien zu seinen Quellen*, ed. W. Beierwaltes (q.v.), pp. 33–54.

Johnson, H.-J. '*Via Negationis* and *Via Analogiae*: Theological Agnosticism in Maimonides and Aquinas'. *Actas del V Congreso Internacional de Filosofía Medieval*. 2 vols. Madrid, 1979, ii, pp. 843–56.

—— 'Why Five Ways? A Thesis and some Alternatives'. *Arts libéraux et philosophie au moyen âge: Actes du quatrième Congrès international de philosophie médiévale, Montréal, 1967*. Montreal/Paris, 1969, pp. 1143–54.

Jones, J. D. 'The Ontological Difference for St Thomas and Pseudo-Dionysius'. *Dionysius*, 4 (1980), 119–32.

Jordan, M. D. 'L'exégèse de la causalité physique chez Thomas d'Aquin'. *Revue thomiste*, 82 (1982), 550–74.

—— 'The Grammar of *Esse*'. *The Thomist*, 44 (1980), 1–26.

—— 'The Modes of Thomistic Discourse: Questions for Corbin's *Le Chemin de la théologie chez Thomas d'Aquin*'. *The Thomist*, 45 (1981), 80–98.

Kenny, A. *The Five Ways: St. Thomas Aquinas' Proof of God's Existence*. London, 1969.

Kovach, F. J. 'Divine Art in Saint Thomas Aquinas'. *Arts libéraux et philosophie au moyen âge: Actes du quatrième Congrès international de philosophie médiévale, Montréal, 1967*. Montreal/Paris, 1969, pp. 663–71.

Kremer, K. *Die neuplatonische Seinsphilosophie und ihre Wirkung auf Thomas von Aquin*. Studien zur Problemgeschichte der Antiken und mittelalterlichen Philosophie 1. Leiden, 1966.

Labbé, Y. 'Logique, métaphysique et théologie: deux ouvrages de Stanislas Breton'. *Rev. sc. ph. th.* 56 (1972), 252–64.

—— 'Le problème de Dieu dans la philosophie de la religion de H. Duméry'. *Rev. sc. ph. th.* 55 (1971), 393–431.

Lafont, G. 'Ecouter Heidegger en théologien'. *Rev. sc. ph. th.* 67 (1983), 371–98.

—— 'Le *Parménide* de Platon et saint Thomas d'Aquin: l'analogie des noms divins et son arrière-plan néoplatonicien'. *Analogie et dialectique: essais de théologie fondamentale*, ed. P. Gisel et Ph. Secretan. Lieux théologiques 3. Geneva, 1982, pp. 53–80.

—— *Peut-on connaître Dieu en Jésus-Christ? Problématique*. Coll. Cogitatio fidei 44. Paris, 1969.

—— *Structures et méthode dans la Somme Théologique de saint Thomas*. Textes et étude théo. Paris/Bruges, 1961.

Lakebrink, B. *Perfectio omnium perfectionum: Studien zur Seinskonzeption bei Thomas von Aquin und Hegel*. Studi tomistici 24. Vatican City, 1984.

Landgraf, A. M. *Einführung in die Geschichte der theologischen Literatur der Frühscholastik*. Regensburg, 1948.

Landry, A.-M. (ed.). *Introduction à l'histoire de la littérature théologique de la scholastique naissante*. Université de Montréal, Publ. de l'Institut d'études médiévales 22. Montreal/Paris, 1973.

Lemaigre, B. M. 'Perfection de Dieu et multiplicité des attributs divins: Pourquoi s. Thomas a-t-il inséré la dispute des attributs divins (*I Sent.*, d. 2, q. 1, a. 3) dans son *Commentaire des Sentences*?' *Rev. sc. ph. th.* 50 (1966), 198–227.

Leo XIII, Pope. 'Aeterni Patris' in St. Thomas Aquinas. *Opera Omnia* (Leonine) i. Rome, 1882, pp. iii–xvi.

—— 'Aeterni Patris'. English trans. in St. Thomas Aquinas, *Summa Theologica*, trans. by the Fathers of the English Dominican Province. 22 vols., London, 1911, i, pp. ix–xxxiii.

Lewy, H. *Chaldean Oracles and Theology*, ed. M. Tardieu. 2nd edn. Paris, 1978.

Lilla, S. 'The Notion of Infinitude in Ps. Dionysius Areopagita'. *Jour. of Theo. Stud.* 31 (1980), 93–103.

Litt, T. *Les corps célestes dans l'univers de saint Thomas d'Aquin*. Philosophes médiévaux 7. Louvain/Paris, 1963.

Lombard, Peter. *Sententiae in IV Libris Distinctae*. Editio tertia. 2 vols. Spicilegium Bonaventurianum 4, 5. Ad Claras Aquas, Grottaferrata, 1971–81.

Lonergan, B. 'Metaphysics as Horizon', in E. Coreth. *Metaphysics*, ed. and trans. J. Donceel. New York, 1968, pp. 197–219.

—— *Verbum: Word and Idea in Aquinas*, ed. D. B. Burrell. Notre Dame, 1967.

Lossky, V. 'Apophasis and Trinitarian Theology'. *In the Image and Likeness of God*, ed. J. H. Erikson and T. E. Bird. St Vladimir's Seminary, 1974, pp. 13–29.

—— *The Mystical Theology of the Eastern Church*, trans. by members of the Fellowship of St Alban and St Sergius. Cambridge/London, 1957.

—— *The Vision of God*, trans. A. Moorhouse. The Library of Orthodox Theology 2. London/Wisconsin, 1963.

Louth, A. *Discerning the Mystery: An Essay on the Nature of Theology*. Oxford, 1983.

—— *The Origins of the Christian Mystical Tradition: From Plato to Denys*. Oxford, 1981.

Lowry, J. M. P. *The Logical Principles of Proclus' ΣΤΟΙΧΕΙΩΣΙΣ ΘΕΟΛΟΓΙΚΗ as Systematic Ground of the Cosmos*. Doctoral Dissertation, Dept. of Classics, Dalhousie Univ., 1976, publ. as Elementa, Schriften zur Philosophie und ihrer Problemgeschichte 13. Amsterdam, 1980.

Luijpen, W. 'Heidegger and the Affirmation of God'. *De Deo in philosophia S. Thomae et in hodierna philosophia: Acta VI Congressus Thomistici Internationalis*. Pont. Acad. Rom. S. Thom. Aquin. 6. 3 vols. Rome, 1965, i, pp. 303–10.

McCabe, H., OP. Appendix 3, 'Signifying Imperfectly'. St. Thomas Aquinas. *Summa Theologiae*. 60 vols. Blackfriars, 1964, iii, pp. 104–5.

McCarthy, D. J. 'Une doctrine en quête d'un auteur'. *Rev. phil. de. Louvain* 66 (1968), 630–60.

McCool, G. A. *Catholic Theology in the Nineteenth Century*. New York, 1977.

—— 'Twentieth-Century Scholasticism'. *Celebrating the Medieval Heritage: a Colloquy on the Thought of Aquinas and Bonaventure*, ed. D. Tracy. *The Journal of Religion*, 58 Supplement (1978), S198–S221.

Macquarrie, J. *In Search of Deity: An Essay in Dialectical Theism*. The Gifford Lectures delivered at the University of St Andrew's in Session 1983–84. London, 1984.

—— *Twentieth-Century Religious Thought: The Frontiers of Philosophy and Theology, 1900—1970*. Rev. edn. London, 1971.

Madec, G. 'L'augustinisme de Jean Scot dans le "De praedestinatione"'. *Jean Scot Érigène et l'histoire de la philosophie*. Colloques internationaux du CNRS 561, Laon, 1975. Paris, 1977, pp. 183–90.

—— 'Le dossier augustinien du *Periphyseon* de Jean Scot (livres i–ii)'. *Recherches augustiniennes*, 15 (1980), 240–64.

—— '"Ego sum qui sum" de Tertullien à Jérôme'. *Dieu et l'être: exégèses d'Exode 3, 14 et de Coran 20, 11–24*, ed. Centres d'études des religions du livre, CNRS. Études augustiniennes. Paris, 1978, pp. 121–39.

—— 'Observations sur le dossier "augustinien" du *Periphyseon*'. *Eriugena: Studien zu seinen Quellen*, ed. W. Beierwaltes (q.v.), pp. 75–84.

Maréchal, J. *Le point de départ de la métaphysique*. 4 vols. Louvain/Paris, 1922–46.

Margerie, B. de. *La Trinité chrétienne dans l'histoire*. Théologie historique 31. Paris, 1975.

Marion, J.-L. *Dieu sans l'être: hors-texte*. Communio. Paris, 1982.

—— 'La vanité d'être et le nom de Dieu'. *Analogie et dialectique: essais de théologie fondamentale*, ed. P. Gisel and Ph. Secretan. Lieux théologiques 3. Geneva, 1982, pp. 17–49.

Maritain, J. *Bergsonian Philosophy and Thomism*, trans. M. L. Andison in collaboration with J. G. Andison. New York, 1955.

—— *Challenges and Renewals: Selected Readings*, ed. J. W. Evans and L. R. Ward. London, 1966.

Mathon, G. 'L'utilisation des textes de saint Augustin par Jean Scot Érigène dans son *De Predestinatione*'. *Augustinus Magister, Actes et Communications du Congrès international augustinien, Paris, 1954*. 3 vols. Paris, 1955, iii, pp. 419–28.

Matthew of Aquasparta. *Quaestiones de fide, Quaestiones Disputatae de fide et de cognitione*. Bibliotheca Franciscana Scolastica Medii Aevi 1. 2nd edn. Quaracchi, 1957.

Maurer, A. A. 'St. Thomas and Changing Truths'. *Atti del Congresso Internazionale Tommaso d'Aquino nel suo settimo centenario*. 9 vols. vi, Naples, 1977, pp. 267–75.

—— *St. Thomas and Historicity*. Aquinas Lecture 1979. Milwaukee, 1979.

—— (editor-in-chief). *St. Thomas Aquinas, 1274–1974: Commemorative Studies*. 2 vols. Toronto, 1974.

—— (trans.). *The Divisions and Methods of the Sciences: Questions V and VI of the Commentary on the De Trinitate*. Toronto, 1963.

Metz, J. B. *Zur Theologie der Welt*. Mainz and Munich, 1968.

—— *Christliche Anthropozentrik: Über die Denkform des Thomas von Aquin*. Munich, 1962.

Minio-Paluello, L. 'La tradition aristotélicienne dans l'histoire des idées'. *Actes du Congrès de Lyon 1958, Association Guillaume Budé*. Paris, 1960, pp. 166–85.

Moltmann, J. *The Trinity and the Kingdom of God: The Doctrine of God*, trans. M. Kohl. London, 1981.

Moore, P. S. *The Works of Peter of Poitiers*. Publ. in Mediaeval Studies, The University of Notre Dame. Notre Dame, Indiana, 1943.

Moreau, C. 'Veritas intellectus et veritas rei selon saint Thomas et Heidegger'. *Sapientia Aquinatis: Communicationes IV Congressus Thomistici Internationalis, Rome, 1955*. Bibl. Pont. Acad. Rom. S. Thom. Aquin. 1 and 2. Rome, 1955, i, pp. 528–36.

Moreau, J. *De la connaissance selon s. Thomas d'Aquin*. Paris, 1975.

— 'Le platonisme dans la *Somme Théologique*'. *Atti del Congresso Internazionale Tommaso d'Aquino nel suo settimo centenario*, 9 vols. Naples, 1975, pp. 238–47.

— 'Le Verbe et la création selon s. Augustin et J. Scot Érigène'. *Jean Scot Érigène et l'histoire de la philosophie*. Colloques internationaux du CNRS, 561, Laon, 1975. Paris, 1977, pp. 201–10.

Murphy, E. F. 'Martin Luther's Marginal Notes to the Sentences of Peter Lombard on the Transmission of Original Sin'. *Science et esprit* 33 (1981), 55–71.

Obertello, L. 'Proclus, Ammonius and Boethius on Divine Knowledge'. *Dionysius*, 5 (1981), 127–64.

O'Brien, D. 'Plotinus and the Gnostics on the Generation of Matter'. *Neoplatonism and Early Christian Thought*, ed. H. J. Blumenthal (q.v.), pp. 108–123.

— 'Plotinus on Evil: A Study in Matter and the Soul in Plotinus' Conception of Human Evil'. *Le Néoplatonisme*. Colloques internationaux du CNRS, Royaumont, 1969. Paris, 1971, pp. 113–46.

O'Brien, T. C. 'The Dionysian Corpus'. Appendix 3. St. Thomas Aquinas. *Summa Theologiae*. Blackfriars, 1975, xiv, pp. 182–93.

— Review of J. Owens, *St. Thomas Aquinas on the Existence of God. The Thomist*, 46 (1982), 644–53.

O'Donovan, O. '*Usus* and *Fruitio* in Augustine, *De Doctrina Christiana* I'. *Jour. of Theo. Studies*, 33 (1982), 361–97.

O'Meara, J. J. 'Eriugena's Use of Augustine in his Teaching of the Return of the Soul and the Vision of God'. *Jean Scot Érigène et l'histoire de la philosophie*. Colloques internationaux du CNRS, Laon, 1975. Paris, 1977, pp. 191–200.

— '*Magnorum Virorum Quendam Consensum Velimus Machinari* (804D): Eriugena's Use of Augustine's *de Genesis ad litteram* in the *de divisione naturae*'. *Eriugena: Studien zu seinen Quellen*, ed. W. Beierwaltes (q.v.), pp. 105–16.

Owens, J. 'Aquinas as an Aristotelian Commentator'. *Commemorative Studies*, ed. A. A. Maurer (q.v.), i, pp. 213–38.

— 'Aquinas and the Five Ways'. *St. Thomas Aquinas on the Existence of God, Collected Papers of Joseph Owens, C.Ss.R.*, ed. J. R. Catan. Albany, NY, 1980, pp. 132–41.

— *The Doctrine of Being in the Aristotelian Metaphysics*. Toronto, 1951.

— 'Existence and the Subject of Metaphysics'. *Science et esprit*, 32 (1980), 255–69.

—— 'Value and Person in Aquinas'. *Atti del Congresso Internazionale Tommaso d'Aquino nel suo settimo centenario*. 9 vols. vii. Naples, 1978, pp. 56–62.

Pannenberg, W. *Basic Questions in Theology*, trans. in part by G. H. Kehm. Library of Philosophy and Theology. 3 vols. London, 1970.

Panofsky, E. *Abbot Suger*. 2nd edn. Princeton, 1979.

Patfoort, A. 'Théorie de la théologie ou réflexion sur le corpus des Ecritures?' *Angelicum*, 54 (1977), 459–88.

Pattin, A. '*Le Liber de Causis*: édition établie à l'aide de 90 manuscrits avec introduction et notes'. *Tijdschrift voor Filosofie*, 28 (1966), 90–203.

Peghaire, J. '*Intellectus' et 'Ratio' selon saint Thomas d'Aquin*. Univ. de Montréal Publ. de l'institut d'études médiévales 6. Paris/Ottawa, 1936.

—— 'L'axiome "Bonum est diffusivum sui" dans le néo-platonisme et l'thomisme'. *Rev. de l'Univ. d'Ottawa*, 1 (1932), section spéc. 5*–30*.

Pegis, A. C. St Thomas Aquinas. *Summa contra Gentiles*, trans. intro., notes. 4 vols. Notre Dame/London, 1975.

—— *The Basic Writings of Saint Thomas Aquinas*. 2 vols. New York, 1945.

Persson, Per Eric. *Sacra Doctrina: Reason and Revelation in Aquinas*, trans. R. Mackenzie. Oxford, 1970.

Petersen, Joan M. *The Dialogues of Gregory the Great in their Late Antique Cultural Background*. Studies and Texts 69. Toronto, 1984.

—— 'Greek Influences on Gregory the Great's Exegesis of Luke 15. 1–10, Hom. Ev. 2. 34'. *Actes du colloque internationale CNRS 'Grégoire le Grand'*, forthcoming.

Pieper, J. 'The Concept of Createdness and its Implications'. *Atti del Congresso Internazionale Tommaso d'Aquino nel suo settimo centenario*. 9 vols. v, Naples, 1977, pp. 20–7.

—— *Introduction to Thomas Aquinas*, trans. R. and C. Winston, London, 1962.

—— *Scholasticism: Personalities and Problems of Medieval Philosophy*, trans. R. and C. Winston. London, 1961.

—— *The Silence of St. Thomas: Three Essays*, trans. D. O'Connor. London, 1957.

Pines, S. 'Les textes arabes dit plotiniens et le courant "porphyrien" dans le néoplatonisme grec'. *Le Néoplatonisme*. Colloques internationaux du CNRS, Royaumont, 1969. Paris, 1971, pp. 303–13.

Piolanti, A. (ed.). *Atti dell'VIII Congresso Tomistico Internazionale*. 8 vols. Studi tomistici 10–17. Vatican City, 1981–2.

—— *Il tomismo come filosofia cristiana nel pensiero di Leone XIII*. Studi tomistici 20. Vatican City, 1983.

Places, Édouard des, SJ. *Études platoniciennes, 1929–1979*. Études préliminaires aux religions orientales dans l'empire romain 90. Leiden, 1981.

—— 'Les *Oracles chaldaïques* et Denys l'Aréopagite'. *Néoplatonisme: mélanges offerts à Jean Trouillard* (q.v.), pp. 291–5.

—— 'La théologie négative de Pseudo-Denys, ses antécédents platoniciens et son influence au seuil du Moyen-Âge'. *Studia Patristica*, xvii(1), ed. E. A. Livingstone. Oxford, 1982, pp. 81–92.

Plotinus. *Opera*, ed. P. Henry et H. R. Schwyzer. Museum Lessianum. Series Philosophia 33, 3 vols. Paris/Brussels, 1951–73.

— Trans. A. H. Armstrong. Loeb Classical Library. 5 vols. of 6. London/Cambridge, 1966–84.

Poitiers, Peter of. *Sententiae Petri Pictaviensis*, ed. P. Moore, M. Dulong, and J. Garvin. 2 vols. Publications in Mediaeval Studies, The University of Notre Dame 7, 11. Notre Dame, Indiana, 1943 and 1950.

Pontificia Università s. Tommaso d'Aquino (Rome). *Rassegna di letteratura tomistica, nuova serie del Bulletin thomiste*. Naples, 1969–82.

Porphyry. *On the Life of Plotinus and the Order of his Books*, in *Plotinus*, trans. A. H. Armstrong. Loeb Classical Library. 5 vol. of 6. London/Cambridge, 1966, i, pp. 2–85.

Pousset, É. 'Une relecture du Traité de Dieu dans la "Somme Théologique" de saint Thomas, I'. *Archives de philosophie* 38 (1975), 559–93.

— 'Une relecture du Traité de Dieu dans la "Somme Théologique" de saint Thomas (fin)'. *Archives de philosophie*, 39 (1976), 61–89.

Proclus. *Commentaire sur la République*, trad. franç. A. M. J. Festugière. Bibl. des textes philosophiques. 3 vols. Paris, 1970.

— *Commentaire sur la Timée*, trad. franç. A. M. J. Festugière. Bibl. des textes philosophiques. 5 vols. Paris, 1966–68.

— *In Platonis Timaeum Commentaria*, ed. E. Diehl. 3 vols. Lipsiae, 1903–6.

— *The Elements of Theology*. A revised text with trans., intro. and commentary by E. R. Dodds. 2nd edn. Oxford, 1963.

— *Théologie platonicienne*, ed. H.-D. Saffrey et L. G. Westerink. Collection des Universités de France. 4 vols. of 6. Paris, 1968–81.

Prümmer, D. *Fontes Vitae S. Thomae Aquinatis*. Fasc. I and II. Toulouse and St. Maximin, 1911 and 1924.

Rachid, A. 'Dieu et l'être selon Al-Farabi: le chapitre de "l'être" dans le Livre des Lettres'. *Dieu et l'être: exégèses d'Exode 3, 14 et de Coran 20, 11–24*, ed. Centre d'études des religions du livre, CNRS. Études augustiniennes. Paris, 1978, pp. 179–90.

Rahner, K. 'Angel'. *Sacramentum Mundi: An Encyclopedia of Theology*, ed. K. Rahner *et al.* 6 vols. i, London, 1968, pp. 27–35.

— 'Theology'. *Sacramentum Mundi: An Encyclopedia of Theology*, ed. K. Rahner *et al.* 6 vols. vi, London, 1970, pp. 233–46.

— 'Remarks on the Dogmatic Treatise "De Trinitate"'. *More Recent Writings*, trans. K. Smyth. *Theological Investigations*. 17 vols. Baltimore/London, 1966, iv, pp. 77–102.

— *Spirit in the World*, trans. from the 2nd German edition by W. Dych. London, 1968.

Richard of St Victor. *La Trinité*, ed. G. Salet. Sources chrétiennes 63. Paris, 1959.

Richards, R. L. *The Problem of an Apologetical Perspective in the Trinitarian Theology of St. Thomas Aquinas*. Analecta Gregoriana 131. Rome, 1963.

Riet, G. van. *L'épistémologie thomiste*. Bibl. phil. de Louvain 3. Louvain, 1946.

— 'Le problème de Dieu chez Hegel'. *De Deo in philosophia S. Thomae et in hodierna philosophia. Acta VI Congressus Thomistici Internationalis*. Bibl. Pont. Acad. Rom. S. Thom. Aquin. 6. 3 vols. Rome, 1965, i, pp. 205–13.

— 'La *Somme contra les Gentils* et la polémique islamo-chrétienne'. *Aquinas and the Problems of his Time*. Mediaevalia Louvaniensia 5. Louvain/The Hague, 1976, pp. 156–60.

Robert, J. D. 'A propos d'un texte capital à Étienne Gilson'. *Revue thomiste*, 80 (1980), 439–55.

Roensch, F. J. *Early Thomistic School*. Dubuque, 1964.

Roland-Gosselin, M.-D. *Le 'De Ente et Essentia' de s. Thomas d'Aquin*. Bibliothèque thomiste 8. Paris, 1948.

Rorem, P. 'The Place of *The Mystical Theology* in the Pseudo-Dionysian Corpus'. *Dionysius*, 4 (1980), 87–98.

— *Biblical and Liturgical Symbol within the Pseudo-Dionysian Synthesis*. Studies and Texts 71. Toronto, 1984.

— 'Iamblichus and the Anagogical Method in Pseudo-Dionysian Liturgical Theology'. *Studia Patristica*, XVII (1), ed. E. A. Livingstone. Oxford, 1982, pp. 453–60.

Roussel, H. and Suard, F. (edd.). *Alain de Lille, Gautier de Châtillon, Jakemart Giélée et leur temps*. Lille, 1980.

Rousselot, P. *L'Intellectualisme de saint Thomas*. 2nd edn. Paris, 1924.

Ruello, F. J. 'La mystique de l'Exode (Exode 3, 14 selon Thomas Gallus, commentateur dionysien, 1246)'. *Dieu et l'être: exégèses d'Exode 3, 14 et de Coran 20, 11–24*, ed. Centre d'études des religions du livre, CNRS. Études augustiniennes. Paris, 1978, pp. 213–43.

— *Les 'Noms Divins' et leur 'raisons' selon saint Albert le Grand commentateur du 'De Divinis Nominibus'*. Bibliothèque thomiste 35. Paris, 1963.

— 'Réflexions sur les intentions et la méthode pédagogiques de saint Thomas dans la *Somme théologique*'. Unpublished thesis, Institut catholique de Paris, Faculté de philosophie, 1945.

— 'Saint Thomas et Pierre Lombard'. *San Tommaso: fonti e riflessi del suo pensiero*, ed. A. Piolanti. Studi tomistici 1. Rome, n.d., pp. 176–209.

Saffrey, H.-D. 'L'état actuel des recherches sur le *Liber de Causis*' comme source de la métaphysique au moyen âge, *Die Metaphysik im Mittelalter*. 2 vols., ed. P. Wilpert. Miscellanea Mediaevalia. Berlin, 1963, ii, pp. 267–81.

— 'La *Théologie platonicienne* de Proclus, fruit de l'exégèse du *Parménide*'. *Rev. de théologie et de philosophie*, 116 (1984), 1–12.

— 'L'Hymne IV de Proclus, prière aux dieux des *Oracles chaldaïques*', *Néoplatonisme: mélanges offerts à Jean Trouillard*. Les Cahiers de Fontenay, 19–22. Fontenay-aux-Roses, 1981, pp. 297–312.

— 'Nouveaux liens objectifs entre le pseudo-Denys et Proclus', *Rev. sc. ph. th.* 63 (1979), 3–16.

Saffrey, H.-D. 'Plan des livres I et II du *De mysteriis* de Iamblique'. *Zetesis, Album amicorum Prof. Dr. Émile de Strycker*. Antwerp/Utrecht, 1973, pp. 281–95.

—— 'Quelques aspects de la spiritualité des philosophes néoplatoniciens, de Jamblique à Proclus et Damascius'. *Rev. sc. ph. th.* 68 (1984), 169–82.

—— 'Théologie et anthropologie d'après quelques préfaces de Proclus'. *Images of Man in Ancient and Medieval Thought, Studia Gerardo Verbeke at amicis et collegis dicata*, ed. F. Boissier *et al.* Symbolae 1. Louvain, 1976, pp. 199–212.

—— 'Un lien objectif entre le Pseudo-Denys et Proclus'. *Studia Patristica* ix, ed. F. L. Cross. Texte und Untersuchungen 94. Berlin, 1966, pp. 98–105.

—— (ed.). *Mémorial A. J. Festugière*, Cahiers d'Orientalisme 10. Geneva, 1984.

Saliba, D. *Étude sur la Métaphysique d'Avicenne*. Paris, 1926.

Saulchoir, Le. *Bulletin thomiste*. 12 vols. Paris, 1924–65.

Schaffer, F. A. *Escape from Reason*. London, 1968.

Schillebeeckx, E. *Revelation and Theology*. Trans. by N. D. Smith of 'Theologie' in *Theologisch Woordenboek*, iii, 1958. London, 1967.

Scotus, John Duns. *De Primo Principio. A Revised Text and Translation* by E. Roche. Franciscan Institute Publications, Philosophy Series 5. New York/Louvain, 1949.

—— *Lectura in Librum Secundum Sententiarum, a distinctione prima ad sextam. Opera Omnia* (Commissio Scotistica), xviii. Vatican City, 1982.

Sheldon-Williams, I. P. 'A Bibliography of the Works of Johannes Scottus Eriugena'. *Jour. of Eccles. History*, 10 (1959), 198–224.

—— 'Eriugena's Greek Sources'. *The Mind of Eriugena*, ed. J. O'Meara and L. Bieler. Dublin, 1973, pp. 1–15.

—— 'Henads and Angels: Proclus and ps.-Dionysius'. *Studia Patristica* xi, ed. F. L. Cross. Texte und Untersuchungen 108. Berlin, 1972, pp. 65–71.

Sillem, E. *Ways of Thinking about God: Thomas Aquinas and Some Recent Problems*. London, 1961.

Smalley, B. *The Study of the Bible in the Middle Ages*. 2nd edn. Oxford, 1952.

Smith, Andrew. *Porphyry's Place in the Neoplatonic Tradition: A Study in Post-Plotinian Neoplatonism*. The Hague, 1974.

Southern, R. W. *Medieval Humanism and Other Studies*. Oxford, 1970.

—— *Platonism, Scholastic Method, and the School of Chartres*. The Stenton Lectures (1978) 12. Reading, 1979.

—— *Saint Anselm and His Biographer*. Cambridge, 1963.

Starnes, C. J. 'Saint Augustine and the Vision of the Truth'. *Dionysius*, 1 (1977), 85–126.

Steel, C. G. *The Changing Self: A Study of the Soul in later Neoplatonism: Iamblichus, Damascius and Priscianus*. Brussels, 1978.

Steenberghen, F. van. 'L'avenir au thomisme'. *Rev. phil. de Louvain* 54 (1956), 201–18.

—— *Dieu caché. Comment savons-nous que Dieu existe?* Essais philosophiques 8. Louvain/Paris, 1961.

—— *Epistemology*, trans. by L. Moonan from the fourth French edition. Louvain/New York, 1970.

—— *Introduction à l'étude de la philosophie médiévale*. Philosophes médiévaux 18. Louvain/Paris, 1974.

—— *The Philosophical Movement in the Thirteenth Century*. Nelson: n.p., 1955.

—— *La philosophie au XIIIᵉ siècle*. Philosophes médiévaux 9. Louvain/Paris, 1966.

Stegmueller, F. *Repertorium Commentariorum in Sententias Petri Lombardi*. Würzburg, 1947.

Stock, B. 'In Search of Eriugena's Augustine'. *Eriugena: Studien zu seinen Quellen*, ed. W. Beierwaltes (q.v.), pp. 85–104.

—— 'The Philosophical Anthropology of Johannes Scottus Eriugena'. *Studi medievali*, 8 (1967), 1–57.

Strauss, Leo. 'On Collingwood's Philosophy of History'. *The Review of Metaphysics*, 5 (1952), 559–86.

Strawson, P. F. 'Semantics, Logic and Ontology'. *Semantik und Ontologie, Neue Hefte für Philosophie*, 8 (1975), 1–13.

Stroick, C. 'Commentaire: la métaphysique de s. Thomas'. *Colloque commemoratif saint Thomas d'Aquin, Église et théologie* 5, 2 (1974), 171–88.

Suermondt, C. S. *Tabulae Schematicae, cum introductione de principiis et compositione comparatis Summae Theologiae et Summae Contra Gentiles S. Thomae Aquinatis*. Rome, 1943.

Sweeney, Leo, SJ. 'Doctrine of Creation in *Liber de Causis*'. *An Étienne Gilson Tribute, Presented by his North American Students with a Response by É. Gilson*, ed. by C. J. O'Neil. Milwaukee, 1959, pp. 274–89.

—— '*Esse Primum Creatum* in Albert the Great's *Liber de Causis et Processu Universitatis*'. *The Thomist*, 44 (1980), 599–646.

—— 'Metaphysics and God, Plotinus and Aquinas'. *Die Metaphysik im Mittelalter*. 2 vols. ed. P. Wilpert. Miscellanea Mediaevalia, Berlin, 1963, ii, pp. 232–9.

Theodoric of Freiberg (attributed). *De subiecto theologiae*. Appendix II, in Berthold of Moosburg. *Expositio super Elementationem Theologicam Procli, 184–221, de animalibus*, ed. L. Sturlese, presentazione E. Massa. Temi e testi 18, Rome, 1974, pp. xci–xcii.

Thillet, P. 'Indices porphyriens dans la théologie d'Aristote'. *Le Néoplatonisme*. Colloques internationaux du CNRS, Royaumont, 1969. Paris, 1971, pp. 293–302.

Thunberg, L. *Microcosm and Mediator: the Theological Anthropology of Maximus the Confessor*. Acta Seminarii Neotestamentici Upsaliensis 25. Lund, 1965.

Trouillard, J., PSS. 'L'âme du *Timée* et l'un du *Parménide* dans le perspective néoplatonicienne'. *Rev. inter. de phil.* 24, no. 92 (1970), 236–51.

—— (ed.). *Études néoplatoniciennes*. Neuchâtel, 1973.

—— 'La μονή selon Proclus'. *Le Néoplatonisme*. Colloques internationaux du CNRS, Royaumont, 1969. Paris, 1971, pp. 229–40.

—— *La mystagogie de Proclus*. Collection d'études anciennes. Paris, 1982.

Trouillard, J., PSS. *Néoplatonisme: mélanges offerts à Jean Trouillard*. Les Cahiers de Fontenay 19–22. Fontenay-aux-Roses, 1981.

—— 'Procession néoplatonicienne et création judeo-chrétienne'. *Néoplatonisme: mélanges offerts à Jean Trouillard* (q.v.), pp. 1–26.

—— *La procession plotinienne*. Paris, 1955.

—— 'Théologie négative et autoconstitution psychique chez les néoplatoniciens'. *Savoir, faire, espérer, hommage à Mgr Henri Van Camp*. Brussels, 1976, pp. 307–20.

—— *L'Un et l'Âme selon Proclus*. Collection des Universités de France. Paris, 1972.

—— (ed.). 'Les fondements du mythe selon Proclos'. *Le Mythe et le symbole de la connaissance figurative de Dieu*, ed. S. Breton *et al.* Philosophie 2. Paris, 1977, pp. 11–37.

Tuilier, A. 'La tradition aristotélicienne à Byzance des origines au VIIᵉ siècle. La formation de la scolastique byzantine'. *Actes du Congrès de Lyon 1958, Association Guillaume Budé*. Paris, 1960, pp. 186–97.

Ulrich of Strasburg. *La 'Summa de Bono' Livre I*. Introduction et édition critique par J. Daguillon. Bibliothèque thomiste 12, Paris, 1930.

—— See Collingwood, F., above.

Vagaggini, Cyprien. 'La hantise de "rationes necessariae" de saint Anselme dans la théologie de saint Thomas'. *Actes du Congrès international du IXᵉ centenaire de l'arrivée d'Anselme au Bec*. Spicilegium Beccense, Le Bec-Hellouin/Paris, 1959, pp. 103–40.

Vaissière, J. de la. 'Le sens du mot "verbe mental" dans les écrits de saint Thomas'. *Archives de philosophie* 3 (1925), 168–75.

Vanier, P. *Théologie trinitaire chez saint Thomas d'Aquin: Évolution du concept d'action notionelle*. Univ. de Montréal Publ. de l'institut d'études médiévales 13. Montreal/Paris, 1953.

Veatch, H. *Aristotle*. Bloomington, 1974.

—— 'St. Thomas' Doctrine of Subject and Predicate: A possible Starting-point for Logical Reform and Renewal'. *Commemorative Studies*, ed. A. A. Maurer (q.v.), ii, pp. 401–22.

—— *Two Logics*. Evanston, 1969.

Vignaux, P. 'Les raisons dans le *Monologion*'. *Rev. sc. ph. th.* 64, 3–25.

—— 'Mystique, scolastique, exégèse'. *Dieu et l'être: exégèses d'Exode 3, 14 et de Coran 20, 11–24*, ed. Centre d'études des religions du livre, CNRS. Études augustiniennes. Paris, 1978, pp. 205–11.

—— *Philosophy in the Middle Ages: An Introduction*, trans. E. C. Hall. Westport, Connecticut, 1959.

—— 'Présentation'. *Dieu et l'être: exégèses d'Exode 3, 14 et de Coran 20, 11–24*, ed. Centre d'études des religions du livre, CNRS. Études augustiniennes. Paris, 1978, pp. 7–13.

—— 'Structure et sens du *Monologion*'. *Rev. sc. ph. th.* 31 (1947), 192–212.

Virgoulay, R. 'Dieu ou l'être? Relecture de Heidegger en marge de J.-L. Marion, *Dieu sans l'être*'. *Recherches de science religieuse*, 72, 2 (1984), 163–98.

Wagar, W. W. 'Modern Views of the Origins of the Idea of Progress'. *The Journal of the History of Ideas*, 28 (1967), 55–70.

Walgrave, J. H. 'The Use of Philosophy in the Theology of Thomas Aquinas'. *Aquinas and the Problems of His Time*. Mediaevalia Lovaniensia 5. Louvain/The Hague, 1976, pp. 161–93.

—— '*Tertia via*'. *Quinque sunt viae*, ed. L. Elders. Studi tomistici 9. Vatican City, 1980, pp. 65–74.

Wallis, R. T. 'Divine Omniscience in Plotinus, Proclus and Aquinas'. *Neoplatonism and Early Christian Thought*, ed. H. J. Blumenthal (q.v.), and R. A. Markus, pp. 223–35.

—— *Neoplatonism*. London, 1972.

Walz, A. *Saint Thomas d'Aquin*, adapt. franç. par P. Novarina. Philosophes médiévaux 5. Louvain/Paris, 1962.

Wéber, É. H. *Dialogue et dissensions entre saint Bonaventure et saint Thomas d'Aquin à Paris (1253–1273)*. Bibliothèque thomiste 41. Paris, 1974.

—— *La controverse de 1270 à l'Université de Paris et son retentissement sur la pensée de s. Thomas d'Aquin*. Bibliothèque thomiste 40. Paris, 1970.

Weisheipl, J. A. *Friar Thomas d'Aquino: His Life, Thought and Works*. Oxford, 1975.

White, Victor. *God the Unknown, and other essays*. London, 1956.

Wilken, R. L. 'Pagan Criticism of Christianity: Greek Religion and Christian Faith'. *Early Christian Literature and the Classical Intellectual Tradition*, ed. W. R. Schoedel and R. L. Wilken. Théologie historique 54. Paris, 1979, pp. 116–34.

Wippel, J. F. *Metaphysical Themes in Thomas Aquinas*. Studies in Philosophy and the History of Philosophy. Washington, 1984.

Wohlman, A. 'L'élaboration des éléments aristotéliciens dans la doctrine thomiste de l'amour'. *Revue thomiste*, 82 (1982), 247–69.

Wojtyła, K. 'The Structure of Self-determination as the Core of the Theory of the Person'. *Atti del Congresso Internazionale Tommaso d'Aquino nel suo settimo centenario*. 9 vols. vii. Naples, 1978, pp. 37–41.

INDEX